Discover the White Mountains of New Hampshire

AMC Guide to the Best Hiking, Biking, and Paddling

Jerry and Marcy Monkman

APPALACHIAN MOUNTAIN CLUB BOOKS
BOSTON, MASSACHUSETTS

Cover Photograph: Jerry and Marcy Monkman
All photographs by the authors unless otherwise noted
Cover Design: Belinda Thresher
Book Design: Mac & Dent
Cartography: Larry Garland and Maptech, Inc.

Distributed by The Globe Pequot Press, Inc., Guilford, CT

ISBN 1-878239-88-0

The paper used in this publication meets the minimum requirements of the American National Standard for Information Sciences—Permanence of Paper for Printed Library Materials, ANSI Z39.48–1984.∞ **Due to changes in conditions, use of the information in this book is at the sole risk of the user.**

✪ Printed on recycled paper using soy-based inks.

Printed in the United States of America.

10 9 8 7 6 5 4 3
07

contents

Introduction viii
Acknowledgments ix
Locator Map x
Map Legend xii

1. White Mountain National Forest: Basic Information 1

Climate 2
Getting There 2
Lodging 3
U.S. Forest Service Information 3
Fees 4
Universal Access 4
Emergencies 5
Choosing Your Trip 5
Hunting Season 5
Logging 6
Don't Drink the Water 6
Backcountry Camping 7
Protect the Resource! 8

2. History 12

Geological History 12
Human History 15

3. Trip Highlights Charts 20

4. Hiking

4. Hiking 34

Hiking Times 35

Trip Ratings 35

Safety and Etiquette 36

Flat and Easy Walks 39

Trip #1: Square Ledge in Pinkham Notch 41

Trip #2: The Roost 44

Trip #3: Cascade Brook and the Basin 47

Trip #4: Stairs, Coosauk, and Hitchcock Falls 51

White Mountain Waterfalls 55

Trip #5: Cascade Path 58

Trip #6: Lonesome Lake 61

Camping and Hiking in Bear Country 64

Trip #7: Mount Willard 66

Trip #8: Greeley Ponds 69

Trip #9: Mount Pemigewasset 72

Trip #10: Lowe's Bald Spot 74

Trip #11: Mount Israel 77

Trip #12: Welch and Dickey Mountains 80

Trail Maintenance 82

Trip #13: Mount Crawford .85

Trip #14: Wildcat River 88

Trip #15: Kearsarge North .92

Trip #16: Caribou Mountain 95

Trip #17: Thoreau Falls 99

Trip #18: Zealand Falls and Zeacliff 102

Trip #19: Mount Moosilauke 107

Glacial Cirques: Remnants of the Ice Age 111

Trip #20: Mount Jefferson via Caps Ridge 112

Trip #21: Mount Webster and Mount Jackson 116

Trip #22: Mount Chocorua 120

The Legend of Chocorua .123

Trip #23: Mahoosucs Adventure:
Goose Eye and Mount Carlo 124

The Appalachian Trail 128

Trip #24: Mount Liberty 131

The Boreal Forest 135

Trip #25: North and South Baldface 137

Trip #26: North Moat and Red Ridge 141

Trip #27: Mount Hight and Carter Dome 144

Trip #28: Franconia Ridge 148

The Alpine Zone 153

Trip #29: Mount Washington via Boott Spur 156

Mount Washington: Tallest, Stormiest, Deadliest 161

Trip #30: Hut to Hut Presidential Traverse 164

AMC Huts: Spending the Night in the
            Backcountry 174

5. Mountain Biking 176

Trip Times 176

Trip Ratings 178

Set a Good Example 178

Safety and Comfort 180

Maps 181

Trip #31: Bartlett Experimental Forest 183

Trip #32: Conway Recreation Trail 186

Trip #33: Lincoln Woods .189

Fall Foliage: Why Leaves Change 193

Trip #34: Chocorua–Tamworth Loop 195

Trip #35: Ellsworth Pond Loop 198

Trip #36: Moose Brook State Park 202

Moose: An Animal Not Soon Forgotten 205

Trip #37: West Side of Loon Mountain 208

Trip #38: Franconia Notch Bicycle Path 212

Trip #39: Sawyer River 216

Missing Predators: Wolves, Mountain Lions,
            and Lynx .220

Trip #40: Lower Nanamocomuck Ski Trail 223

Trip #41: Mineral Site and Moat Mountain 226

Trip #42: Bog Brook Eddy 230

Trip #43: Slippery Brook Road 233
The Northern Hardwood Forest 236
Trip #44: Rob Brook Road 237
Trip #45: Wild River .241
Tracking: Reading the Signs of Nature 245
Trip #46: Livermore Road 247
Trip #47: Flat Mountain Pond 250
Federally Designated Wilderness 255
Trip #48: Province Pond 257
Trip #49: Beebe River Road 260
Trip #50: Tunnel Brook 263
Biking on Ski Trails .268

6. Quietwater Paddling 270
Safety and Etiquette 270
Paddling Times and Distances 273
Trip #51: Upper Kimball Pond 274
Trip #52: Mountain Pond 276
Amphibious Exploration 278
Trip #53: Chocorua Lake 281
Trip #54: Conway Lake 283
The Common Loon: Symbol of Wilderness 286
Trip #55: Long Pond 289
Trip #56: Lake Tarleton 291

7. Whitewater Paddling 294
Safety 295
Etiquette and the Environment 298
Local Paddling Groups 298
Trip #57: Pemigewasset River—
Woodstock to Thornton 300
The Pemigewasset: A River Restored 303

Trip #58: Pemigewasset River—
Woodstock Whitewater 305
Trip #59: Ammonoosuc River—
Littleton to Lisbon 309
Cold and Fastwater: Trout and Salmon Habitat . . .313
Trip #60: Androscoggin River—
Northern Forest Adventure 315
The Northern Forest 318
Trip #61: Saco River—
North Conway to Conway 319

8. Other Activities 323

Appendix A: Recommended Reading 328
Appendix B: Environmental Organizations 330
Appendix C: Lodging 331
Appendix D: Outfitters 346
About the Authors 352
About the Appalachian Mountain Club 353
Leave No Trace 354

introduction

NEW HAMPSHIRE'S WHITE MOUNTAINS are a special place for us. It is where we first learned to hike after moving to New England from the very flat land around Chicago. A visit to Zealand Falls was soon followed by our first foray above treeline on Mount Jefferson. We were in awe that a place so beautiful was so close to our new home. The vastness of the Pemigewasset Wilderness Area and the drama of the glacial cirques of the northern Presidentials got us hooked on exploring the White Mountains as often as possible, and now these places feel like familiar stomping grounds, though no less awesome than during those first visits.

"The Whites" are well known for their spectacular scenery and rugged topography. More than 7 million people a year visit the region—that's more people than those who visit such well-known national parks as Yosemite and Grand Canyon. The most popular activities include ascending Mount Washington by foot, car, or cog railway, paddling the gentle waters of the Saco River, fishing for trout below the Old Man of the Mountain in Franconia Notch, and, yes, shopping the outlet malls of North Conway. However, this book celebrates the fact that the White Mountains have a lot more to offer than the usual tourist destinations. Exploring a place in different ways lets you see things from different perspectives, which is why we encourage you to discover the region on your bike, in a boat, and on your own two feet. Along the way, you might find tiny plants that live nowhere else in the world, giant moose that make your heart race, and waterfalls that soothe your soul.

acknowledgments

MANY PEOPLE PROVIDED substantial input in support of this book. Mark Russell, our former editor at the Appalachian Mountain Club, signed us up for this project and played an important role in developing the ideas that resulted in *Discover the White Mountains of New Hampshire*. Beth Krusi took over for Mark and, along with Ellen Gibson-Kennedy and Belinda Desher, has been invaluable in seeing this book to completion. Other AMC'ers that helped out were Tim Levesque, the AMC White Mountain Trails Supervisor, and several members of the AMC New Hampshire Paddlers, especially Tom Todd, Mike Jacobs, Dennis Belliveau, Bill Lowman, and Bruce Healy. We would especially like to thank Prijon Kayaks and John and Mitchell at Canoe King in Ossipee.

We would like to thank Steve Smith of the Mountain Wanderer bookstore, Peter Minnich at Red Jersey Cyclery, and Dan Gardoqui of White Pine Programs. Our friend Ned Therrien was gracious enough to share his extensive knowledge of the United States Forest Service, and Forest Service personnel proved to be invaluable resources, especially Eric Swett, Karl Roenke, and Steve Fay.

We also want to say thank you to all of our friends who helped us explore the White Mountains, because it was always more fun to be sharing the experience: Tom, Jane, and Eddie Ferrini, Liz Fowler, Lee Fairbanks (hope the ankle's better), John and Sarah Muller, Mike Herlihy, Jay Hoyt, Tim Clairmont (hope the stitches healed), Mark Russell and Ola Frank, and Darren Almeida and Sara.

Of course, none of this would have happened without the loving support of our families.

locator map

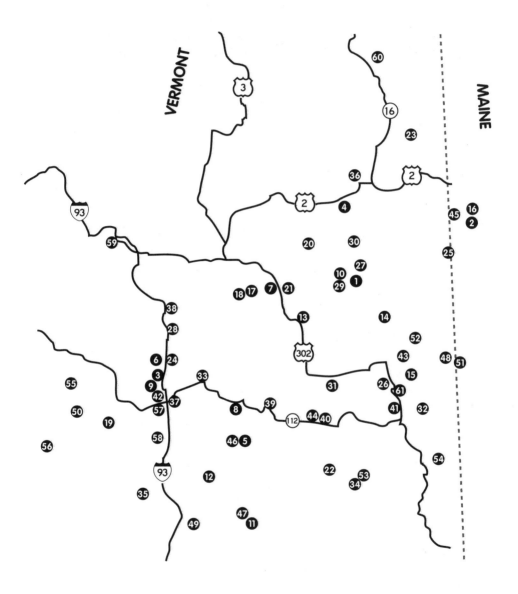

Trips

1. Square Ledge in Pinkham Notch
2. The Roost
3. Cascade Brook and the Basin
4. Stairs, Coosauk, and Hitchcock Falls
5. Cascade Path
6. Lonesome Lake
7. Mount Willard
8. Greeley Ponds
9. Mount Pemigewasset
10. Lowe's Bald Spot
11. Mount Israel
12. Welch and Dickey Mountains
13. Mount Crawford
14. Wildcat River
15. Kearsarge North
16. Caribou Mountain
17. Thoreau Falls
18. Zealand Falls and Zeacliff
19. Mount Moosilauke
20. Mount Jefferson via Caps Ridge
21. Mount Webster and Mount Jackson
22. Mount Chocorua
23. Mahoosucs Adventure: Goose Eye and Mount Carlo
24. Mount Liberty
25. North and South Baldface
26. North Moat and Red Ridge
27. Mount Hight and Carter Dome
28. Franconia Ridge
29. Mount Washington via Boott Spur
30. Hut to Hut Presidential Traverse
31. Bartlett Experimental Forest
32. Conway Recreation Trail
33. Lincoln Woods
34. Chocorua–Tamworth Loop
35. Ellsworth Pond Loop
36. Moose Brook State Park
37. West Side of Loon Mountain
38. Franconia Notch Bicycle Path
39. Sawyer River
40. Lower Nanamocomuck Ski Trail
41. Mineral Site and Moat Mountain
42. Bog Brook Eddy
43. Slippery Brook Road
44. Rob Brook Road
45. Wild River
46. Livermore Road
47. Flat Mountain Pond
48. Province Pond
49. Beebe River Road
50. Tunnel Brook
51. Upper Kimball Pond
52. Mountain Pond
53. Chocorua Lake
54. Conway Lake
55. Long Pond
56. Lake Tarleton
57. Pemigewasset River—Woodstock to Thornton
58. Pemigewasset River—Woodstock Whitewater
59. Ammonoosuc River—Littleton to Lisbon
60. Androscoggin River—Northern Forest Adventure
61. Saco River—North Conway to Conway

LEGEND

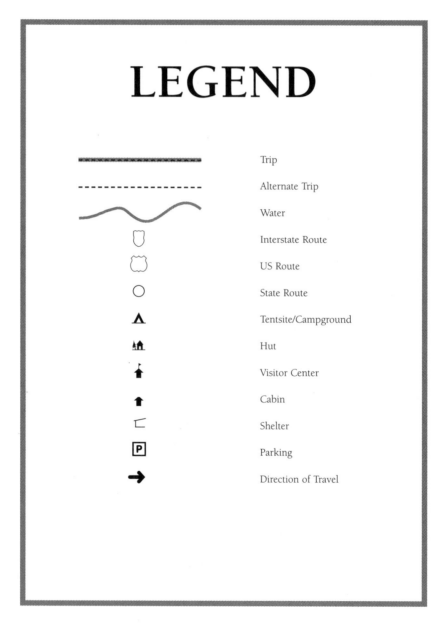

▪▪▪▪▪▪▪▪▪▪▪▪▪▪	Trip
- - - - - - - - - -	Alternate Trip
～～～	Water
⛉	Interstate Route
⬭	US Route
○	State Route
▲	Tentsite/Campground
⛪	Hut
⛿	Visitor Center
⬆	Cabin
⊏	Shelter
🅿	Parking
➜	Direction of Travel

1

White Mountain National Forest
basic information

THE WHITE MOUNTAINS have been drawing tourists to their lofty heights since the mid-1800s, when most visitors made the trip from cities to the south by train or horse-drawn carriage to spend a month or more taking in the fresh air and sublime views. Today's visitors might spend only the weekend or a couple of weeks, but they are still enticed by the incredible scenery provided by the highest peaks in the Northeast, which culminate in the summit of Mount Washington at 6,288 feet. Hiking is the traditional and most popular outdoor sport in the area, and, with more than 1,200 miles of trail to choose from, hikers can visit the mountains again and again without hiking the same stretch of trail twice. Of course, the beauty of places like the above-treeline world of Franconia Ridge or the Presidential Range ensures that most hikers will visit those places over and over again. While there are few water-based miles of recreation in the Whites, it is still a great place to enjoy a quiet paddle in a mountain setting or the adrenaline rush of whitewater. And with the relatively recent addition of knobby tires and shock-absorbing suspension to bicycles, mountain biking has become a new and exciting way to enjoy both the frontcountry and portions of the backcountry in the White Mountains.

Chapters 4 through 7 give detailed descriptions of hiking, biking, and paddling trips, from one-hour excursions to all-day adventures, while Chapter 8 provides information for participating in other activities. The rest of this introductory chapter provides some basic information you can use to get started on your visit to the White Mountains.

Climate

The White Mountains are notorious for their bouts of bad weather anytime of the year, with storms seeming to come out of nowhere. Despite this reputation, the weather in the area is generally like that of the rest of northern New England. The winters are long and cold, with daytime highs in the twenties and thirties and lows in the tens and below. The average winter snowfall is around 100 inches. Springs are usually wet and muddy, with daytime highs in the forties and fifties and lows in the twenties and thirties. Summers are warm with afternoon thunderstorms fairly common, particularly at higher elevations. Average highs are in the seventies and eighties with lows in the fifties and sixties. Fall is cool with occasional heavy rains. Highs are in the fifties and sixties and lows are in the thirties and forties. These averages, however, are only for the valleys. As you gain elevation in the mountains, the temperature can drop dramatically (often by 30 degrees), the winds can get very strong, and rain, sleet, or snow can fall even on a day when it is sunny in the valleys. Current weather forecasts can be obtained by calling the AMC weather line at 603-466-2721 (option 4) or the National Weather Service at 603-225-5191.

Getting There

The White Mountains are readily accessible by car, with the major access routes being I-93, NH 16, US 2, and US 302. Several airlines service the airports in Manchester, New Hampshire, and Portland, Maine, both of which are approximately a 90-minute drive from the mountains. Bus service to several locations in the White Mountains is provided by Concord Trailways. For a schedule, call 800-639-3317 or visit their website at www.concordtrailways.com.

Once in the Whites, you can take advantage of the AMC Hiker Shuttle, which provides transportation between various AMC facilities and trailheads for a flat fee. The shuttle runs only in the summer, but it is a great way to plan one-way trips without the need to spot a car. For a current schedule or to make reservations, contact the AMC at 603-466-2727 or visit the AMC website, www.outdoors.org.

Lodging

Literally hundreds of choices for lodging exist in and around the White Mountains. They range from basic campgrounds to very expensive, luxurious hotels and inns. The appendix to this book has a campground listing as well as resources for finding other accommodations.

U.S. Forest Service Information

To request information about the White Mountains before your trip, you can contact the U.S. Forest Service at: White Mountain National Forest, P.O. Box 638, Laconia, NH 03247; 603-528-8721; TTY 603-528-8722; www.fs.fed.us/r9/white/. Once in the Whites, you can visit one of five regional ranger stations:

Ammonoosuc Ranger Station, located 1.0 mile from the intersection of US 3 and US 302 on Trudeau Road in Bethlehem, New Hampshire

Androscoggin Ranger Station, located 0.5 mile south of US 2 on NH 16 in Gorham, New Hampshire

Evans Notch Ranger Station, located on US 2 and Bridge Street in Bethel, Maine

Pemigewasset Ranger Station, located on NH 175 in Plymouth, New Hampshire—take Exit 25 on I-93

Saco Ranger Station, located on NH 112 (Kancamagus Highway), just west of NH 16

A U.S. Forest Service information center is also located in Lincoln, New Hampshire, on NH 112, just off of Exit 32 on I-93. In addition to these Forest Service offices, the AMC Pinkham Notch Visitor Center is an excellent source of visitor information. It is located on NH 16 about 20.0 miles north of Conway and 11.0 miles south of Gorham.

Fees

Recently, the Forest Service has instituted a parking pass program, which requires cars parked at trailheads and along most roads in the national forest to display a White Mountain National Forest parking pass. In 2001, annual passes for $20 and one-week passes for $5 are available at Forest Service offices, Pinkham Notch Visitor Center, and selected outfitters. Self-serve pay stations are located at many parking areas, where you can pay a one-day, $3 fee to park. Ninety-five percent of parking fees go back to the White Mountain National Forest for recreation services and facilities repairs. National forest campground fees range from $12 to $16 per site per night depending on the facilities. Some backcountry sites also have fees, which are usually under $10. State campground fees usually range from $15 to $20 per night.

Universal Access

The Forest Service and State of New Hampshire campgrounds with universally accessible facilities are listed in the appendix. The Forest Service is constantly adding accessible facilities, and they can mail you a list of these facilities as well as a list of suggested wheelchair-friendly hikes. Just call the Forest Service headquarters at 603-528-8721, TTY 603-528-8722. One great option for visitors with disabilities is the Franconia Notch Bicycle Path, a paved path that is accessible from most of the parking areas along the Franconia Notch Parkway—see trip #38.

Emergencies

In an emergency situation, you should call 911, as New Hampshire has recently implemented a statewide 911 system. Backcountry accidents and search and rescue situations can also be reported to the New Hampshire State Police at 800-852-3411, the U.S. Forest Service at 603-528-8721, or the AMC at Pinkham Notch at 603-466-2727.

Choosing Your Trip

The 61 hiking, biking, and paddling trips in this book provide a variety of outdoor experiences. Before heading out on the trail or on the water, you should decide what the focus of your trip is (play-boating, mountain views, wildlife watching, etc.). You should also decide how strenuous a trip you and your group are willing and able to complete. The trip highlights charts following this introduction have an easy to follow listing of all the trips, including their difficulty, length, and trip highlights. Once you have narrowed down your choices, read the detailed trip descriptions in the individual hiking, biking, and paddling chapters to get a better idea of what the trip entails and what you might encounter.

Hunting Season

Hunting is allowed in the White Mountain National Forest. Hunting accidents are rare in New Hampshire, but everyone in your group, including dogs, should wear at least one piece of blaze-orange clothing during hunting season, particularly during November when deer hunters are allowed to hunt with rifles. Hunting seasons are set by the New Hampshire Fish and Game Department and are posted on their website: www.wildlife.state.nh.us. In general, the various hunting seasons are as follows:

- Deer: archery—middle of September through middle of December; muzzle-loader—end of October through first week of November; regular firearms (shotguns and rifles)—early November through early December

- Black bear: early September through early December

- Moose: nine days, starting on the third Saturday in October

- Turkey: archery—middle of September through middle of December; Archery and shotgun—May

- Birds and small mammals: usually early October through December

Logging

The White Mountain National Forest is managed for multiple uses, including timber harvesting. While you will most likely never encounter a logging operation while hiking or paddling, many of the bike trips in this book use active logging roads. While traveling these roads, be prepared to move aside for logging vehicles. Logging has been around for more than 150 years in the White Mountains, and the White Mountain National Forest sees a relatively low amount of harvesting compared to other national forests.

Don't Drink the Water

While the water in many White Mountain streams is probably safe to drink, there is no way to tell a safe water source from a contaminated one. Even water bubbling up from a spring can contain bacteria, viruses, or protozoa that can cause illness. If you are just out for the day, the easiest thing to do is bring enough water with you. If you are camping or prefer to fill up on an "as needed" basis, use one of the following procedures for purifying your water:

- Boiling—boiling water for one to three minutes is a surefire way of killing any diseases that may be in the water. The down side is having to set up a stove and then wait for the water to boil and cool down before drinking.

- Filtering—using a portable water filter is a convenient way to get potable water. There are several different kinds of filters— some use glass, carbon, or ceramic elements to strain the nasties out of the water. These filters do not rid the water of viruses which are rare in the American backcountry but do take care of bacteria and protozoa and are fine for the White Mountains—just make sure the filter element has a pore size of 0.2 microns or smaller. If you want extra protection, buy a filter that also passes the water through a layer of iodine, which will kill viruses.

- Chemical Treatments—dropping a few tablets of a chemical purifier into your water such as Potable Aqua or Polar Pure is a simple, lightweight water purification solution. The down side is that your water will have an unpleasant iodine taste. This can be somewhat covered up with powdered drinks like Gatorade or Tang. Be sure to add your powdered drink *after* the chemical purifier has had sufficient time to work—usually thirty minutes to two hours. Also, chemical treatments cannot kill *cryptosporidium*, a protozoan which can cause flulike symptoms, including diarrhea and severe bloating. We carry Potable Aqua in our first-aid kit for emergency purposes on day hikes when we don't want to carry the extra weight of a filter.

Backcountry Camping

The trips in this book are all day trips, but several trips pass by backcountry campsites or shelters that are good places to spend a night in the woods, away from the crowds. The appendix lists all of the official backcountry sites in the White Mountain National Forest. Camping is also allowed anywhere in the forest, with the following exceptions:

- No camping or wood or charcoal fires are allowed within 0.25 mile of any hut, shelter, cabin, picnic area, campground, or trailhead. This rule is also in effect near most roads in the national forest, as well as near popular waterfalls and ponds.

- The 0.25-mile restriction is reduced to 200 feet in designated wilderness areas and in posted Forest Protection Areas along popular trails, as well as a few other locations. Before a backcountry trip, you should confirm the location of Forest Protection Areas with a ranger station or by visiting the Forest

Service website at www.fs.fed.us/r9/white/recreation/land_
above/backcountry_rules.html.

- Camping and hiking group size is limited to ten people in designated wilderness areas.

- No camping or wood or charcoal fires are allowed within the Bartlett Experimental Forest, Mount Chocorua Scenic Area, Greeley Ponds Scenic Area, or the islands in Long Pond.

- No wood or charcoal fires are allowed in the Great Gulf Wilderness Area, and no camping is allowed between the intersection of the Great Gulf and Sphynx Trails and Spaulding Lake.

- No camping in Tuckerman or Huntington Ravines (above or below treeline) except at the Harvard Mountain Club Cabin (December 1–March 31 only) and Hermit Lake Shelters (no dogs allowed overnight). No wood or charcoal fires are allowed at any location in either ravine.

- Camping is allowed in the alpine zone (where trees are less than eight feet tall) *only* on two or more feet of snow and not on frozen bodies of water. No wood or charcoal fires are allowed above treeline.

Protect the Resource!

The White Mountains are one of the most visited natural areas in the United States. With 7 million visitors entering the national forest every year, it sees more use than national parks such as Yellowstone or Yosemite. With that many people enjoying the White Mountains' limited resources, it is imperative that everyone learn and adhere to Leave No Trace principles. These principles were developed and are updated regularly by Leave No Trace in order to promote and inspire responsible outdoor recreation. How we use the forest now determines what the forest will be like in the future. Whether you are hiking, biking, or paddling, follow these principles:

Plan ahead and prepare

When going into the backcountry, plan a trip that you know everyone in your group can finish. Be prepared for unexpected events by having extra food, water, and clothing. A well-planned day will prevent the need for an unnecessary night out in the woods, where you may be forced to build fires and trample delicate vegetation. Keep your group size to ten or less, splitting into smaller groups if necessary (this is required in designated wilderness areas). Try to avoid travel in wet and muddy conditions, and use extra care when in the delicate alpine zone. Planning ahead also means confirming that you are traveling and/or camping in an area where it is legal to do so.

Camp and travel on durable surfaces

When hiking, try to stay on trails and rocks. Stay in the center of the trail, even when it is wet and muddy. Use your boots! Trails are hardened sites where use should be concentrated. Avoid contributing to the widening and braiding of trails. Hiking off-trail into pristine areas is allowed, but requires greater understanding and effort and is especially discouraged above treeline. First, consider if hiking off-trail is necessary. If you decide to hike off-trail use durable surfaces such as rock, gravel, or grasses. Spread your group out, take different routes, and avoid places where unofficial "social" trails are just beginning to show. While mountain biking, always stay on the trail. Camping in the backcountry should be at designated sites, sites which have already been impacted, or 200 feet from trails and water sources. Avoid moderately impacted sites where your visit could create more damage.

Dispose of waste properly

Pack out *all* that you bring in. This includes any and all food you may drop while eating. Urinate at least 200 yards from any water source and pack out your used toilet paper. To dispose of solid human waste in the backcountry, dig an individual "cathole" at least 200 yards from a trail or water source. Organic topsoil is preferable to sandy mineral soil. Dig a hole four to eight inches deep and about six inches in diameter. After use, mix some soil into the cathole with a stick and cover with the remainder of the soil. Disguise the hole by covering it with leaves or other brush. Pack out your toilet paper in an odor-proof bag. It is especially important not to pollute near any watercourse, as it probably leads to a campground or town water source.

Leave what you find

Leave all natural and historical items as you find them. There is much human history in and around the White Mountains that should be left for future visitors to enjoy. Eating a few blueberries on a hike or adding a wild mushroom to a camp dinner is OK, but it is illegal to harvest any forest product for commercial purposes without a permit from the Forest Service. Before picking any wild edibles, consider the number of other people who might be using the area and decide if you will be negatively impacting an important food source for wildlife.

Minimize campfire impacts

Use a lightweight, backpacking stove when in the backcountry. Try to build campfires only in designated fire pits in campgrounds and picnic areas.

Respect wildlife

Remain quiet while in the backcountry, and give animals enough space so that they feel secure. While watching wildlife, if you notice them changing their behavior, it is most likely because you are too close. In that case, back off and give the animals space. Avoid nesting or calving sites and *never* attempt to feed any wildlife, even those cute little red squirrels. For low-impact wildlife-watching tips, visit Watchable Wildlife's website, www.watchablewildlife.org.

Be considerate of other visitors

Stay quiet. Refrain from using cell phones and radios. When hiking, take rests on the side of the trail so that other hikers do not have to walk around you. When on the water, remember that sound carries a long, long way. Dogs are allowed on all trails in the national forest, but they must be under control, either verbally or on a leash. Leashes are required in campgrounds.

You can learn more about the Leave No Trace program by visiting their website, www.lnt.org, or by writing them at Leave No Trace, P.O. Box 997, Boulder, CO 80306. A good book for learning more about ethics in the backcountry is *Backwoods Ethics: Environmental Issues for Hikers and Campers* by Laura and Guy Waterman, published by Countryman Press.

2
history

WHILE EXPLORING THE WHITE MOUNTAINS, you will see the clues that tell us the region is constantly changing. In some places, the forest canopy has been destroyed by recent storms, creating a brighter forest where a new generation of trees will grow. Old cellar holes and stone walls are spread throughout what is now wilderness, marking the locations of former farms and logging towns. Glacial cirques like Tuckerman Ravine and U-shaped valleys like Crawford Notch are reminders that the White Mountains were covered in ice 18,000 years ago. Sharp-eyed visitors might even notice sedimentary rocks that indicate the entire region was under an inland sea 500 million years ago. While we include pieces of history throughout this book, the following chapter serves as a brief summary of the forces, both natural and human, that have shaped the White Mountains as they are today.

Geological History

Five-hundred million years ago, all of New Hampshire lay under a vast ancient ocean known as the proto-Atlantic. The North American continent ended around the present day eastern border of Vermont.

Over millions of years, sedimentary rock formed at the bottom of this ancient ocean. Between 500 million and 300 million years ago, multiple mountain-building events took place as the European and African continents merged with the North American continental plate. First, what is known as the Taconian event created an ancient mountain range. As ancient Europe moved across the Atlantic, it pushed a volcanic chain of islands, much like Japan and the Philippines, into the North American continent. The pressures of this collision transformed sedimentary rocks like sandstone, shale, and limestone into much harder metamorphic rocks like quartzite, schist, gneiss, and marble. By the end of this collision, around 435 million years ago, new mountains stood in Vermont and far western New Hampshire; however, the rest of what would become the White Mountains still lay at the bottom of the ocean.

Much of the mountains built during the Taconian event eroded away into the proto-Atlantic, creating new layers of sedimentary rock over what would become the rest of New Hampshire. Between 335 and 375 million years ago, the European and African plates eventually collided with North America in what is known as the Acadian mountain-building cycle or Acadian Orogeny. This event created a mountain range where the White Mountains now stand. Again, sedimentary rocks were metamorphosed into much harder rocks, the most resistant of which is still visible today and is known as Littleton schist. The Presidential Range consists of Littleton schist, which was much more resistant to erosion than other rocks. According to this picture of history, New Hampshire and the White Mountains were once part of Africa or Europe.

The mountain building did not end with the Acadian Orogeny, however. As the continents once again separated to re-form the Atlantic Ocean about 200 million years ago, the earth's crust was stretched and fractured, allowing magma to bubble up from deep within the earth. This is when most of New Hampshire's granite was formed in underground magma plutons and above ground in volcanic lava flows. The most common rocks from this era include Moat volcanics (still seen on Moat Mountain), Conway granite, Mount Osceola granite (most of Mount Chocorua), and Winnepesaukee granite. The Moat volcanics once covered most of the White Mountains in more than 9,000 feet of rock, but it has mostly eroded away. Conway granite is now the most common granite in the area. It formed underground in a huge sea of lava, which as it hardened became what is now known as the White Mountain batholith. The granite of this batholith now forms the base of the White Mountains.

Millions of years of erosion have taken place since these mountain-building events, leaving behind a mountain range with a complex composition. Sedimentary rocks have completely disappeared from the New Hampshire landscape, leaving a mixture of igneous rocks, like granite and basalt, and metamorphic schists and gneisses. Since schists are the most durable of these rocks, they make up the tallest peaks, while granite is more common on lower peaks. Over the last 2 or 3 million years, much of the erosion in New England has occurred during periods of heavy glaciation. During this time frame, there have been several periods of glaciation, known as ice ages, where all of New Hampshire was covered in a layer of ice, sometimes more than a mile thick.

The last ice age, known as the Wisconsin glaciation, peaked around 18,000 years ago when a continental ice sheet reached as far south as Long Island. All of the White Mountains were completely covered with ice, and their smooth, rounded summits are a result of glacial scouring. Tongues of ice carved through weaker rocks to form the U-shaped valleys of Franconia Notch, Zealand Notch, and Crawford Notch. As the ice retreated, small remnant glaciers remained on the colder north and east facing slopes. These alpine glaciers eventually carved out several glacial cirques including Tuckerman Ravine and Madison Gulf. The ice sheet also left behind huge boulders that it carried for miles. One of these "glacial erratics" is Glen Boulder, which can be seen from NH 16 as you approach Pinkham Notch from the south.

The ice completely retreated from the White Mountains at some point between 12,000 and 14,000 years ago. For a while, the area resembled the high arctic, where only lichens and small tundra plants could survive. Remnants of this tundra community still exist in the White Mountains above treeline. As the climate slowly warmed, the composition of plant species began to change. Conifers like spruce and fir first grew in the recently thawed soil. Over time, hardwoods moved in: first birch and aspen, then beech, maple, and oak. About 3,000 years ago, the current make up of the forests was reached, with northern hardwood forests common at lower elevations and boreal forests dominant above 3,000 feet. Since that time, the landscape has continued to be shaped by wind, water, and people.

Human History

The White Mountains probably became suitable for human habitation around 12,000 years ago. There is very little evidence of early human habitation from this period. The only artifacts discovered to date are from seven sites, which date from about 8,000 to 10,000 years ago. At that time, the area was similar to the arctic in climate, and it is impossible to determine whether people lived year-round in the White Mountains or just passed through at certain times of year. Eventually, Native Americans settled in the more hospitable climes of river valleys like the Saco, Pemigewasset, and Ammonoosuc.

By the time Europeans arrived in the area, various bands of the Abenaki Indians lived in the White Mountains, cultivating corn to supplement a diet of wild game, fish, and native plants. The names of some of these Abenaki tribes and their chiefs are now names used for various places in the area—Penacook, Pequawket, Pemigewasset, Kancamagus, Passaconaway, and Chocorua. Although European settlers did not settle the White Mountains in great numbers until the late eighteenth century, most Abenakis died of diseases from early European contact. Most of the remaining Native Americans fled to Quebec in the early eighteenth century as a result of white persecution, the most notable of which was a massacre along the Baker River in 1712. Today the largest communities of Abenakis are in eastern Maine and Quebec.

The first recorded reference to the White Mountains is in notes made by the Italian explorer Giovanni da Verrazano, who sailed along the New England coast in 1524. In 1604, Samuel de Champlain also described what must have been the White Mountains, which he saw from Casco Bay on the Maine coast. The Whites appeared on early maps of the area as the White Hills or Crystal Hills until a 1677 map called them the White Mountains. They remained relatively unexplored through early colonial history due mostly to the hostilities between the English, the Native Americans, and the French. These hostilities culminated in King Philip's War in 1675, and the French and Indian Wars in the mid-1700s. The area was not considered safe to settle until the treaty signed at the end of the French and Indian Wars established the border between English and French land in 1763.

The earliest white settlements were in the valleys on the outskirts of the mountains—places like Lancaster, Tamworth, and Sandwich. The heart of the White Mountains, Crawford Notch, was settled by the legendary Crawford family in 1791 after a route through the notch was discovered by a hunter from Lancaster. The Crawford's homestead became a stopping point for travelers through the mountains, and the family became well-known as mountain guides. Abel Crawford and his son, Ethan Allen, built the first trail up Mount Washington in the 1820s. This trail, the Crawford Path, is considered the oldest continuously used footpath in the United States. By the 1840s, the Crawfords were guiding tourists to the summits of the Presidentials on horseback.

By 1851, when a passenger railroad to Gorham was completed, the White Mountains had become a popular tourist destination. Tourists from cities like Boston and New York visited the Whites for extended vacations—sometimes all summer—in order to breathe the purifying air and take in the "sublime" views. Mountain climbing was usually done on horseback, and there were only bridle trails on a few mountains, most notably Mount Washington, Mount Lafayette, Mount Moosilauke, Mount Moriah, Mount Kearsarge, and Mount Osceola. Those who lived in the area were mostly farmers, climbing mountains such as the Moats in order to pick berries. The wool industry was also a major contributor to the economy, although it peaked in the 1840s.

During the next 50 years, the Whites became one of the premier tourist destinations in the world. More than 200 hotels were built in the region, which eventually could accommodate up to 12,000 guests. Grand hotels, accommodating up to 400 guests each, provided visitors with luxurious amenities such as gas lighting and lawn tennis. These hotels also provided guided hiking services, and hiking trails began to proliferate. It was during this time that the AMC and other hiking clubs were formed, providing the impetus to develop a comprehensive system of trails. With the advent of the automobile, people began taking shorter vacations and these grand hotels fell out of favor. Most eventually burned to the ground. Two remain: The Mount Washington Hotel in Bretton Woods and The Balsams in Dixville Notch.

The railroads brought not only tourists to the area, but timber barons who saw the potential of the forest. In 1850 there were 376 miles of railroad in all of New Hampshire, and while the state as a whole was at its lowest percentage of forest coverage, most of the unsettled, rugged peaks of the White Mountains were still covered by virgin boreal and northern hardwood forests. In 1867, with hopes of jump-starting the post-Civil War economy, Governor Walter Harriman sold all of the state's land in the White Mountains to timber speculators for $27,000. By 1880 there were 1,200 miles of railroads in the state and the race to cut trees in the Whites was underway. It is ironic that the first wave of nature appreciation and tourism in the Whites coincided with the virtual destruction of most of the area's forest, but that is exactly what happened.

During the next 50 years, railroads were built into most of the remote valleys of the White Mountains and, except for a very few small pockets of old-growth, all of the forest was cut. Lumber barons such as George Van Dyke and J.E. Henry showed no mercy to the forest. Clearcutting was the method of choice though less accessible areas were "high-graded," removing only the largest, most valuable trees. In addition, large fires started primarily by the railroads and fueled by massive amounts of logging debris, consumed tens of thousands of acres of cutover and uncut land. By 1900 New Hampshire was the most intensively lumbered state in the country, with as much as 750 million board feet a year harvested. As a comparison, recent annual timber harvests across the state average 300 million board feet, with the White Mountain National Forest supplying about 8 percent of this total.

All this timber harvesting did create a boom in the economies of surrounding towns as saw mills and paper mills were established in large numbers. The populations of places like Berlin, Lincoln, and Conway grew considerably during the timber era. However, the unsustainable practices of the lumber barons caused the forest to be played out, and, while harvesting continues to this day, most of the logging railroads ceased operations by the end of World War I. The last railroad, which penetrated deep into what is now the Pemigewasset Wilderness Area and supplied timber to the mills in Lincoln, completed its last run in 1948. Today you can still find the railroad ties for this line if you hike or bike the Wilderness Trail (a.k.a. Lincoln Woods Trail) along the East Branch of the Pemigewasset River.

The clearcutting and extensive forest fires (over 200,000 acres burned in 1903 alone) of the late nineteenth and early twentieth centuries had a direct influence on the way forests are managed in the eastern U.S. today. In 1901, the Society for Protection of New Hampshire Forests (SPNHF) formed with the specific purpose of saving the White Mountains from further exploitation. A decade of lobbying by SPNHF and other groups, including the AMC, resulted in the passage of the Weeks Act in 1911. This law allowed the federal government to purchase private land east of the Mississippi for purposes of establishing national forests, and by 1912 more than 70,000 acres of New Hampshire had been set aside as the White Mountain National Forest.

Today the White Mountain National Forest consists of almost 800,000 acres of multiple-use forest. There are more than 1,200 miles of hiking trails, and millions of people visit the forest to hike, bike, paddle, fish, camp, and hunt. From high points above the forest, like Zeacliff or Mount Crawford, it is hard to believe that the surrounding forest was a virtual treeless wasteland less than 100 years ago. Today the mountains and notches are covered in thick forests of spruce and fir, or yellow birch, beech, and sugar maple. Bears and moose are common, and peregrine falcons nest on cliffs throughout the national forest. As you pass through these mountains, enjoy the fresh fir-scented air, the wildlife, and the incredible views. It can be a little overwhelming to think that the White Mountains have been 500 million years in the making, but that makes it easier to understand the need to leave them as we find them for future generations.

trip highlights chart

SPORT	TRIP #	TRIP	REGION	DIFFICULTY	DISTANCE
Walking		Wilderness Trail	Kancamagus	Easy	5.8 mi. up and back
Walking		Great Gulf Link Trail	Pinkham Notch	Easy	2.0 mi. up and back
Walking		The Flume	Franconia	Easy	2.0 mi. round-trip
Walking		Sabbaday Falls	Kancamagus	Easy	0.6 mi. up and back
Walking		Rocky Gorge & Falls Pond	Kancamagus	Easy	0.9 mi. round-trip
Walking		Ammonoosuc Lake	Crawford Notch	Easy	2.0 mi. round-trip
Walking		Lost Pond	Pinkham Notch	Easy	0.5 mi. up and back
Hiking	1	Square Ledge in Pinkham Notch	Pinkham Notch	Easy	1.0 mi. up and back
Hiking	2	The Roost	Evans Notch	Easy	1.8 mi. round-trip
Hiking	3	Cascade Brook & the Basin	Franconia	Easy	2.0 mi. up and back
Hiking	4	Stairs, Coosauk, & Hitchcock Falls	Northern Presidentials	Easy	2.0 mi. up and back
Hiking	5	Cascade Path	Waterville Valley	Easy	3.0 mi. round-trip

ELEVATION	ESTIMATED HIKING TIME	FEATURES	PAGE
Minimal	3.5 hrs.	A great walk in the woods next to the Pemigewasset River.	39
Minimal	1.5 hrs.	An easy hike along the Peabody River.	39
Minimal	1.5 hrs.	A popular walk over gravel trails and boardwalks to the Flume Gorge.	39
Minimal	45 min.	An easy hike with interpretive signs to the base of Sabbaday Falls.	39
Minimal	1 hr.	A gentle, scenic walk to an impressive gorge.	39
Minimal	1.5 hrs.	A nice walk to this scenic lake with a view of the Presidentials.	40
Minimal	1 hr.	An easy walk along the Ellis River to Lost Pond with great views of Huntington Ravine on Mount Washington.	40
500 ft.	45 min.	A great leg-stretcher from Pinkham Notch Visitor Center to excellent views of the notch and Mount Washington.	41
550 ft.	1 hr. 15 min.	A steep but short climb to excellent views of the Evans Notch area.	44
500 ft.	1.5 hrs.	An easy family hike in Franconia Notch to waterfalls and countless cascades.	47
650 ft.	2 hrs.	A great family hike in spring with wildflowers and waterfalls.	51
750 ft.	2 hrs.	An easy family hike to a series of waterfalls near Waterville Valley.	58

trip highlights chart

SPORT	TRIP #	TRIP	REGION	DIFFICULTY	DISTANCE
Hiking	6	Lonesome Lake	Franconia	Easy	3.2 mi. up and back
Hiking	7	Mount Willard	Crawford Notch	Easy	3.2 mi. up and back
Hiking	8	Greeley Ponds	Kancamagus	Easy	4.4 mi. up and back
Hiking	9	Mount Pemigewasset	Franconia	Easy	3.6 mi. up and back
Hiking	10	Lowe's Bald Spot	Pinkham Notch	Moderate	4.4 mi. up and back
Hiking	11	Mount Israel	Waterville Valley	Moderate	4.2 mi. up and back
Hiking	12	Welch & Dickey Mountains	Waterville Valley	Moderate	4.4 mi. round-trip
Hiking	13	Mount Crawford	Crawford Notch	Moderate	5.0 mi. up and back
Hiking	14	Wildcat River	Pinkham Notch	Moderate	6.5 mi. round-trip
Hiking	15	Kearsarge North	Conway	Moderate	6.2 mi. up and back

ELEVATION	ESTIMATED HIKING TIME	FEATURES	PAGE
950 ft.	2 hrs.	An easy family hike in Franconia Notch to a high mountain lake with views of Franconia Ridge.	61
900 ft.	2 hrs.	A popular hike to a spectacular view of Crawford Notch.	66
500 ft.	2.5 hrs.	A relatively flat hike to the Greeley Ponds Scenic Area.	69
1,150 ft.	2.75 hrs.	Great views for the effort. A good first hike for families interested in exploring White Mountain peaks.	72
900 ft.	2.75 hrs.	A short, moderate hike from Pinkham Notch to good views of Mounts Adams and Madison, and Wildcat Mountain. Good for kids with some hiking experience.	74
1,700 ft.	3 hrs.	A moderate hike to excellent views of the Sandwich Range and the Lakes Region.	77
1,800 ft.	3 hrs.	A moderate hike to relatively small peaks with big views.	80
2,100 ft.	4 hrs.	A moderate climb to unique views of the Presidential Range and the Presidential Range–Dry River Wilderness Area.	85
700 ft.	4 hrs.	A great half-day walk through the woods.	88
2,600 ft.	4.5 hrs.	Close to North Conway with 360-degree views, including an excellent look at Mount Washington.	92

trip highlights chart

SPORT	TRIP #	TRIP	REGION	DIFFICULTY	DISTANCE
Hiking	16	Caribou Mountain	Evans Notch	Moderate	7.0 mi. round-trip
Hiking	17	Thoreau Falls	Crawford Notch	Moderate	9.2 mi. up and back
Hiking	18	Zealand Falls & Zeacliff	Crawford Notch	Moderate	8.2 mi. up and back
Hiking	19	Mount Moosilauke	Franconia	Moderate	7.4 mi. up and back
Hiking	20	Mount Jefferson via Caps Ridge	Northern Presidentials	Strenuous	5.0 mi. round-trip
Hiking	21	Mount Webster & Mount Jackson	Crawford Notch	Strenuous	6.5 mi. round-trip
Hiking	22	Mount Chocorua	Conway	Strenuous	7.5 mi. round-trip
Hiking	23	Mahoosucs Adventure: Goose Eye & Mount Carlo	North Country	Strenuous	7.7 mi. round-trip
Hiking	24	Mount Liberty	Franconia	Strenuous	8.0 mi. up and back
Hiking	25	North & South Baldface	Evans Notch	Strenuous	9.7 mi. round-trip
Hiking	26	North Moat & Red Ridge	Conway	Strenuous	10.0 mi. round-trip

ELEVATION	ESTIMATED HIKING TIME	FEATURES	PAGE
1,900 ft.	4.5 hrs.	A hike through a mature northern hardwood forest to great views of the Caribou–Speckled Mountain Wilderness Area.	95
500 ft.	5 hrs.	A relatively flat hike through good wildlife habitat to mountain views and Thoreau Falls.	99
1,750 ft.	5.5 hrs.	A moderate day hike to wildlife-rich beaver ponds, Zealand Falls, and excellent views of the Pemigewasset Wilderness Area.	102
2,450 ft.	6 hrs.	Cascading streams lead the way to New Hampshire's westernmost alpine peak.	107
2,700 ft.	4.5 hrs.	A quick ascent to rocky ridges, alpine vegetation, and spectacular views of Mount Washington and the Northern Presidentials.	112
2,500 ft.	4.5 hrs.	A hike high above Crawford Notch with excellent views and a visit to the upper reaches of Silver Cascade.	116
2,600 ft.	6 hrs.	A scenic loop hike to one of the most photographed mountains in New England.	120
2,700 ft.	6 hrs.	A rugged hike to spectacular views in the wild and woolly Mahoosuc Range.	124
3,150 ft.	6 hrs.	A climb to excellent views on the bald summit of Mount Liberty.	131
3,600 ft.	7 hrs.	A spectacular day hike with more than 3.0 miles of hiking above treeline.	137
2,900 ft.	8 hrs.	Open ridge walking, great views, and close to North Conway.	141

trip highlights chart

SPORT	TRIP #	TRIP	REGION	DIFFICULTY	DISTANCE
Hiking	27	Mount Hight & Carter Dome	Pinkham Notch	Strenuous	10.2 mi. round-trip
Hiking	28	Franconia Ridge	Franconia	Strenuous	8.9 mi. round-trip
Hiking	29	Mount Washington via Boott Spur	Pinkham Notch	Very Strenuous	9.5 mi. round-trip
Hiking	30	Hut to Hut Presidential Traverse	Pinkham Notch to Crawford Notch	Very Strenuous	23.2 mi. one-way without summits; 25.5 mi. including all summits

SPORT	TRIP #	TRIP	REGION	AEROBIC LEVEL	TECHNICAL DIFFICULTY
Biking	31	Bartlett Experimental Forest	Crawford Notch	Easy	Easy to Moderate
Biking	32	Conway Recreation Trail	Conway	Easy	Easy
Biking	33	Lincoln Woods	Kancamagus	Easy	Easy except for crossing the Pemi
Biking	34	Chocorua–Tamworth Loop	Conway	Moderate	Easy
Biking	35	Ellsworth Pond Loop	Waterville Valley	Moderate	Moderate to Difficult

ELEVATION	ESTIMATED HIKING TIME	FEATURES	PAGE
3,600 ft.	8 hrs.	A strenuous all-day hike to Carter Dome and the spectacular views from Mount Hight.	144
4,000 ft.	8 hrs.	This spectacular loop over Mount Lafayette and Mount Lincoln includes the longest above-treeline hike in the White Mountains outside of the Presidential Range.	148
4,300 ft.	8 hrs.	A climb up New England's tallest peak, with plenty above-treeline hiking and awesome views.	156
6,500 ft. without summits; 9,600 ft. including all summits	3–4 days	Three days of spectacular views on the largest piece of alpine real estate in the eastern United States.	164

DISTANCE	ELEVATION	ESTIMATED BIKING TIME	FEATURES	PAGE
4.8 mi. round-trip	400 ft.	1 hr.	A smooth ride through beautiful forest followed by a fun and bumpy stretch of single-track.	183
6.0 mi. up and back	200 ft.	1.5 hrs.	An easy ride through tall pines next to the Saco River.	186
6.4 mi. round-trip	300 ft.	1.5 hrs.	An easy ride along the rushing waters of the Pemigewasset River.	189
11.4 mi. round-trip	600 ft.	1.5 hrs.	An easy ride on gravel roads through the tranquil forests of Tamworth.	195
6.4 mi. round-trip	400 ft.	1.5 hrs.	A bumpy ride past bogs and streams and through the wild forests on the southern slopes of Mount Kineo.	198

trip highlights chart

SPORT	TRIP #	TRIP	REGION	AEROBIC LEVEL	TECHNICAL DIFFICULTY
Biking	36	Moose Brook State Park	Northern Presidentials	Moderate	Moderate
Biking	37	West Side of Loon Mountain	Franconia	Moderate	Moderate
Biking	38	Franconia Notch Bicycle Path	Franconia	Moderate	Easy
Biking	39	Sawyer River	Kancamagus	Easy	Moderate
Biking	40	Lower Nanamocomuck Ski Trail	Kancamagus	Moderate	Moderate
Biking	41	Mineral Site & Moat Mountain	Conway	Moderate	Easy to Difficult (with easy alternative)
Biking	42	Bog Brook Eddy	Franconia	Moderate	Difficult
Biking	43	Slippery Brook Road	Conway	Strenuous	Moderate
Biking	44	Rob Brook Road	Kancamagus	Moderate	Moderate
Biking	45	Wild River	Evans Notch	Moderate	Moderate

DISTANCE	ELEVATION	ESTIMATED BIKING TIME	FEATURES	PAGE
4.0 mi. round-trip	600 ft.	1.75 hrs.	A climb through moose country with a fun downhill return.	202
5.0 mi. up and back	800 ft.	2 hrs.	Sometimes bumpy but with good views and a long, exhilarating downhill.	208
18.4 mi. up and back	600 ft.	2.5 hrs.	An easy ride on a paved bike path through Franconia Notch—one of the most scenic places in the White Mountains.	212
9.4 mi. round-trip	300 ft.	2–3 hrs.	A good mixture of single-track and gravel roads with excellent wildlife-watching opportunities.	216
8.4 mi. up and back	800 ft.	2.5 hrs.	One of the more scenic back-country rides in the White Mountains.	223
8.6 mi. round-trip	1,000 ft.	2–3 hours	A fast downhill run over rocky single-track, followed by miles of riding on quiet forest roads.	226
6.5 mi. up and back	1,000 ft.	2.5 hrs.	A somewhat technical ride to a high-elevation bog and good views of Franconia Ridge.	230
12.5 mi. up and back	1,000 ft.	2–3 hrs.	Excellent forest scenery combined with moderate elevation gain and 6.0 miles of downhill riding.	233
12.5 mi. round-trip; 15.8 mi. with optional single-track	200 ft.; 500 ft. with optional single-track	3–4 hrs.	Easy woods riding on a gravel road with the option for some adventurous single-track.	237
16.8 mi. up and back	800 ft.	3 hrs.	An easy ride on a dirt road next to the Wild River, followed by technical riding into the deep backcountry of the Wild River valley.	241

trip highlights chart

SPORT	TRIP #	TRIP	REGION	AEROBIC LEVEL	TECHNICAL DIFFICULTY
Biking	46	Livermore Road	Waterville Valley	Strenuous	Moderate
Biking	47	Flat Mountain Pond	Waterville Valley	Moderate	Difficult
Biking	48	Province Pond	Conway	Strenuous	All Levels of Difficulty
Biking	49	Beebe River Road	Waterville Valley	Moderate	Easy
Biking	50	Tunnel Brook	Franconia	Strenuous	All Levels of Difficulty

SPORT	TRIP #	TRIP	REGION
Quietwater Paddle	51	Upper Kimball Pond	Conway
Quietwater Paddle	52	Mountain Pond	Conway
Quietwater Paddle	53	Chocorua Lake	Conway
Quietwater Paddle	54	Conway Lake	Conway

DISTANCE	ELEVATION	ESTIMATED BIKING TIME	FEATURES	PAGE
10.0 mi. up and back	1,400 ft.	3 hrs.	A steady but scenic climb through a beautiful forest next to the rushing waters of Avalanche Brook.	247
16.4 mi. up and back	1,500 ft.	5 hrs.	A technical ride with good views along the edge of the Sandwich Range Wilderness Area.	250
13.7 mi. round-trip	1,600 ft.	4–5 hrs.	Exciting downhills, mountain views, and a visit to a remote pond make up for the long climbs on this challenging ride.	257
17.2 mi. up and back	1,100 ft.	5.5 hrs.	A long ride with plenty of opportunities for riverside photo and snack stops.	260
17.0 mi. round-trip	2,200 ft.	5 hrs.	A difficult but scenic ride through the rich wildlife habitat west of Mount Moosilauke.	263

DISTANCE	ESTIMATED PADDLING TIME	FEATURES	PAGE
3.4 mi. round-trip	2 hrs.	An easy paddle with good mountain views and excellent bird-watching opportunities.	274
1.7 mi. round-trip plus 0.3-mi. portage	1 hr.	A paddle on a remote pond with excellent views of the surrounding mountains.	276
3.3 mi. round-trip	2 hrs.	Loons, pines, and spectacular views of Mount Chocorua.	281
7.5 mi. round-trip	4 hrs.	Mountain views and miles of varied wildlife-filled shoreline.	283

trip highlights chart

SPORT	TRIP #	TRIP	REGION	
Quietwater Paddle	55	Long Pond	Western Whites	
Quietwater Paddle	56	Lake Tarleton	Western Whites	

SPORT	TRIP #	TRIP	REGION	DIFFICULTY
Whitewater Paddle	57	Pemigewasset River —Woodstock to Thornton	Franconia	Flatwater, Quickwater, Class I
Whitewater Paddle	58	Pemigewasset River —Woodstock Whitewater	Franconia	Class I, Class II, one short Class III section (easily portaged)
Whitewater Paddle	59	Ammonoosuc River —Littleton to Lisbon	Western Whites	Quickwater, Class I, Class II
Whitewater Paddle	60	Androscoggin River —Northern Forest Adventure	North Country	Class I, Class II+
Whitewater Paddle	61	Saco River —North Conway to Conway	Conway	Flatwater, Quickwater, Class I

DISTANCE	ESTIMATED PADDLING TIME	FEATURES	PAGE
2.5 mi. round-trip	1.5 hrs.	An easy paddle on one of New Hampshire's most scenic ponds.	289
3.5 mi. round-trip	2 hrs.	Views of Mount Moosilauke and a paddle along some of New Hampshire's recently protected undeveloped shoreline.	291

DISTANCE	ESTIMATED PADDLING TIME	FEATURES	PAGE
12.3 mi.	5 hrs.	A long, enjoyable paddle through the beautiful White Mountain countryside.	300
4 mi.	2.5 hrs.	An adventurous stretch of whitewater with good views of Franconia Ridge.	305
6.8 mi.; 9.7 mi. with alternate trip	3 hrs.	Relatively easy rapids are followed by good bird-watching opportunities.	309
2 mi.	1.5 hrs.	A short but exciting stretch of almost nonstop rapids in the Great North Woods region of New Hampshire.	315
8.5 mi.	4 hrs.	An easy paddle close to town, with great scenery.	319

4

hiking

HIKING IN NEW HAMPSHIRE'S White Mountains is one of the oldest outdoor sports activities in America. By the 1850s, tourists were flocking to the White Mountains to hike Mount Washington and other peaks. Those early visitors enjoyed the same rewards that today's hikers find: incredible views from the highest mountains in the northeast, lush forested valleys filled with wildlife, serene mountain ponds, and thunderous waterfalls. While hiking in the White Mountains, you can study alpine flora left over from the last ice age, watch an otter at play in a backcountry pond, and traverse a knife-edge ridge with 2,000 vertical feet between you and the valley floor. Hundreds of miles of hiking trails in the White Mountains allow for just about any kind of hiking experience, from a one- or two-hour hike to a waterfall or a several day exploration of the high ridges. We have suggested 30 hikes in this chapter that will take you to some of the most scenic spots in the White Mountains. If you have an insatiable appetite for White Mountain hiking, you should also pick up a copy of the *AMC White Mountain Guide*, which describes in detail over 500 trails in the White Mountains.

Hiking Times

Our hiking times are based on estimates in the *White Mountain Guide*, and our own experiences as average 30-something hikers carrying 15 to 30 pounds of gear. As a general guideline, the *White Mountain Guide* estimates thirty minutes for each 0.5 mile traveled and thirty minutes for every 1,000 feet of elevation gain traveled. Obviously, these times can vary based on the weather, physical fitness, and how much gear you stuff into your pack. While we think these times are useful for planning a trip, your hiking times will undoubtedly vary from ours, and you should always be prepared to spend a longer time outdoors than planned due to factors such as weather and fatigue.

Trip Ratings

Trip ratings vary in difficulty based on mileage, elevation gain, and trail conditions. *Easy* trips are suitable for families with kids; however, even hikes listed as easy may have short sections of significant climbing or rough footing—the White Mountains are a rugged place and easy is a relative term. *Moderate* hikes entail more mileage than easy hikes, usually between 5.0 and 10.0 miles, and can involve as much as 2,500 feet of elevation gain. The hikes in this chapter listed as moderate will challenge most hikers at some point along the way, but they can still be fun for older children who have experience hiking steep and rocky trails, and are willing to hike for more than a few hours. *Strenuous* trips usually take an entire day to complete due to the significant mileage and elevation gain involved, as well as the possibility for one or more scrambles over steep rock faces. Only hikers in good physical condition with some hiking experience should consider undertaking a strenuous trip. At the beginning of this chapter is a list of *Flat and Easy Walks* that are suitable for people of all abilities who are looking for a trip without elevation gain.

Safety and Etiquette

- Select a trip that is appropriate for everyone in the group. Match the hike to the abilities of the least capable person in the group.

- Plan to be back at the trailhead before dark. Determine a turn-around time and stick to it—even if you have not reached your goal for the day.

- Check the weather. Weather in the White Mountains is notoriously changeable and potentially dangerous. It is not uncommon to be hiking above treeline and suddenly experience conditions with visibility of only a few yards. Combine this with high winds and wet weather and you are suddenly in a life-threatening situation. Lightning is also a serious threat above treeline—take shelter if you hear thunder or see thunderstorms approaching. Rain and fog can make steep trails over rock ledges dangerous. We have needed our fleece, Gore-Tex, wool hats, and mittens during every month of the year in the White Mountains, so do not assume that a hike to the summit in July is going to be shorts and T-shirt weather. Know the weather forecast before you begin your hike, monitor the sky for changing weather, and be prepared to alter your route or end your hike early. For daily weather updates, you can call the AMC weather and trail information line at 603-466-2721 (option 4).

- Bring a pack with the following items:
    Water—two or more quarts per person depending on the weather and length of the trip (and water purification items for long trips)
    Food—Even for a short one-hour hike, it is a good idea to bring some high-energy snacks like nuts, dried fruit, or snack bars. Bring a lunch for longer trips.
    Map and compass—and know how to use them!
    Flashlight
    Extra clothing—rain gear, sweater, hat
    Sunscreen
    First-aid kit
    Pocketknife

Waterproof matches and a lighter
Binoculars for wildlife viewing (optional)

- Wear appropriate footwear and clothing. Wear wool or synthetic hiking socks and comfortable, waterproof hiking boots that give you good traction and ankle support. Bring rain gear even in sunny weather since unexpected rain, fog, and wind is possible at any time in the White Mountains. Avoid wearing cotton clothing, which absorbs sweat and rain, making for cold, damp hiking. Polypropylene, fleece, silk, and wool are all good materials for keeping moisture away from your body and keeping you warm in wet or cold conditions.

In addition to practicing the Leave No Trace techniques described in this book's introduction, it is also a good idea to keep the following things in mind while hiking:

- Try not to disturb other hikers. While you may often feel alone in the wilderness, wild yelling or cell phone usage will undoubtedly upset another person's quiet backcountry experience.

- When you are in front of the rest of your hiking group, wait at all trail junctions. This avoids confusion and keeps people in your group from getting lost or separated.

- If you see downed wood that appears to be purposely covering a trail, it probably means the trail is closed due to overuse or hazardous conditions.

- If a trail is muddy, walk through the mud or on rocks, never on tree roots or plants. Having waterproof boots will keep your feet comfortable, and by staying in the center of the trail you will keep the trail from eroding into a wide "hiking highway."

- If you decide to take an impromptu swim in a trailside stream or pond, be sure to wear sturdy sandals or old tennis shoes to protect your feet and give you traction on slippery surfaces. Also, wipe off sunscreen and bug spray to avoid polluting water that animals, plants, and other hikers depend on.

By taking the above precautions, you can spend your trip focusing on the pleasures of exploring the wilderness that exist in the White Mountains. Most of the hikes in this book will take you through multiple natural habitats, giving you the opportunity to see a variety of flora and fauna. You probably won't see something as exciting as a moose on every trip, but you will always be surrounded by the wonders of nature, whether it is the fresh tracks of an otter in the mud next to a stream, the junglelike sounds of the northern hardwood forest in the spring, or the delicate details of alpine azalea growing on the slopes of Mount Washington.

Flat and Easy Walks

WILDERNESS TRAIL. This 9.0-mile-long trail provides access to the heart of the Pemigewasset Wilderness Area. The first 2.9 miles (also called the Lincoln Woods Trail) are basically flat with good footing and parallel the East Branch of the Pemigewasset River. You can hike any amount of time along this trail for a nice "walk in the woods" experience. At the 2.9-mile mark the trail reaches the wilderness boundary and Franconia Brook. A rough side trail on the left leads to Franconia Falls (often very crowded and a day permit is now required to visit the falls). The Wilderness Trail begins at the Lincoln Woods parking area on NH 112, 4.1 miles east of I-93.

GREAT GULF LINK TRAIL. This 1.0-mile-long trail follows the Peabody River for much of its length. If an easy walk in the woods with some time spent sitting next to a mountain stream is what you crave, this is a good choice. The trail begins at the Dolly Copp Campground, north of the AMC Pinkham Notch Visitor Center on NH 16.

THE FLUME. This 2.0-mile loop hike is a major tourist destination in Franconia Notch; there may be crowds, but it is still a rewarding walk over gravel trails and boardwalks to the Flume—one of the more interesting gorges in the White Mountains. The trail also visits Avalanche Falls and the Pool, a circular formation in the Pemigewasset River that is 100 feet in diameter and 40 feet deep. Access to the Flume is at the Flume Gorge Visitor Center, off Exit 1 of the Franconia Notch Parkway (I-93), north of Lincoln. There is an admission fee.

SABBADAY FALLS. It is only 0.3 mile from the Kancamagus Highway (NH 112) to the base of Sabbaday Falls. Interpretive signs describe the geological processes that formed the small gorge, pools, and potholes found along the trail. The trailhead is located at a parking area on the south side of the road, about 15.0 miles west of the intersection of NH 112 and NH 16 in Conway.

ROCKY GORGE AND FALLS POND. This 0.9-mile loop over Rocky Gorge and around Falls Pond is relatively flat with very good footing. Rocky Gorge is a small but impressive gorge that squeezes the rushing waters of the Swift River through rock walls that are only 15 feet apart. The loop around Falls Pond (on the Lovequist Loop) is a scenic walk through hemlock, spruce, and hardwood forests. The parking area for this hike is on the north side of the Kancamagus Highway, 9.0 miles west of NH 16 in Conway.

AMMONOOSUC LAKE. Two miles of easy hiking take you to this scenic lake as well as views of the Presidentials. From the AMC Crawford Hostel in Crawford Notch, follow the Around-the-Lake Trail, which loops around the lake. At about 0.3 mile, you will reach a side trail to the Red Bench overlook. Follow this trail for twenty minutes to a red bench with views of Mount Washington. Return to the Around-the-Lake Trail to finish your walk.

LOST POND. This 0.5-mile trail starts across NH 16 from the AMC Pinkham Notch Visitor Center. It parallels the Ellis River and ends at Lost Pond, where you will have good views of Huntington Ravine on Mount Washington.

Square Ledge in Pinkham Notch

Rating: **Easy**

Distance: **1.0 mile up and back**

Elevation Gain: **500 feet**

Estimated Time: **45 minutes**

Maps: **AMC White Mountain Map #1, USGS Mount Washington and Carter Dome Quadrangles**

A great leg-stretcher from Pinkham Notch Visitor Center to excellent views of the notch and Mount Washington.

SQUARE LEDGE IS A ROCKY outcropping on the western side of Wildcat Mountain. Perched about 500 feet above NH 16 and the AMC Pinkham Notch Visitor Center, Square Ledge provides an excellent opportunity for visitors at Pinkham Notch to make a quick hike to close-up views of Mount Washington, which rises 4,200 feet above the floor of the notch only 3.0 miles away. While the hike is only 0.5 mile each way, 500 feet is gained in elevation, with the last 50 yards being surprisingly steep. Nonetheless, this is a good hike for families with kids who have experience hiking and are anxious to get out and explore the wilderness.

The hike begins on the Lost Pond Trail, across NH 16 from the visitor center. Just after crossing a beaver pond on a wooden bridge, turn left onto the Square Ledge Trail. In 0.1 mile you reach a side trail, which leads 50 yards to "Ladies' Lookout," an obstructed view of Mount Washington and the visitor center from just above the highway. Continuing on the Square Ledge Trail, you will discover that even short, relatively easy trails in the White Mountains can be rugged. Rocks and tree roots fill the pathway as you climb moderately up the side of Wildcat Mountain. About halfway to Square Ledge, you pass under the aptly named Hangover Rock. As you continue climbing at a moderate pace, you reach the base of Square Ledge at about 0.4 mile. From here the trail leads you steeply up through a narrow cleft in the mountain, which is filled with loose rocks and spindly birch and spruce.

As you emerge from the cleft, you are at the top of Square Ledge and rewarded with excellent views of Mount Washington, Tuckerman Ravine, and Pinkham Notch. Pinkham Notch, now home to the AMC White Mountain headquarters, was once a common walking route for college students in the 1860s and 1870s who walked from Massachusetts up through Pinkham Notch, returning via Crawford or Franconia Notch. If these students climbed any of the peaks, it was most likely Chocorua, Kearsarge, Washington, and the Southern Presidentials. They would usually travel in groups of twelve or more, with names such as "the Pemigewasset Perambulators," "the Oatmeal Crusaders," or simply "the Bummers." In some ways, this was a precursor to today's common quest of thru-hiking the Appalachian Trail.

Directions

This hike begins on the Lost Pond Trail directly across NH 16 from the AMC Pinkham Notch Visitor Center. The visitor center is on NH 16, about 12.0 miles north of US 302 in Glen and 11.0 miles south of US 2 in Gorham.

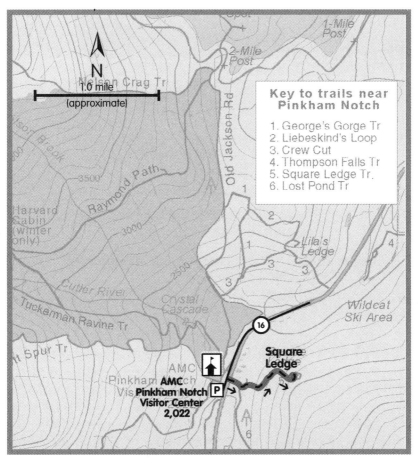

Key to trails near
Pinkham Notch

1. George's Gorge Tr
2. Liebeskind's Loop
3. Crew Cut
4. Thompson Falls Tr
5. Square Ledge Tr.
6. Lost Pond Tr

SQUARE LEDGE IN PINKHAM NOTCH

The Roost

Rating: **Easy**

Distance: **1.8 miles round–trip**

Elevation Gain: **550 feet**

Estimated Time: **1 hour 15 minutes**

Maps: **AMC White Mountain Map #5, USGS Speckled Mountain (Maine) Quadrangle**

A steep but short climb to excellent views of the Evans Notch area.

COMPARED TO THE REST of the White Mountains, Evans Notch is remote, out-of-the-way, and one of the less visited portions of the White Mountain National Forest. Straddling the Maine-New Hampshire border, the notch provides access to some excellent hiking, biking, and camping. This trip makes a short but steep climb to the Roost, a small peak at the northern end of the notch with great views to the south and west. The Roost sits high above the Wild River, a beautiful mountain stream that was once a major route for loggers 100 years ago. Today the forest along the Wild River and throughout Evans Notch has recovered well and seems as wild as it gets.

From the small parking area on the west side of ME 113 just north of Wild River Road, walk north on 113 over the bridge that crosses Evans Brook. The Roost Trail is across the street just after the bridge. The trail immediately climbs very steeply, although the footing is good and the climbing is not technically difficult. The ascent soon moderates as you climb gradually through a beautiful northern hardwood forest that includes northern red oaks and a few very large white pines. At 0.3 mile you cross a small brook and climb more steeply for the remaining 0.2 mile to the summit of the Roost, which is covered in a forest of mixed conifers.

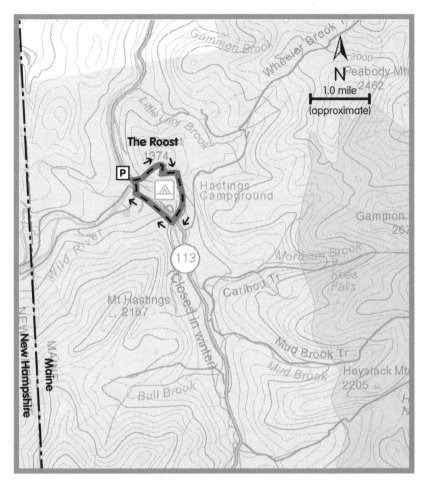

THE ROOST

There are no views from the summit, but a side trail leads down and to the right for about 150 yards to open ledges. These ledges have excellent views of Mount Moriah, North and South Baldface (see trip #25), Royce Mountain, and the Wild River (see trip #45). Blueberries, checkerberries, and fragrant white pines have found enough soil to grow in isolated pockets. The ledges are composed of metamorphic schist, and you can see where the rock was bent and folded by pressures deep within the earth's crust. Shiny mica and quartz crystals sparkle in the sun when not covered by gray, green, or black lichens. To continue this trip, hike back up to the summit of the Roost.

From the summit, follow the Roost Trail southeast (on your right as you face the trail sign). The trail descends this side of the Roost much more moderately than it climbed to the summit. The trail levels out as you reach Evans Brook, which is lined by dark green hemlock. Cross the brook and then turn right as the trail follows an old woods road. As the trail crosses another brook, look for an old cellar hole on the left. This area was once the town of Hastings, Maine, during the logging boom on the Wild River in the late 1800s. The town and the logging trains are long gone, with the building now being done by beaver. The trail can be very wet at times due to recent beaver activity, and you should be able to see trees that have been cut recently or gnawed on by these large rodents.

The Roost Trail ends on ME 113, which was built by the Civilian Conservation Corps in 1936. Turn right on ME 113 to complete your loop. The parking area is 0.6 mile on the left.

Directions

From the intersection of US 2 and ME 113 in Gilead, Maine, head south on ME 113. In 3.0 miles, park in the small parking area on the right just before Wild River Road.

Trip #3

Cascade Brook and the Basin

> Rating: **Easy**
>
> Distance: **2.0 miles up and back**
>
> Elevation Gain: **500 feet**
>
> Estimated Time: **1.5 hours**
>
> Maps: **AMC White Mountain Map #2, USGS Franconia and Lincoln Quadrangles**
>
> **An easy family hike in Franconia Notch to waterfalls and countless cascades.**

THIS HIKE IN FRANCONIA NOTCH is a great family hike, as it follows Cascade Brook for nearly 1.0 mile, visiting two waterfalls and numerous cascades along the way. Excellent views can also be seen from spots where the brook cuts a wide swath through the forest. The elevation gain is easy to tackle for enthusiastic kids who love exploring the mountains, although the footing can be rough at times due to exposed tree roots. The falls are most spectacular in the spring, but, in very high water, the crossing of the brook at Kinsman Falls can be too much for smaller children. Since both Lonesome Lake and Kinsman Pond feed Cascade Brook, it has plenty of water throughout most of the year. For a longer day hike, this trip can be combined with trip #6, the Lonesome Lake hike (see alternate description at the end of this trip).

From either the northbound or southbound parking area on the Franconia Notch Parkway, follow signs to the Basin, an impressive circular pool of water in the Pemigewasset River that was carved into the rock by thousands of years of rushing water. For this hike you will want to use the Basin-Cascade Trail, which starts at an intersection of trails just to the west of the Basin. At the trail junction follow the Basin-Cascade Trail toward Lonesome Lake. You will

Hobblebush decorate the shore along the Pemigewasset River.

stay on this trail for the entire hike. Almost immediately the trail begins to parallel Cascade Brook, which will be on your left. Water falls in beautiful cascades over smooth rock, and the ledges next to the water provide good views to the east. On a sunny day, you may find that you have no need to explore farther than the first 0.25 mile, but if you do, you will find ever more dramatic cascades, and ever fewer people.

A side trail soon leads left to the base of a wide, unnamed waterfall that is worth a look. The trail climbs moderately to the top of these falls, where there are more good views. The forest next to the brook varies; you will see hardwoods and conifers, as well as flowery shrubs like hobblebush and shadbush. The trail continues to climb moderately over a rough trail that can be slippery in wet weather due to exposed tree roots. You will pass a seemingly endless series of cascades, small waterfalls, calm pools, and even a small gorge on your way to the base of Kinsman Falls, where the trail crosses Cascade Brook about 0.5 mile from the Basin. This crossing can be difficult in high water. Try crossing yourself before letting small children forge ahead. Kinsman Falls is a series of ten-foot cascades where the water plunges from pool to pool before being forced through a small gorge for the final drop.

Continue hiking on the Basin-Cascade Trail for a moderate climb to Rocky Glen Falls at 0.9 mile. This is our favorite waterfall of the trip. At Rocky Glen Falls water tumbles over a series of falls through a narrow gorge of gray rock, which is topped by the cool green of balsam fir and red spruce. Viewing the falls from the bottom of the gorge is a refreshing experience, as the temperature can be much cooler than in the surrounding forest from the cold mountain water chilling the air. Continuing up the trail you get different views of the falls. This trip ends at the junction with Cascade Brook Trail. For one final look at the falls, follow the bank of the brook south from this trail junction for about 60 yards to the top of the falls. Be careful: it is a long, rocky ride down if you slip and fall. To return to the parking area, retrace your steps down the Basin-Cascade Trail.

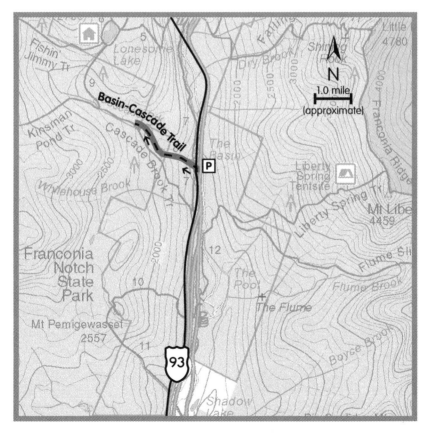

CASCADE BROOK AND THE BASIN

Alternate Trip

To combine this trip with the Lonesome Lake trip, turn right onto the Cascade Brook Trail when you reach the end of the Basin-Cascade Trail. From this point it is 1.3 miles and 650 feet of elevation gain to Lonesome Lake and the Fishin' Jimmy Trail. At the junction with the Fishin' Jimmy Trail, turn left to head to Lonesome Lake Hut, or turn right to follow the shore of the lake to the Lonesome Lake Trail, which will take you down to Lafayette Campground. From the campground, you can take either the Pemi Trail or the Franconia Notch Bicycle Path 1.9 miles back to the Basin parking area.

Directions

This hike begins from the exit marked "The Basin" on the Franconia Notch Parkway, just north of the Flume Gorge Visitor Center and about 6.0 miles north of NH 112 in Lincoln. Separate parking areas are on the northbound and southbound sides of the highway. Either parking area is OK.

Stairs, Coosauk, and Hitchcock Falls

Rating: **Easy**

Distance: **2.0 miles up and back**

Elevation Gain: **650 feet**

Estimated Time: **2 hours**

Maps: **AMC White Mountain Map #1, USGS Mount Washington Quadrangle**

A great family hike in spring with wildflowers and waterfalls.

THIS HIKE ON THE LOWER END of the Howker Ridge Trail visits three waterfalls along a mile of Bumpus Brook, a stream that begins on the upper slopes of Mount Madison. This is a great hike for families, particularly in May when the brook is running high and the wildflowers are in full bloom. Later in the summer the falls tend to be less impressive, particularly Stairs Fall that practically disappears, so wait for a heavy rain if you plan to do this hike long after the snow has melted. While the hike is rated easy, the elevation gain is 650 feet, so expect to breathe heavily once in a while. However, the trail surface is in good shape with good footing and moderate grades. Since there is a lot to explore along most of this hike, you can easily turn around when the kids get tired without feeling like you have missed much.

Leaving the south side of Pinkham B Road, the Howker Ridge Trail coincides with the Randolph Path for about 30 yards. Soon after crossing an abandoned railroad bed, turn left where the two trails diverge, continuing on the Howker Ridge Trail. The trail climbs gradually through a forest recovering from several years of

Coosauk Fall, Bumpus Brook

logging and soon crosses an old logging road. The Howker Ridge
Trail continues straight across the road and comes to the banks of
Bumpus Brook, about 0.4 mile from the parking area. Bumpus Brook
is named after the Bumpus family, some of the earliest settlers of this
area. With the brook on the left, the trail begins to climb moderately.
In high water, the cascades along this lower section of the brook are

worth visiting, even if you do not plan to continue to the falls higher up.

In spring, you will be surrounded by many of the wildflowers that are common in the lower forests of the White Mountains, finding yourself in a forest of green accented by red, white, yellow, and pink. These flowers include red and painted trilliums, wild lily-of-the-valley, trout lilies, clintonia, bellwort, wild oats, rose twisted stalk, and Indian cucumber. Keep your eyes and ears open for songbirds such as American redstart, Canada warblers, black-throated blue warblers, and hermit thrushes, which forage amongst the understory of striped maple and hobblebush. On a lucky day you might even spot a snowshoe hare or a moose.

You soon reach an outlook to Stairs Fall, which tumbles 15 feet over a natural rock staircase from a tributary on the opposite side of Bumpus Brook. In high water, the waterfall is about 10 feet wide and water splashes in all directions, but when the mountains dry out, it is a disappointing trickle. Just beyond Stairs Fall is the Devil's Kitchen, a beautiful, richly shaded gorge with 40-foot-high rock walls. Bumpus Brook runs through the center of the gorge, while hemlock trees lean over the gorge from the banks above. Keep an eye on small children while viewing the Devil's Kitchen from above, as the drop-off is sudden.

Next, you come to an outlook to Coosauk Fall, which like Stairs Fall drops into Bumpus Brook from a tributary on the opposite bank. Coosauk Fall may be the most picturesque of the three waterfalls on this trip. It falls about 40 feet in a delicate, thin stream, framed by hemlock and birch trees and surrounded by lush ferns. According to *The White Mountains: Names, Places, and Legends* by John T. B. Mudge, Coosauk Fall was named by William Peek, a summer resident of Randolph, New Hampshire, who mistakenly thought the Abenaki Indian word "coos" meant "rough." Coos is generally thought to mean "place of pines."

Continuing on toward Hitchcock Fall, the Howker Ridge Trail passes both the Sylvan Way and Kelton Trail. Continue straight at both intersections and climb moderately away from Bumpus Brook and through more wildflower habitat. The trail crosses a few small streams before returning to Bumpus Brook at the foot of Hitchcock Fall 1.0 mile from the parking area. Hitchcock Fall is a tall waterfall that plunges about 60 feet over large boulders. Tall cliffs protect the banks on both sides of the stream, making it somewhat difficult to explore the upper reaches of the falls; however, resting on the rocks at the base of the falls is a great way to spend a lunch break. The Howker Ridge Trail crosses the brook at this point on its way to the summit of Mount Madison (a very strenuous four-hour hike from here). This trip, however, ends at Hitchcock Fall.

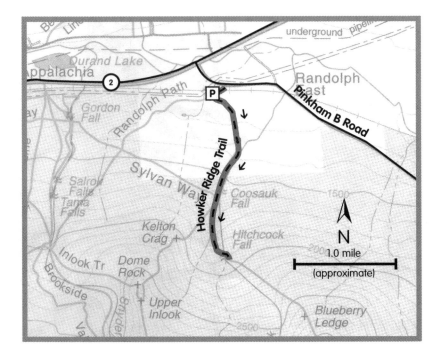

STAIRS, COOSAUK, AND HITCHCOCK FALLS

Directions

From the western intersection of NH 16 and US 2, head west on US 2 for 4.5 miles and turn left onto Pinkham B Road (also called Dolly Copp Road). The parking area for the Howker Ridge Trail is on the right in another 0.2 mile.

white mountain waterfalls

HUNDREDS OF WATERFALLS and cascades flow throughout the White Mountains. More than 100 of these are notable or visited enough to have been named. Other than the summits of the area's mountains, waterfalls are the most popular natural feature to be sought out by visitors to the Whites, and several of the hiking trips in this book visit waterfalls on the way to a summit or as a destination. The tallest waterfall in New Hampshire is Arethusa Falls, where the waters of Bemis Brook tumble almost 200 feet over a wall of reddish-brown granite. In the high water of spring, even the smallest of falls seems to possess incredible power as thousands of gallons of water pulse through narrow cracks in the bedrock or over ledges of broken and tilted granite. The following list is a small sample of some of the White Mountains' more notable waterfalls:

Falls visited by trips in this book:

- Kinsman and Rocky Glen Falls: These two falls are part of a 1.0-mile-long string of cascades and small gorges in Franconia Notch. See trip #3.

- Stairs, Coosauk, and Hitchcock Falls: Another nice set of cascades and small gorges, located on the lower slopes of Mount Madison. See trip #4.

- Waterville Cascades: Waterfalls and swimming holes for the whole family near Waterville Valley. See trip #5.

- Thoreau Falls: Remote falls in the Pemigewasset Wilderness Area. See trip #17.

- Zealand Falls: A popular spot next to an AMC hut with

Arethusa Falls, tallest waterfall in New Hampshire

excellent views of the Pemigewasset Wilderness Area. See trip #18.

- Silver Cascade and Flume Cascade: Two long ribbons of water that fall for hundreds of feet over a series of ledges in Crawford Notch. These impressive falls can be seen from the road, less than 1.0 mile south of

Crawford Depot. Trip #21 visits a 40-foot waterfall, which is part of Silver Cascade, high up the slopes of Mount Jackson.

- Diana's Baths: Small cascades fill numerous inviting swimming holes. See trip #26.

- Stairs, Swiftwater, and Cloudland Falls: An increasingly impressive series of waterfalls in Franconia Notch reached via the Falling Waters Trail. See trip #28.

- Crystal Cascade: A beautiful 80-foot cascade tucked away near Pinkham Notch on the Tuckerman Ravine Trail. See trip #29.

Other Notable Waterfalls:

- Arethusa Falls: The tallest waterfall in the White Mountains is a 1.3-mile hike in from Crawford Notch on the Arethusa Falls Trail. In spring, the roar of the water is impressive.

- Sabbaday Falls, Lower Falls, and Rocky Gorge: These waterfalls are all short, easy walks from parking areas along NH 112 (Kancamagus Highway).

- Glen Ellis Falls: A popular, easy to reach waterfall in Pinkham Notch, which is a short walk from NH 16.

- Bridal Veil Falls: This 80-foot drop in Coppermine Brook on Cannon Mountain is well worth the 2.5-mile hike (with 1,100 feet of elevation gain) on the Coppermine Trail.

If you get the desire to spend a summer or two visiting waterfalls, check out the excellent guidebook *Waterfalls of the White Mountains* by Bruce, Doreen, and Daniel Bolnick, published by Backcountry Publications.

Trip #5

Cascade Path

> Rating: **Easy**
>
> Distance: **3.0 miles round-trip**
>
> Elevation Gain: **750 feet**
>
> Estimated Time: **2 hours**
>
> Maps: **AMC White Mountain Map #3,**
> **USGS Mount Tripyramid Quadrangle**
>
> **An easy family hike to a series of waterfalls near Waterville Valley.**

THIS EASY HIKE close to Waterville Valley combines woodland hiking with waterfall exploration and views from the top of Snows Mountain. The area is filled with ski trails and walking paths, so you will need to pay attention to stay on the right trail. Detailed maps of the area can be purchased at the Jugtown Deli in Waterville Valley if you want to have an extra level of information. The highlight of the hike is the series of cascades and waterfalls along Cascade Brook, which is best visited in the spring when the water is high, although kids will find this hike interesting at any time of year. Spring is also a good time to catch the woods full of wildflowers.

To get to the Cascade Path, follow the ski trail at the northeast end of the parking lot up the grassy hill and into the woods, where the trail is a wide gravel road. Continue straight past the Lower Wishbone and Snows Mountain ski trails, as well as an unmarked trail on the left. Shortly after the unmarked trail, turn left onto the well-marked Cascade Path. The trail enters a forest of mostly small trees, which are growing in a recently logged area. The loggers did, however, leave a few large yellow birch, American beech, and sugar maple, and the trail soon enters a more mature forest. At 0.5 mile continue straight past the Elephant Rock Path

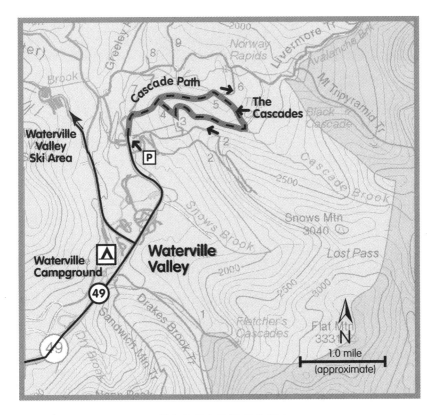

CASCADE PATH

(you will use the Elephant Rock Path on the return trip). The trail then begins a gradual descent toward Cascade Brook. The forest becomes more interesting as you will find trilliums, clintonia, bunchberry, and a variety of ferns like long beech fern, Massachusetts fern, and spinulose wood fern.

At about the 1.0-mile mark the trail crosses a small brook on a wooden bridge and then turns right to follow a wide ski trail. The climactic effects of Cascade Brook can be seen here as you enter a grove of moisture-loving hemlock trees. After traveling 100 yards on the ski trail, turn right to stay on the Cascade Path (left would take you over a wooden bridge and to Norway Rapids). You will now be walking with Cascade Brook on your left. Even here the brook is enchanting as it flows over small boulders through a forest of deep green. You soon reach the first waterfall: a dramatic 40-foot drop in a gorge of fractured rock ledge tilted at a 30-degree angle. The dark rock is covered by moss and surrounded by the deep green and brown of hemlock trees. At this point you can choose to hike on either side of the brook; although the right side seems to be the best traveled, either side provides excellent views of the upcoming waterfalls.

After the first waterfall the trail gets steeper and a little rougher. The Cascade Path ends at the Snows Mountain Ski Trail, 1.7 miles from the parking area. Along the way you will pass three more waterfalls and several smaller cascades, as well as several swimming pools (cold, cold, water). In a couple of spots the trail comes near some steep drop-offs, so you will want to keep an eye on small children. Once you reach the Snows Mountain Ski Trail, turn right and follow the ski trail through a beautiful beech and birch forest that is filled with moose tracks and sometimes signs of black bear. Wildflowers abound here during spring, especially red trilliums. When you reach the top of Snows Mountain and the ski lift, you will have good views down to the village of Waterville Valley and across the valley to Mount Tecumseh and Mount Osceola.

To return to the parking area, follow the ski trail on the right down the mountain for about 200 yards. Turn right onto the Elephant Rock Path, which leads past Elephant Rock (yes, a large rock) for 0.3 mile to the Cascade Path. Turn left onto the Cascade Path, following it back to its end. Turn right onto the ski trail and follow it back to the parking area.

Directions

From I-93, take Exit 28 and head east toward Waterville Valley on NH 49. Take NH 49 all the way into Waterville Valley (around 11.0 miles) and follow the road as it makes a long left turn around a golf course, and then a right hand turn onto Valley Road. Follow the signs for Waterville Valley Trails. Just past a sign that denotes the end of NH 49, turn right into the parking lot for the ski area. The Cascade Path begins from the northeast corner of the parking lot.

Trip #6

Lonesome Lake

> Rating: **Easy**
>
> Distance: **3.2 miles up and back**
>
> Elevation Gain: **950 feet**
>
> Estimated Time: **2 hours**
>
> Maps: **AMC White Mountain Map #2,
> USGS Franconia Quadrangle**
>
> **An easy family hike in Franconia Notch to a
> high mountain lake with views of Franconia
> Ridge.**

LONESOME LAKE is one of those special places in the White Mountains, where families and friends build backcountry vacation memories that are never forgotten. Perhaps it is the rustic comfort of Lonesome Lake Hut, or the friendly conversations that begin there over a cup of hot chocolate. Most likely it is the incredible setting: the beautiful blue waters of the lake are surrounded by a rich green spruce-fir forest, and in the distance rising above the trees is the rugged, sharp-edged outline of Franconia Ridge, looking more like the Rockies than New England. It is also relatively easy to get to Lonesome Lake. The well-graded path of Lonesome Lake Trail enables you to climb the 950 feet to the hut in a little more than an hour. This is a good hike for families, and Lonesome Lake Hut is the AMC "family hut," so it makes a great place to take children for their first overnight experience in the backcountry. It is a popular place in summer; if you plan on spending the night, you will need to make reservations well in advance.

The hike to Lonesome Lake begins from Lafayette Campground in Franconia Notch State Park. The Lonesome Lake Trail is about 50 yards south of the shower building on the back road

Lonesome Lake, New Hampshire

of the campground. The trail begins in a mature northern hardwood forest typical of the lower slopes in Franconia Notch. Birch, beech, and maple are the dominant trees, and if you look carefully at the smooth bark of the beech trees, you might find the claw marks of black bears, which depend on beechnuts for a large part of their diets. Though you are unlikely to see one on your hike, bears are common in this area and can sometimes be seen on the ski slopes of Cannon Mountain foraging for raspberries.

The trail climbs moderately for the most part, although there are a few steep sections, especially after the trail makes a sharp right. After this right the forest slowly makes a transition from northern hardwoods to a forest of fir and paper birch. When you reach the height-of-land, you have entered the boreal zone where the air is filled with the sweet smell of red spruce and balsam fir. At this point the trail levels out and you soon reach a trail junction near the eastern shore of Lonesome Lake. Turn left and follow the Cascade Brook Trail, which follows the eastern shore of the lake and has good views of the Kinsmans. At the next trail junction continue straight on what is now the Fishin' Jimmy Trail. You soon come to Lonesome Lake Hut. Below the hut is a small dock where you can sit and soak in the views of Franconia Ridge or take a plunge into the lake, which averages three to 6 feet in depth and is 12 feet at its deepest.

While in the hut, pick up information for a self-guided nature tour of the area. In addition to the boreal forest, an extensive boggy area is also near the hut and provides a good place for bird watching or plant study. Plants such as leatherleaf, Labrador tea, and sheep laurel are common here, and you can also find the insectivorous, sticky-leaved sundew in nutrient poor soils around the bog. To complete the hike, follow the Around-Lonesome-Lake Trail from the hut. This trail takes you along the western shore of the lake, over bog bridges with views of the Cannon Balls, and back to the Lonesome Lake Trail. Turn right on the Lonesome Lake Trail and follow it back down to Lafayette Campground. For a longer day hike, you can combine this trip with a hike along Cascade Brook (see trip #3).

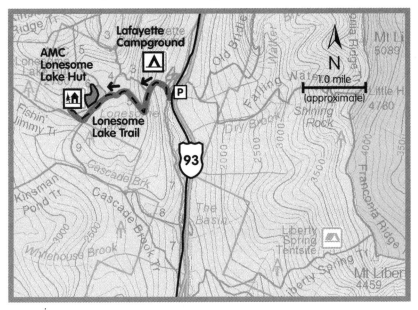

LONESOME LAKE

Directions

From the Franconia Notch Parkway (I-93), follow signs to Lafayette Campground, 7.6 miles north of NH 112. Park in the hiker parking area at the Lafayette Campground in Franconia Notch State Park. The only exit for the campground is on the southbound side of the parkway, but hiker parking is available on the northbound side.

camping and hiking in bear country

Black bears are common in the White Mountains, although hikers rarely see them. More timid than their larger cousins the grizzly bears (which do *not* live in the White Mountains), black bears are mostly vegetarians, feeding on nuts, fruits, grasses, and insects. Black bears can grow to be six feet long and weigh as much as 450 pounds, though they average around 300 pounds. Though not true hibernators, black bears do experience a significant slowdown in their metabolism during the winter. In general, they sleep for five to seven months, denning in caves, burrows, or even the hollowed-out trunks of large trees. Females give birth to their cubs during this winter downtime. While rare, it is possible to encounter a bear in winter.

While you are unlikely to encounter bears while hiking, you may see signs of them. Beech trees often have scars in their bark made by the claws of bears that climb the trees for their nuts in the fall. A bear's footprints are large and exciting to find, measuring up to seven inches long and four inches across, with five distinct toes and claws visible above a rounded, triangular shaped foot.

If you do see a bear while hiking, do *not* approach it: not to get a better look, not to take a picture, not for anything. Slowly back away and find another route to where you are going. Most likely the bear will run at the sight of you. Sometimes black bears can be frightened away by making a lot of noise and throwing rocks in its vicinity, but, of course, don't throw rocks *at* the bear.

Seeing more than the hind end of a black bear while hiking in the White Mountains is extremely rare. More common are bear visits to campgrounds, both in the backcountry and next to roads. Follow these precautions when camping in bear country to ensure your safety, the safety of future campers, and the safety of the bears (once they get a taste of human food, bears can rarely resist sampling it again and often end up being relocated or destroyed because they lose their fear of humans in an attempt to get more).

- Hang food from a high branch that will not support a bear's weight, at least 12 feet off the ground and 6 feet from the tree's trunk.

- Wrap trash and odorous foods in sealed plastic bags or other sealed containers to conceal smells. Hang *all* trash and food as well as other items such as sunscreen, insect repellent, and toiletries that can attract animals.

- Keep a clean cooking area and fire pit. Grease and food scraps will attract bears. If you can, cook at least 100 yards from your tent.

- Remove the clothes you've worn while cooking; they hold food odors and attract bears. Hang such clothing with your pack.

- Never store food in your tent. This will keep rodents out of your tent as well as bears.

- If a bear gets your stuff, don't attempt to get it back.

- Report any bear encounters to the nearest forest ranger or ranger station.

We have never had a bear encounter in the White Mountains, and if you follow these precautions you will most likely enjoy sleep-filled, bear-free camping.

Mount Willard

> **Rating: Easy**
>
> **Distance: 3.2 miles up and back**
>
> **Elevation Gain: 900 feet**
>
> **Estimated Time: 2 hours**
>
> **Maps: AMC White Mountain Map #3, USGS Crawford Notch Quadrangle**
>
> **A popular hike to a spectacular view of Crawford Notch.**

THIS HIKE MAY HAVE THE BEST effort-to-view ratio in the White Mountains, as its relatively easy climb brings you to wonderfully scenic views of Crawford Notch. While this hike is rated easy, 900 feet of elevation gain will seem difficult if you are unaccustomed to regular physical activity. However, if you are used to hiking and looking for an easy day, or if you want to bring along kids anxious to climb their first mountain, this is a great choice. Of course, the relative ease of this hike does draw the crowds; so to ensure a more peaceful experience, hike Mount Willard at times other than summer and fall weekends. Getting an early start helps. Sitting alone in the sun on the ledges of Mount Willard early on a summer morning is one of the more relaxing experiences in the White Mountains.

The Mount Willard Trail begins across the railroad tracks from the Crawford Depot Visitor Center, where it coincides with the Avalon Trail for about 100 yards (you can follow the Avalon Trail to Mount Avalon if you are up for a longer, more strenuous hike to less crowded views of Crawford Notch). At its junction with the Mount Avalon Trail, the Mount Willard Trail turns left and winds its way through a mixed forest as it parallels a brook and climbs moderately. In spring and summer you might find warblers foraging for insects

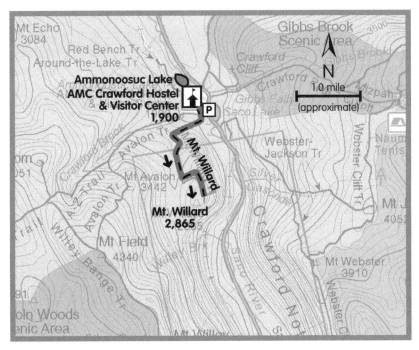

MOUNT WILLARD

amongst the hobblebush, trilliums, and trout lilies. On your right at
0.5 mile you will find Centennial Pool, a basin of cool water sitting
at the base of a small waterfall that tumbles ten feet over square, fractured rocks.

After Centennial Pool, the trail leaves the brook and continues on a moderate grade over a pathway eroded from years of use as
a carriage road and hiking trail. At times the footing is a bit rough
due to exposed rocks, but for the most part the hiking is relatively
easy. As you get higher, the forest becomes dominated by paper birch
with an understory of balsam fir. Many of the birch trees are severely
bent over as a result of the 1998 ice storm. The trail makes a long,
moderate ascent of the western side of the mountain before turning
sharply left, then right on its way to the summit, with the last 400
yards being an easy, mostly flat walk. As you reach the summit, you
will emerge from the forest onto several acres of wide-open ledges
with spectacular views to the south of Crawford Notch.

Crawford Notch is a classic **U**-shaped valley, carved by a
glacier during the last ice age 15,000 to 18,000 years ago. On the

eastern side of the notch, the Webster Cliffs rise dramatically from the floor of the notch and mark the southern extent of the ridge that forms the Southern Presidentials. On the western side of the notch is the Willey Range, with Mount Willey and Mount Field rising almost 3,000 feet from the Saco River visible at the bottom of the notch. From this perspective it is easy to picture a river of ice flowing between the peaks. In addition to the great views, you are likely to see white-throated sparrows, slate-colored juncos, ravens, and possibly a soaring hawk while you are soaking in the sun on the granite ledges.

To complete your hike, just retrace your steps back down the Mount Willard Trail.

Directions

Parking for the Mount Willard Trail is at the AMC Crawford Hostel in Crawford Notch, which is on US 302 8.5 miles south of US 3 in Twin Mountain and 21.0 miles north of NH 16 in Glen.

Trip #8

Greeley Ponds

> Rating: **Easy**
>
> Distance: **4.4 miles up and back**
>
> Elevation Gain: **500 feet**
>
> Estimated Time: **2.5 hours**
>
> Maps: **AMC White Mountain Map #3, USGS Mount Osceola Quadrangle**
>
> **A relatively flat hike to the Greeley Ponds Scenic Area.**

IF YOU ARE LOOKING FOR AN EASY DAY OF HIKING in the woods and the opportunity to eat lunch on the shores of a mountain pond, this is the hike for you. This hike to upper and lower Greeley Ponds only climbs 500 feet in 2.2 miles. It is a scenic woods walk as it crosses several small brooks while passing through a typical New England northern hardwood forest. Both ponds have stretches of gravel shoreline, where you can kick back, soak up some sun, and stare at the cliffs of East Osceola or Mount Kancamagus. While this trip description describes the northern approach from the Kancamagus Highway, it is also possible to hike in to Greeley Ponds from the Waterville Valley area by beginning on the southern end of the Greeley Ponds Trail at Livermore Road.

The Greeley Ponds Trail leaves the Kancamagus at a fairly level grade and soon crosses the south fork of Hancock Branch, a tributary of the Pemigewasset River. After crossing the stream, the trail begins a gradual climb to the height-of-land between the Hancock Branch and Greeley Ponds. This height-of-land is reached at the trail's intersection with the Mount Osceola Trail, 1.3 miles from the Kancamagus. (A very strenuous side trip up East Osceola is possible on the Mount Osceola Trail—the summit is reached after climbing 1,800 feet in only 1.5 miles.) As you continue on the

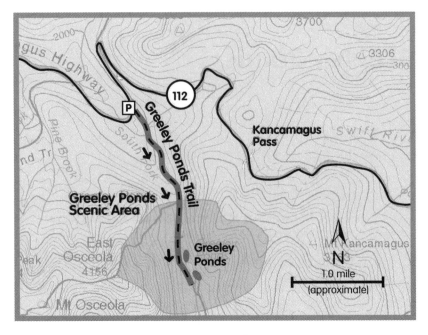

GREELEY PONDS

Greeley Ponds Trail, you begin a gradual descent into the Mad River watershed. The ponds are actually the source of the Mad River, which flows south to form what is now known as Waterville Valley. Immediately after passing a large boulder, be sure to stay to the right at the fork with the Greeley Ponds cross-country ski trail.

At about 1.6 miles, you reach the upper pond and a side trail leads left to a gravel beach on the pond's northern shore. Another trail at the south end of the pond leads to an open area with views of Mount Osceola. From the south end of the upper pond, the Greeley Ponds Trail continues over a wet and rocky trail through a northern hardwood forest and past an occasional sphagnum bog. About 0.3 mile after leaving the upper pond, you reach the northern end of the lower pond, which is the bigger of the two. A side trail at the north end of the pond leads to a gravel beach, which is a great place to sit and watch for mergansers and other ducks as they swim amongst the silvery, gnarled trunks of standing dead spruce and white pine. These trees were killed when the pond was enlarged by beaver activity several years ago.

One more resting spot on this pond is in a cove about 300 yards south of the gravel beach. Just turn left on the short side path, which begins in a grove of paper birch. This secluded little cove provides a great view of the cliffs on the western shoulder of Mount Kancamagus, which is named after Chief Kancamagus, "the Fearless One," who led a raid on Dover, New Hampshire, in 1686. The Greeley Ponds Trail continues another 2.9 miles to Livermore Road in Waterville Valley, but to complete your hike, turn around here and retrace your steps to the Kancamagus Highway.

Directions

Take Exit 32 on I-93 in Lincoln and travel east on NH 112 (Kancamagus Highway) for about 9.0 miles. The Greeley Ponds Trail hiking area will be on the right, approximately 0.25 mile past a parking area for the Greeley Ponds cross-country ski trail.

Trip #9

Mount Pemigewasset

> Rating: **Easy**
>
> Distance: **3.6 miles up and back**
>
> Elevation Gain: **1,150 feet**
>
> Estimated Time: **2 hours, 45 minutes**
>
> Maps: **AMC White Mountain Map #2, USGS Lincoln Quadrangle**
>
> **Great views for the effort. A good first hike for families interested in exploring White Mountain peaks.**

MOUNT PEMIGEWASSET, also known as Indian Head, is a small peak with a large treeless rock ledge that provides excellent views for a moderate effort. Pemigewasset is an Abenaki Indian word meaning "rapidly moving," which well describes the nearby Pemigewasset River. Pemigewasset was also a name given to a tribe of Native Americans that lived in the area during the seventeenth and eighteenth centuries. Two trails lead to the summit of Mount Pemigewasset: the Indian Head Trail and the Mount Pemigewasset Trail, both of which climb the peak from US 3 in Lincoln. This hike follows the Mount Pemigewasset Trail, which leaves from the Flume Gorge Visitor Center and entails 400 less feet of elevation gain than the alternate route.

From the north end of the Flume Gorge Visitor Center parking lot, follow the Franconia Notch Bicycle Path (see trip #38 for a description of this bike path) for about 150 yards to the Mount Pemigewasset Trail. Turn left onto the Mount Pemigewasset Trail. The trail crosses under US 3, passes a stream over a wooden bridge, and then tunnels under I-93. You soon leave civilization behind as you climb moderately through a northern hardwood forest filled with large yellow birch and American beech. The trail meanders over streams and past wildflowers, which, depending on the season, can

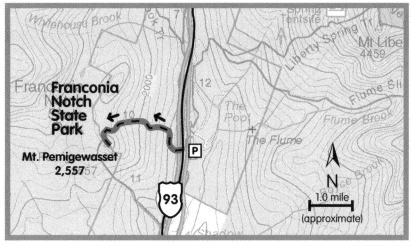

MOUNT PEMIGEWASSET

include trout lilies, trilliums, star flowers, and rose twisted stalk. Shrubs include hobblebush, whose showy white flowers bloom in late May and early June. To keep the kids interested, tell them what animals live in a northern hardwood forest: deer, bears, wild turkeys, ruffed grouse, and porcupines.

As you near the summit, the hardwoods are replaced by a spruce-fir forest, and at 1.7 miles the Indian Head Trail enters from the right.. At 1.8 miles you suddenly emerge from the forest onto rock ledges (keep an eye on small children here) with excellent views to the south and west. After just an hour and a half of moderate hiking, you are looking out at Kinsman Ridge, Mount Moosilauke, Mount Osceola, and the peaks in the southern part of the Pemigewasset Wilderness Area. To get a view of Franconia Ridge to the northeast, continue past the first ledges to the true summit, which is on your left. On your way back down, be sure to stay to the right at the trail junction with the Indian Head Trail just below the ledges.

Directions

Parking for this trail is on US 3 at the Flume Gorge Visitor Center in Franconia Notch State Park. To get on US 3, you can take either Exit 33 on I-93 or Exit 1 on the Franconia Notch Parkway, which is 3.8 miles north of NH 112 in Lincoln.

Trip #10

Lowe's Bald Spot

> Rating: **Moderate**
>
> Distance: **4.4 miles up and back**
>
> Elevation Gain: **900 feet**
>
> Estimated Time: **2 hours, 45 minutes**
>
> Maps: **AMC White Mountain Map #1, USGS Mount Washington Quadrangle**
>
> **A short, moderate hike from Pinkham Notch to good views of Mounts Adams and Madison, and Wildcat Mountain. Good for kids with some hiking experience.**

LOWE'S BALD SPOT is an outcropping of rock that rises above the surrounding spruce to provide excellent views across the Great Gulf Wilderness. Its relatively low elevation and its proximity to the AMC Pinkham Notch Visitor Center make this a popular short hike. One scramble over steep rock near the top and the 900 feet of elevation gain results in some sections requiring substantial exertion; nonetheless, this is a good hike for families with hiking experience. This can be a fun hike for kids and adults as it crosses several small streams, passes through two forest types, and ends up with rewarding views from a prime wilderness lunch spot. Lowe's Bald Spot is most likely named after Charles Lowe, an early guide in the White Mountains who built the first trail up Mount Adams in 1875 and 1876.

The hike begins on the Old Jackson Road, a hiking trail that leaves from the Tuckerman Ravine Trail about 50 yards from its start at the AMC Pinkham Notch Visitor Center. The Old Jackson Road heads north, making a gentle ascent through a northern hardwood forest and crossing a small stream. The trail crosses several cross-country ski trails, and at 0.4 mile crosses a bridge and turns left (the

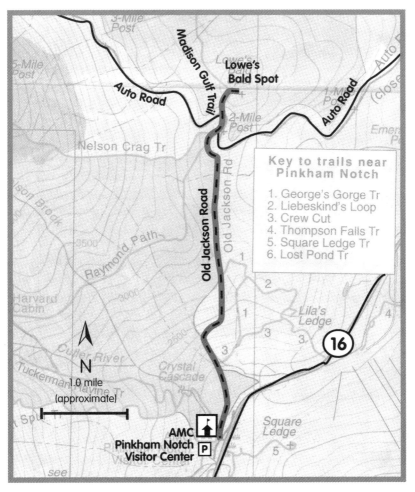

LOWE'S BALD SPOT

Link is a ski trail that leads to the right at this point). After this left turn the trail begins a moderately steep climb, crosses another brook, and turns right for a long stretch of straight hiking that alternates between moderate climbs, descents, and flat sections.

In this section, the trail follows the contour line at the 2,600-foot level of Mount Washington, with the northern hardwood forest floor dropping quickly to the east. With the canopy of trees near eye-level to your right and the forest floor above you to the left, you can listen for a variety of woodland songbirds such as American redstart, white-throated sparrows, and hermit thrushes. After crossing several small brooks, the trail reaches a larger brook, makes a sharp left turn, and climbs steeply up a set of impressively placed rock stairs. At the top of these stairs, the trail turns right and continues at a relatively flat grade. The trail gets a little rockier as it passes the Raymond Path and the Nelson Crag Trail on its way to the Mount Washington Auto Road at 1.9 miles. This is the end of the Old Jackson Road.

Cross the auto road and enter the Great Gulf Wilderness via the Madison Gulf Trail. Notice how the forest has changed to one filled with conifers: red spruce and balsam fir. You are now in the boreal forest, which is the dominant forest in Canada and along the United States-Canadian border. Turn right on the spur path 0.2 mile from the road, which leads to the summit of Lowe's Bald Spot. This 0.1-mile stretch of steep climbing to the open ledges above is the hardest part of the hike, with a scramble over a rock wall. Once at the top, you are rewarded with outstanding views across the Great Gulf Wilderness Area to Mount Adams and Mount Madison. The steep and impressive headwall of Madison Gulf can be seen between the two peaks. Madison Gulf is a glacial cirque formed by a glacier that flowed into the Great Gulf. Views to the north and east are also good from the summit's ledges, which are populated by scrubby spruce, blueberries, and sheep laurel.

This is an out-and-back hike, so to complete your trip just retrace your steps back down the Madison Gulf Trail and Old Jackson Road.

Directions

This hike begins behind the trading post at the AMC Pinkham Notch Visitor Center. The visitor center is on NH 16, about 12.0 miles north of US 302 in Glen and 11.0 miles south of US 2 in Gorham.

Mount Israel

Rating: **Moderate**

Distance: **4.2 miles up and back**

Elevation Gain: **1,700 feet**

Estimated Time: **3 hours**

Maps: **AMC White Mountain Map #3,
  USGS Center Sandwich Quadrangle**

**A moderate hike to excellent views of the
Sandwich Range and the Lakes Region.**

MOUNT ISRAEL STANDS at the southern edge of the national forest, rising above the pastoral setting of rural New Hampshire towns that fill the gap between the lakes and the mountains. Despite its relatively low summit, which stands no higher than 2,630 feet, Mount Israel has excellent views of the surrounding mountains as well as the Lakes Region to the south. The hike via the Wentworth Trail is more ambitious than you would expect, climbing 1,700 feet through a variety of forest types, including one of the more beautiful stands of northern red oak in northern New Hampshire. Mead Base, where the trail begins, is an Explorer Scout Camp that is used as a base for a variety of outdoor activities, including trail maintenance.

This hike follows the Wentworth Trail for its entire length. The trail begins behind and to the left of the main building at Mead Base, climbing moderately through a mixed forest that fills with the colors of wildflowers in the spring. On your way up the mountain, you are likely to spot pink lady's slippers, star flowers, wild lily-of-the-valley, wood sorrel, trilliums, violets, columbines, and other flowers growing beneath shrubs like hobblebush and striped maple. After a spring rain, you should also keep your eyes open for red efts, the land form of the aquatic red-spotted newt. Red efts are 1 1/2 to

A northern red oak near the Mount Israel trailhead in Sandwich, New Hampshire.

3 3/8 inches long and their bright orange color stands out dramatically against the leaf litter on the forest floor. In the red-spotted newt's life cycle, efts are the stage between the larval stage and adulthood. Once red efts turn into newts, they can only breathe underwater through their gills.

The Wentworth Trail turns right at a stream crossing and angles up the south side of the mountain, paralleling a stone wall before turning left and following a brook while climbing moderately. The trail turns right again, leaving the brook at 0.8 mile, and winds its way up the mountain via switchbacks. Soon, northern red oaks are practically the only trees in the forest on the rocky southwest side of the mountain. The oaks create a high canopy that allows occasional glimpses to the southwest of Squam Lake. At 1.5 miles the trail passes under a rocky cliff on the right. A side trail on the left leads ten yards to good views of the Lakes Region. The Wentworth Trail makes a right turn and climbs steeply to attain the ridgeline above the cliff. After this short, steep climb, you will find the hiking easier as you enter a spruce-fir forest and more level terrain.

The ridge walk through the dark green conifers is relatively flat and easy, until you make a short climb to a rocky knob that lies to the west of the true summit. From here, excellent views of the mountains are to the north. As you continue toward the summit, you

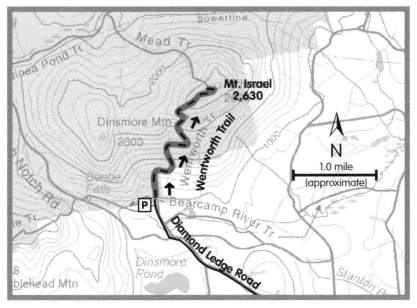

MOUNT ISRAEL

re-enter the forest, which occasionally thins out as you walk over gray rock ledges lined with veins of quartz and covered with reindeer lichen. Just below the summit, you will pass the Mead Trail on your left, which leads 1.7 miles to Sandwich Notch Road. A short climb brings you to the summit of Mount Israel, which has excellent 180-degree views to the north, particularly of the Sandwich Range. While on the summit, you are likely to see dark-eyed juncos, yellow-rumped warblers, and the signs of coyote.

Directions

From the intersection of NH 113 and NH 109 in Center Sandwich, head west on NH 113 for a few hundred yards and turn right (north) onto Grove Street toward Sandwich Notch Road, following a sign for Mead Base. In 0.5 mile take the left fork (straight) onto Diamond Ledge Road. In 1.0 mile the road turns to gravel. One mile after this point, take the right fork, staying on Diamond Ledge Road and continuing to follow signs for Mead Base. Mead Base will be in another 0.4 mile at the end of the road. Park in the lot on the left.

Welch and Dickey Mountains

Rating: **Moderate**

Distance: **4.4 miles round-trip**

Elevation Gain: **1,800 feet**

Estimated Time: **3 hours**

Maps: **AMC White Mountain Map #3,
      USGS Waterville Valley Quadrangle**

**A moderate hike to relatively small peaks
with big views.**

WELCH AND DICKEY MOUNTAINS were two of the earliest mountains visited regularly by summer tourists. In the 1850s, Nathaniel Greeley, who had pioneered in Waterville Valley in the 1830s, created a system of trails in the area for visitors to his inn. This was the first true system of trails in the White Mountains. Today the Welch-Dickey Loop Trail is a popular hike with families because it has good views for a relatively low amount of effort, as most of the hike follows moderate grades. Welch and Dickey Mountains are well below 3,000 feet in elevation, but they both have several open rocky ledges. Naturalists also will enjoy this hike because of its high diversity of trees, including one of only four stands of jack pine in New Hampshire. The hike is close to Waterville Valley and is one of the first White Mountain hikes reached from Boston via I-93. This is a great hike to do in the off-season, when the crowds are nonexistent and the weather on higher peaks may be uncertain.

The Welch-Dickey Loop Trail leaves the north end of the parking lot and immediately offers you the choice of climbing Welch or Dickey Mountains; either direction loops over both peaks. This trip describes the route in a counterclockwise direction, climbing Welch Mountain first in order to hike up its steep south ridge, which

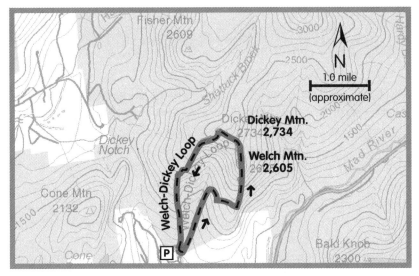

WELCH AND DICKEY MOUNTAINS

is preferable to climbing down it. Following the right fork of the trail quickly brings you to a beautiful rushing stream surrounded by hemlock trees. The trail follows the brook for 0.5 mile before turning right and heading south and east toward the south ridge of the peak. At 1.3 miles you reach the first open ledges on the hike in an area filled with revegetation zones marked by stone circles. The maintainers of this trail are attempting to encourage the regrowth of the subalpine plants that usually grow here but die off when trampled by hikers. Please use care when hiking over these ledges.

From these first ledges, the trail climbs steeply over rock for 0.6 mile, passing in and out of the trees on its way to the summit of Welch Mountain. The summit ledges provide excellent views in most directions, especially down into the Mad River valley. They also provide the opportunity to study the southernmost occurrence of jack pine in New Hampshire. Jack pine is a very common tree in the boreal forests of Canada, but it is relatively rare in New Hampshire. Its one-inch-long needles grow in bundles of two, and are easily distinguished from the much longer needles of the more common red and white pines you will also find in this area. Jack pines are highly resistant to fire and they actually depend on fire to reproduce, as the extreme heat of a forest fire is needed to open up their cones and release their seeds.

trail maintenance

THE WHITE MOUNTAINS have more than 1,200 miles of hiking trails, all of which require varying amounts of work to keep them in good shape. This is a fairly daunting task to manage, and in fact several different organizations, including the U.S. Forest Service, the Appalachian Mountain Club, the Randolph Mountain Club, Wonalancet Outdoor Club, and others, maintain White Mountain trails through a combination of professional trail crews and volunteers. With over 7 million people a year visiting the White Mountains, trail maintenance has become increasingly important for resource protection. Maintenance now focuses on preventing erosion and guiding hikers in such a way as to prevent damage to the surrounding environment. On difficult sections of trail, maintenance is also important to keep trails as safe as possible.

Appalachian Mountain Club volunteers, as well as the AMC professional trail crew, maintain about 350 miles of trails in the Whites, including 105 miles of the Appalachian Trail. It is important to note the AMC does not own these trails, but rather maintains them in cooperation with the Forest Service. From late spring through late summer, 18 professional trail maintainers work in four groups doing a lot of the heavy maintenance like building rock steps, water bars, and bridges. This maintenance also includes keeping over 800 backcountry trail signs (none of which are at trailheads or on the Appalachian Trail) up-to-date and in good condition.

Anyone can volunteer for trail maintenance, and it is a great way to give a little back to the outdoors. It can also be a fun way to spend a day or more in the mountains, getting to know the intricate details of one or more trails. For a ten-week period in the summer, the AMC Camp Dodge near Pinkham Notch hosts a trail maintenance program, where AMC members, age 16 and older, volunteer to work with one of three trail crews for a few days, a week, or two weeks. The AMC also runs an Adopt-A-Trail program, with more than

A trail crew uses a pulley system to move boulders over fragile vegetation.

170 volunteers maintaining their own sections of 108 White Mountain trails. The Camp Dodge trail maintenance program is a great way to learn trail maintenance techniques. The AMC also publishes a comprehensive book on the subject, *The Complete Guide to Trail Building and Maintenance* by Carl Demrow and David Salisbury. To volunteer to do trail maintenance with the AMC or to apply for a professional trail crew position, visit the AMC website, www.outdoors.org, or call Pinkham Notch Visitor Center at 603-466-2721 for more information.

From the summit of Welch Mountain, the Welch-Dickey Loop Trail continues north to Dickey Mountain. On the way, it first descends into an open area between the peaks populated by red spruce and shrubs that are typical in the ledgy areas of New England: sheep laurel, rhodora, blueberries, and pin cherry. Silvery mats of reindeer lichen are also common. At 2.4 miles after a short but steep climb, you reach the summit of Dickey Mountain, which has open ledges on all sides of its wooded summit. You have good views of the nearby Sandwich Range and Franconia Ridge, which are about 15.0 miles to the north. In fall, the summits of both mountains are good places to watch for migrating hawks, falcons, and monarch butterflies.

The trail continues by descending the rocky ledges of Dickey Mountain's west ridge. Views are abundant from these ledges as you hike in and out of the trees. If you look closely, you can see glacial striations in the ledges. These striations were created when boulders trapped under glacial ice carved lines in the rock as the ice moved over the mountain. These ledges are also home to a spruce forest that provides good habitat for spruce grouse, a rare cousin of the common ruffed grouse found at lower elevations. Just before entering the forest for good, you traverse a long ridge of bare rock perched over the northwest wall of the valley that sits between Welch and Dickey. Excellent views can be seen from here of Welch Mountain and the northern hardwood forest below.

Below this last ledge the trail makes a moderate descent to the trailhead for the final 1.2 miles. During this time the forest becomes a northern hardwood forest rich in northern red oaks, whose acorns provide an important food source for many animals, including white-tail deer, wild turkeys, and black bears. Other trees you can find here include sugar maple, American beech, yellow birch, mountain ash, large-tooth aspen, and Eastern hophornbeam.

Directions

From I-93, take Exit 28 and head east toward Waterville Valley on NH 49. In 5.6 miles turn left onto Upper Mad River Road. In 0.6 mile turn right onto Morris Road, following signs for the Welch-Dickey Loop Trail. In another 0.6 mile turn right onto a gravel road, which leads 50 yards to the parking area for the Welch-Dickey Loop Trail.

Trip #13

Mount Crawford

Rating: **Moderate**

Distance: **5.0 miles up and back**

Elevation Gain: **2,100 feet**

Estimated Time: **4 hours**

Maps: **AMC White Mountain Map #3, USGS Stairs Mountain and Bartlett Quadrangles**

A moderate climb to unique views of the Presidential Range and the Presidential Range–Dry River Wilderness Area.

MOUNT CRAWFORD is a relatively low peak just to the south of Crawford Notch. It is the first peak reached by hikers using the Davis Path, which makes a 15.0-mile ascent of Mount Washington through the Presidential Range–Dry River Wilderness Area. The peak is just one of several landmarks in the area named after the legendary Crawford family, who were the first settlers in Crawford Notch and provided mountain hospitality and guide services to travelers in the area for much of the nineteenth century (see the history section of this book for more information about the Crawfords). The hike up Mount Crawford begins on US 302, along the banks of the Saco River, and climbs steadily to the summit, which has excellent 360-degree views.

To start your hike, follow the gravel road at the north end of the parking lot for about 100 yards to a footbridge over the Saco River. This is the beginning of the Davis Path, which was built in 1845 by Nathaniel Davis, Ethan Crawford's son-in-law. The Davis Path is also the beginning link in the Cohos Trail, a new long-distance trail that starts in Crawford Notch and ends at the Quebec border. On the other side of the river, the trail crosses private property and passes many unmarked side trails and woods roads: keep an eye out for signs that

Mount Crawford, just off the Davis Path and Cohos Trail

help you stay on the right path, which follows telephone lines for a short distance before entering the White Mountain National Forest. At this point, you will notice you have entered a northern hardwood forest that includes many northern red oak. While it is most often associated with the oak-hickory forests to the south and west of the White Mountains in northern New England and Canada, northern red oak is often found in low-elevation northern hardwood forests. Like most oaks they can grow to be tall, stately trees, producing bumper crops of acorns every three or four years.

The trail crosses an often dry, rocky stream just before it enters the Presidential Range–Dry River Wilderness Area. This stream might look like the namesake of the wilderness area, but the Dry River actually lies to the north and west of Mount Crawford, where it drains the southern slopes of the Presidential Range. After crossing the stream, the Davis Path climbs moderately, increasing in steepness as you gain elevation. At 0.9 mile, the trail makes a sharp right-hand turn and follows a zigzag course on its way to the ridge between Mount Hope and Mount Crawford. Conifers become more common as you climb, and by the time you reach the ridgeline, you are in a pure boreal forest.

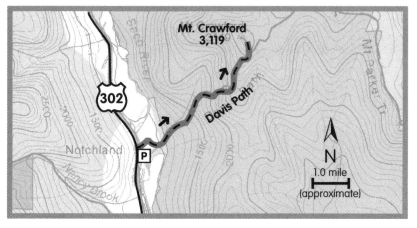

MOUNT CRAWFORD

The trail follows the ridge to the north, and at 1.9 miles you reach the first of several open ledges on your way to the summit. Views are particularly good to the south and west, with Mount Carrigain the dominant peak. At 2.2 miles turn left onto the Mount Crawford spur path. The spur path climbs steeply over bare rock ledges for most of its 0.3 mile to the summit. Small spruce trees, as well as sheep laurel, creeping snowberry, and alpine willows populate the summit area. Ledges on each side of the summit provide views in all directions. The views of Mount Washington and the Southern Presidentials are excellent, as the high alpine peaks rise above the vast forests of the Dry River valley and the long craggy ridge of the Dry River Range.

To complete your hike, follow the Mount Crawford spur path and Davis Path back to your car. If you feel like exploring the area a little farther, you can continue north on the Davis Path from the Mount Crawford spur path for 0.7 mile. At this point you will reach a ledgy outlook on Crawford Dome, which provides good views of the steep, rocky east side of Mount Crawford.

Directions

From the intersection of US 302 and NH 16 in Glen, follow US 302 west for 12.1 miles. The parking area for the Davis Path will be on the right.

Trip #14

Wildcat River

> Rating: **Moderate**
>
> Distance: **6.5 miles round-trip**
>
> Elevation Gain: **700 feet**
>
> Estimated Time: **4 hours**
>
> Maps: **AMC White Mountain Map #5, USGS Jackson Quadrangle**
>
> **A great half-day walk through the woods.**

THIS HIKE IS PERFECT when it just seems necessary to take a good long walk in the woods. The trails that explore the upper reaches of the Wildcat River and its tributary, Bog Brook, follow easy grades through a forest that harbors moose, partridge, warblers, and pileated woodpeckers. This trip is a particularly good choice on a cool, drizzly day as the forest trees protect you from the rain and wind, and the ferns and shrubs living below the canopy appear to drip with rich, saturated greens. A wet and diverse habitat means a good variety of wildflowers bloom here in spring and early summer, but realize that these trails often traverse wet and boggy ground, making spring hiking a muddy (not to mention buggy) experience. By late summer and fall, however, the trail is drier and the bugs are less numerous. *Please note that there is only room for two cars at the trailhead.*

This hike begins on the Bog Brook Trail, which leaves Carter Notch Road 5.5 miles north of Jackson. The trail begins by following an old woods road through young second growth forest. Stay to the right as the road passes another old road on the left. Soon the Bog Brook Trail resembles a normal hiking path as it begins a gradual descent to Wildcat Brook. As you cross Wildcat Brook, you will notice the forest is now a northern hardwood forest, dominated by

Bog Brook meanders along the Bog Brook Trail.

beech, birch, and maple. The trail crosses another brook before reaching and crossing the Wildcat River. All of these stream crossings can be difficult in high water but pose no difficulty at normal water levels. Shortly after crossing the river, turn left onto the Wildcat River Trail (0.7 mile from the parking area). The trail climbs gently as it parallels the river, crosses a gravel road, and makes its way to the confluence of Bog Brook and the Wildcat River. All of the streams

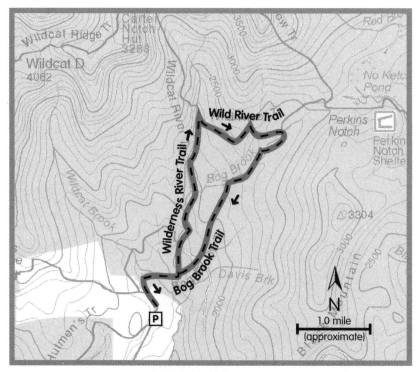

WILDCAT RIVER

on this trip drain the southern slopes of Wildcat Mountain. (The northern side of Wildcat is home to a downhill ski area, famous for late season snows and up-close views of Mount Washington.)

You enter a more mature forest as the trail makes some short, steep climbs before crossing Bog Brook. Growing thick beneath tall sugar maple and yellow birch is an understory of hobblebush and striped maple (also called moose maple). Moose, as well as deer, beaver, and rabbits, eat the striped bark of these small trees, especially in winter. It is on this part of the trip where you may start seeing signs of moose such as tracks and droppings. In the spring you might find wildflowers such as trout lilies, wood sorrel, red and painted trilliums, and bunchberries. In late summer you will find goldenrod and asters on the sunnier sections of the trail.

After crossing Bog Brook the Wildcat River Trail climbs gradually and passes a small cascade shortly before its intersection with the Wild River Trail, 2.6 miles from the parking area. The Wild

River Trail is just under 10.0 miles long and is used as the main route between the AMC Wild River Camp in Evans Notch and the AMC Carter Notch Hut. For this hike, turn right on to the Wild River Trail for 1.1 miles of flat walking through a mixture of hardwoods, boreal forests, and boggy meadows. After the second brook crossing, turn right on to the Bog Brook Trail for the final 2.8 miles of the trip. The trail follows Bog Brook much of the way. Look for sphagnum moss growing beneath the forest of spruce to the left of the brook. These small "forested wetlands" are often filled with water in spring and are an important part of the forest, recharging groundwater and providing vital breeding habitat for amphibians.

Bog Brook drains a bog, making the Bog Brook Trail prone to mud and erosion. About halfway between the Wild River Trail and the parking area, the trail has been reclaimed by the bog. Follow the relocated trail to the left of its original course for about 100 yards. After this relocation, the trail descends gradually to a logging road and then makes a short climb before returning to the trailhead.

Directions

From NH 16A in downtown Jackson, go north on NH 16B (across from the Jackson Library and Jackson Community Church). Follow NH 16B north for 2.1 miles. At this point, continue straight on Carter Notch Road. (NH 16B turns right and crosses the river.) In 2.2 miles the road becomes a gravel road, which is suitable for two-wheel drive. In another 0.7 mile a small parking area for the Bog Brook Trail will be on the right. This trailhead can only accommodate two cars. The gravel portion of Carter Notch Road may not be passable in winter. To avoid the three stream crossings at the beginning of the hike, you can drive to the gravel logging road (Fire Road 233) just beyond the trailhead and park where the road crosses Bog Brook (the second bridge).

Trip #15

Kearsarge North

Rating: **Moderate**

Distance: **6.2 miles up and back**

Elevation Gain: **2,600 feet**

Estimated Time: **4.5 hours**

Maps: **AMC White Mountain Map #5, USGS North Conway East Quadrangle**

Close to North Conway with 360–degree views, including an excellent look at Mount Washington.

KEARSARGE NORTH in Intervale is popular with the North Conway crowd because of its proximity to town and its excellent views from an abandoned fire tower (Kearsarge South is actually in southwestern New Hampshire near Mount Monadnock). The *AMC White Mountain Guide* calls Kearsarge North "one of the finest viewpoints in the White Mountains." Also called Mount Pequawket, Kearsarge had a building on its summit as early as 1845, and was one of the few mountains in the Whites climbed regularly by tourists in the mid-nineteenth century. Its current fire tower was built in 1951 and is now listed on the National Historic Fire Lookout Register, although it is no longer used for fire detection. The views from its elevated glassed-in room and surrounding porch attract numerous visitors on summer and fall weekends. For a quiet hike, make this trip early in the morning or during the week.

This hike climbs the mountain via the Mount Kearsarge North Trail, which starts at a parking area on the north side of Hurricane Mountain Road. The trail begins in a typical second growth northern hardwood forest and passes a few houses in the first 0.25 mile. For much of the first half of the hike, the trail parallels a brook,

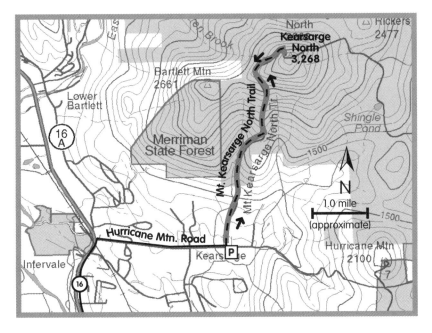

KEARSARGE NORTH

which is just out of view yet still within earshot. As you enter the national forest, you pass through a grove of conifers—mainly hemlock and red pine. The thick canopy of these trees prevents the growth of smaller trees, making it possible to see for a long distance through the forest. After 1.1 miles the trail turns left and begins a steep climb up the south side of Kearsarge.

As you hike over rocky ledges, you will start to see occasional views to the south and west toward North Conway, the Moat Mountains, and Mount Chocorua. At 2.4 miles you crest the ridge and circle around the west side of the mountain where you enter a cool, dark, and moist spruce-fir forest. The footing gets rougher as the trail climbs moderately over rocks and roots. You reach open ledges about 200 yards below the summit, where you are surrounded by stunted spruce, fir, and birch. At 3,268 feet Kearsarge North is well below treeline, but the fire tower on its summit rises above the surrounding forest to provide sweeping views in all directions. The state of New Hampshire operated the first fire tower on Kearsarge North in 1909. The current tower ceased operation in 1968, when the use of airplanes for fire detection replaced the need for lookouts.

View of Mount Washington from inside the fire tower on Kearsarge North.

You may want to hike out on the Weeks Brook Trail if you are able to spot a car on Fire Road 317, which is several miles east of the Mount Kearsarge North Trail trailhead. The Weeks Brook Trail passes through some interesting terrain, but it is sometimes hard to follow and should only be used by experienced hikers with a good map. If you are unable (or unwilling) to spot a car, you should return via the Mount Kearsarge North Trail.

Directions

From NH 16 in Intervale, head east on Hurricane Mountain Road, which leaves the highway just north of the "scenic view" parking area. The trailhead for the Mount Kearsarge North Trail is on the left, 1.5 miles from NH 16.

Trip #16

Caribou Mountain

> Rating: **Moderate**
>
> Distance: **7.0 miles round-trip**
>
> Elevation Gain: **1,900 feet**
>
> Estimated Time: **4.5 hours**
>
> Maps: **AMC White Mountain Map #5, USGS Speckled Mountain (Maine) Quadrangle**
>
> **A hike through a mature northern hardwood forest to great views of the Caribou-Speckled Mountain Wilderness Area.**

THIS HIKE TAKES YOU THROUGH the 12,000-acre Caribou–Speckled Mountain Wilderness on the way to the summit of Caribou Mountain. While Caribou is a relatively low peak (2,800 feet), its summit is bare and provides views in all directions. Caribou is in the less visited Maine portion of the White Mountain National Forest. While you will see other hikers on a summer weekend, you are much more likely to encounter long moments of solitude than in the Presidentials or on Franconia Ridge. The unique perspective from the summit also makes this a nice change of pace from bagging all of those 4,000-footers to the west.

For this trip you will complete the loop made by the Caribou and Mud Brook Trails, both of which begin from the Caribou Mountain parking area on ME 113. Begin your hike on the Caribou Trail, which leaves from the northeast corner of the parking lot. You immediately enter a beautiful, mature northern hardwood forest that is rich with sugar maple and feathery-needled hemlock. Except for the area near the summit, you will be walking through various versions of this forest for the entire hike. The trail descends gradually to cross Morrison Brook over a wooden bridge. It then climbs gradually before

Caribou–Speckled Mountain Wilderness from the top of Caribou Mountain.

crossing the brook and becoming steeper. Typical of a northern hardwood forest in northern New England, the understory on this part of the hike is populated by hobblebush, striped maple, and wildflowers such as wood sorrel, bunchberries, and trilliums.

Two miles from the parking area, the trail crosses the brook at Kees Falls, where the water drops 25 feet over a moss-covered rock wall into a deep, circular pool. At this point you will begin to notice that the forest canopy was heavily damaged by the 1998 ice storm. The storm injured or destroyed scores of birch and beech trees, but the understory is taking advantage of the extra sunlight reaching the forest floor, growing thick and bushy. After Kees Falls the trail crosses the brook several times before climbing steeply to its junction with the Mud Brook Trail in a col between Caribou and Gammon Mountains (3.0 miles from the parking area). A boggy area to the left of the trail junction is frequented by moose, as is much of the forest adjacent to the Mud Brook Trail.

Turn right on the Mud Brook Trail for a steady 0.6-mile climb to the summit. Along the way, the hardwood forest gives way to a boreal forest of spruce and fir mixed with some paper birch and mountain ash. Caribou Mountain's summit is a large open area of granite ledges with scattered small spruce and fir, pin cherry, sheep

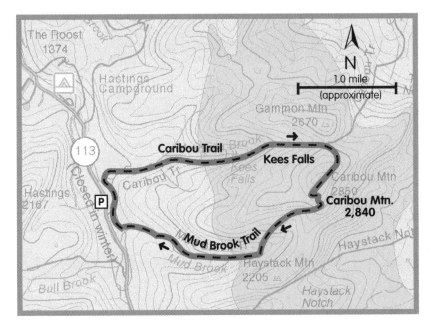

CARIBOU MOUNTAIN

laurel, and blueberries. Views are in all directions: the Mahoosucs to the north, the Baldface and Carter ranges to the west, Kezar Lake to the south, and the rest of Maine to the east. The view of the thickly forested and roadless Caribou–Speckled Mountain Wilderness Area to the south is particularly impressive. From the summit, follow the Mud Brook Trail, which drops down to the south for several yards before turning right and traversing the open west ridge of the mountain.

The trail descends steeply into spruce and fir for about fifteen minutes before providing one last good viewpoint from an open ledge looking south. The trail continues a steep descent through boreal forest before the grade eases and you reach the first of several brook crossings. By this time, you are once again in a storm-damaged northern hardwood forest. While unsightly at first, extensive storm damage in a well-protected wilderness area can actually benefit the forest by knocking down weaker trees, creating habitat for a variety of wildlife, and giving surviving trees the opportunity to grow bigger and stronger than they would have in a forest thick with

competing trees. The remainder of the hike becomes easier as the trail flattens out on its way back to the parking area.

Directions

From the easternmost intersection of NH 16 and US 2 in Gorham, New Hampshire, drive east on US 2 for 11.1 miles and turn right on ME 113 in Gilead. The parking area will be 4.7 miles on the left.

Trip #17

Thoreau Falls

Rating: **Moderate**

Distance: **9.2 miles up and back**

Elevation Gain: **500 feet**

Estimated Time: **5 hours**

Maps: **AMC White Mountain Map #2,
USGS Crawford Notch Quadrangle**

**A relatively flat hike through good
wildlife habitat to mountain views and
Thoreau Falls.**

WITH ITS SUNNY ROCK LEDGES and excellent views of Mount Bond, Thoreau Falls is a popular destination on hot summer days, but its relatively long distance from the nearest road keeps the number of visitors down to a tolerable level. It can be reached from either Crawford Notch or the end of Zealand Road, and both routes have their highlights. We prefer the trip in from Zealand Road: the walk along the rockslide on Whitewall Mountain is one of the most scenic valley hikes in the White Mountains. This trip shares its beginning with the Zealand Falls/Zeacliff hike, and in fact a long day hike combining the two trips is possible (see the description of trip #18 for more details). There is not much climbing on this trip (only 500 feet of elevation gain), but the hike is rated as moderate due to its 9.2-mile length.

You begin your hike on the Zealand Trail, which starts at the end of Zealand Road. The trail begins as a wide path that climbs gradually through a mixed forest of spruce, fir, maple, and birch. After about 0.4 mile you cross a wooden bridge and climb through a grove of spruce trees over a heavily eroded trailbed. (Please try to stay on the trail here by following the blue blazes). You will soon hear the Zealand River on your left. After making a close approach to the river at 0.8 mile, the trail turns to the right and continues a gradual climb. After crossing the river on a wooden bridge, you begin to walk through an area of beaver activity that lasts for almost 1.0 mile. The trail passes alder thickets and over wooden bridges and occasionally you will have good views of Zealand Mountain and Zeacliff to the southwest.

Just before reaching a junction with the A-Z Trail at 2.3 miles, you pass the largest of the beaver ponds, where there are at least two large beaver lodges and frog song is common. Various species of flycatchers and swallows can be seen feeding on insects above the ponds, and warblers and vireos are common in the surrounding forest. With a little luck, you might even see a moose in this area. Continue straight on the Zealand Trail and you will soon come to Zealand Pond, which will be on your right. After crossing the outlet of the pond on a wooden bridge, the trail follows the eastern shore of the pond before ending at its intersection with the Ethan Pond Trail and the Twinway, 2.5 miles from the parking area.

To go to Thoreau Falls, take the left fork, which is the Ethan Pond Trail. The Ethan Pond Trail, part of the Appalachian Trail, follows a straight course through a forest of paper birch with a few spruce and fir trees. Signs of moose are common on this section of trail. The trail is built on an old railroad bed, which was constructed in the 1880s in order to transport lumber out of the heart of what is now the Pemigewasset Wilderness Area. At one point the railroad tracks went as far as Shoal Pond and Ethan Pond. Today the wide, level hiking trail is all that is left of the railroad, although you might run across an occasional railroad spike.

About 1.0 mile past the Zealand Trail, the Ethan Pond Trail emerges from the forest and passes under a huge rockslide on the side of Whitewall Mountain. Large white boulders are piled up on either side of the trail. Excellent views can be seen here through Zealand Notch to Mount Carrigain and Mount Hancock, as well as up to the cliffs on Whitewall Mountain and Zeacliff. Looking back, you can just make out Zealand Falls Hut, about 1.5 miles away. Continue straight past the junction with the Zeacliff Trail, 3.8 miles from the parking area. About 0.3 mile after the trail re-enters the woods, turn right onto the Thoreau Falls Trail for a 150-yard walk to the falls.

The falls are in a beautiful wilderness setting, with the water tumbling away from you in a graceful S-curve toward the East

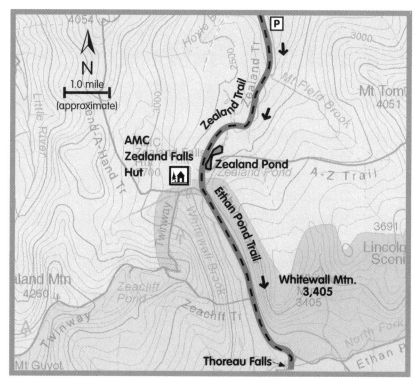

THOREAU FALLS

Branch of the Pemigewasset River. Rising into view across the valley are the thickly forested slopes of Mount Bond and Mount Guyot. The ledges at the top of the falls are a comfortable place to soak in the scenery, but they are well worn and slippery and care should be taken, especially with children. The falls are named after Henry David Thoreau, but, ironically, there is no evidence that he ever visited this part of the White Mountains. To complete your hike, walk back to the Ethan Pond Trail and turn left, following it and the Zealand Trail back to the parking area.

Directions

From the intersection of US 3 and US 302 in Twin Mountain, follow US 302 south for 2.2 miles and turn right onto Zealand Road. The parking area is at the end of Zealand Road, 3.5 miles from US 302.

Zealand Falls and Zeacliff

Rating: **Moderate**

Distance: **8.2 miles up and back**

Elevation Gain: **1,750 feet**

Estimated Time: **5.5 hours**

Maps: **AMC White Mountain Map #2,
        USGS Crawford Notch Quadrangle**

A moderate day hike to wildlife–rich beaver ponds, Zealand Falls, and excellent views of the Pemigewasset Wilderness Area.

THIS WAS OUR FIRST HIKE in the White Mountains, and we return time and time again to take in the incredible beauty of the Zealand valley. All kinds of wildlife habitat are on this hike, including a hardwood forest, beaver swamps, a mountain pond, a thick boreal forest, and a high-elevation bog. Signs of moose are common and the birdlife is extremely varied. You can see multitudes of warblers and flycatchers as well as grouse, woodcock, and ducks, and migrating birds of prey such as osprey and merlin in the fall. This trip also visits the AMC Zealand Falls Hut, which is situated next to the ledges of Zealand Falls—a great place to sit and take in the views of the Zealand valley. The hike from the hut to Zeacliff is a steep one, but the views from the top of the cliff are some of the best in the White Mountains.

You begin your hike on the Zealand Trail, which starts at the end of Zealand Road. The trail begins as a wide path that climbs gradually through a mixed forest of spruce, fir, maple, and birch. After about 0.4 mile you cross a wooden bridge and climb through a grove of spruce trees over a heavily eroded trailbed. (Please try to

Sitting on Zeacliff overlooking the Pemigewasset Wilderness Area.

stay on the trail here by following the blue blazes.) You will soon hear the Zealand River on your left. After making a close approach to the river at 0.8 mile, the trail turns to the right and continues a gradual climb. After crossing the river on a wooden bridge, you begin to walk through an area of beaver activity that lasts for almost 1.0 mile. The trail passes alder thickets and over wooden bridges and occasionally you will have good views of Zealand Mountain and Zeacliff to the southwest.

Just before reaching a junction with the A-Z Trail at 2.3 miles, you pass the largest of the beaver ponds, where there are at least two large beaver lodges and frog song is common. With a little luck, you might even see a moose in this area. Continue straight on the Zealand Trail and you will soon come to Zealand Pond, which will be on your right. Beaver dams are on either side of the bridge that spans the outlet of the pond, and a quiet hiker visiting the pond at dawn or dusk can most likely spot a beaver swimming. After the bridge, the trail follows the eastern shore of the pond before ending at its intersection with the Ethan Pond Trail and the Twinway. To make your way to the hut and the falls, follow the Twinway to the right for a short, but steep climb.

Zealand Falls Hut is one of two AMC huts open year-round (the other is Carter Notch Hut), and it makes a great destination during any season. The ledges of Zealand Falls provide excellent views across Zealand Pond to Mount Tom, across Whitewall Brook to Whitewall Mountain, and through Zealand Notch to the heart of the Pemigewasset Wilderness. This is definitely one of the best views for the effort in the White Mountains. The falls themselves are more than picture-worthy, whether in spring with blooming shad-bush and pin cherry, during fall foliage season, or in winter when the falls freeze and the spruce lining the brook are covered in fluffy snow. If the sun is out, you will have a hard time picking yourself up off the granite to begin the climb up to Zeacliff.

To reach Zeacliff, follow the Twinway as it passes the left side of the hut and crosses the brook (twice) before beginning a moderate, and sometimes steep, climb up the north side of Zeacliff. Most of the forest on this leg of the hike is filled with paper birch and balsam fir. In fall, the woods have a yellow glow as the sun filters through the leaves of the birch trees. In spring, you will find the understory filled with false hellebore, hobblebush, clintonia, wild lily-of-the-valley, and a variety of ferns. Sometimes the footing is rough, but it is never difficult. As you get higher up, the fir start to push out the birch, and by the time you near the top of the cliff, you are in a boreal forest of fir and spruce.

Soon after the trail levels out, about 1.1 miles above the hut, follow a side path on the left marked "view." Here you will find the ledges of Zeacliff and their spectacular views down into Zealand Notch and across to the Willey Range, with Mount Washington visible in the distance. Most of the wide expanse of the 45,000-acre Pemigewasset Wilderness Area lies below you. One of the largest roadless areas in the eastern United States, this wilderness area was

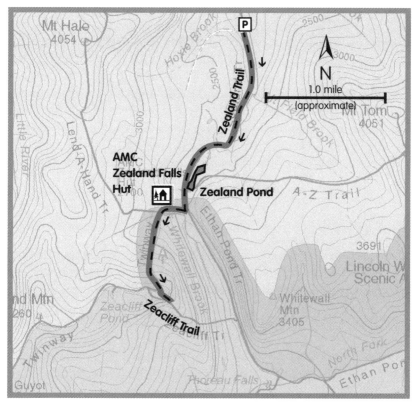

ZEALAND FALLS AND ZEACLIFF

once one of the most heavily logged and burnt-over forests in New Hampshire. The destruction that occurred in this area at the end of the nineteenth century inspired groups like the AMC and the Society for the Protection of New Hampshire Forests to lobby Congress for the creation of the White Mountain National Forest. In 1911 they succeeded when Congress passed the Weeks Act, preserving the White Mountains as a national forest.

Once you have taken in the views from the cliff, you can begin your trip back down to the hut or spend some time looking at the plants living in the high-elevation bog, which can be found on the Twinway just past the side trail to the cliff. Here you will find rhodora, sheep laurel, Labrador tea, and cotton grass, growing through a thick mat of sphagnum moss. Since this is an up-and-back trip, complete your hike by retracing your steps back to the parking area.

Alternate Trip

This trip can easily be combined with the trip to Thoreau Falls (trip #17) to make a long day hike. From the summit of Zeacliff, continue on the Twinway away from the hut for about 0.25 mile and turn left onto the Zeacliff Trail. Follow the Zeacliff Trail for 1.4 miles to the Ethan Pond Trail and turn right to head toward Thoreau Falls (from this point on, follow the description in trip #17). *A word of caution:* the Zeacliff Trail is extremely steep and can be dangerous to descend in wet or icy weather or with a heavy pack.

Directions

From the intersection of US 3 and US 302 in Twin Mountain, follow US 302 south for 2.2 miles and turn right onto Zealand Road. The parking area is at the end of Zealand Road, 3.5 miles from US 302.

Trip #19

Mount Moosilauke

> Rating: **Moderate**
>
> Distance: **7.4 miles up and back**
>
> Elevation Gain: **2,450 feet**
>
> Estimated Time: **6 hours**
>
> Maps: **AMC White Mountain Map #4, USGS Mount Moosilauke and Mount Kineo Quadrangles**
>
> **Cascading streams lead the way to New Hampshire's westernmost alpine peak.**

MOOSILAUKE is the Algonquin Indian word for bald place. It is a fitting name for this open, rounded peak, which is the westernmost above-treeline summit in the White Mountains. Mount Moosilauke is a significant landmark for northbound hikers of the Appalachian Trail, as it is the first bald peak they encounter north of Virginia. The mountain is also important to Dartmouth College, which owns about half of the mountain and maintains most of its trails. This hike begins next to the college's Ravine Lodge at the southeastern base of the mountain, and climbs to the summit via the Gorge Brook Trail. The moderate grades and scenic qualities of this trail make it popular, and heavy traffic has created some rough footing at the beginning of the hike; however, the trailbed is smoother after the first mile. An option exists to make this a loop hike, by walking down Mount Moosilauke's south ridge and returning via the Moosilauke Carriage Road and Snapper Trail.

Walk along the old gravel roadbed that extends from the end of Ravine Lodge Road to reach the Gorge Brook Trail. In about 50 yards, turn left onto a trail that leads down to the Baker River. Cross the river on the bridge and turn left onto the Gorge Brook Trail on the other side of the river. The Baker River, which flows into the

On the summit of Mount Moosilauke.

Pemigewasset River, was used extensively for logging operations in the late nineteenth century. Logs harvested on Mount Moosilauke were floated down the river to mills in Plymouth. The last old-growth spruce logs harvested from the mountain were used to build the Ravine Lodge in 1937 and 1938. The remaining old-growth forest on the mountain was destroyed soon after by the 1938 hurricane.

The Gorge Brook Trail soon reaches a junction with the Hurricane Trail; turn right to stay on the Gorge Brook Trail. The trail climbs steadily over rocks and roots as it parallels Gorge Brook. After crossing the brook on a wooden bridge at 0.6 mile, the Gorge Brook Trail turns right while the Snapper Trail goes to the left. Stay on the Gorge Brook Trail, which continues to parallel the brook, climbing moderately. During this part of the hike, you are treated to the constant sounds of rushing water as Gorge Brook flows from cascade to cascade. At 1.3 miles the trail crosses the brook for the last time and heads due west for a while before turning north and climbing the southeastern ridge of the mountain.

Following the moderate grade of an old logging road, the trail soon brings you to an outlook with good views to the southeast. The forest changes to spruce-fir, indicating you are one habitat zone below the alpine world of Mount Moosilauke's summit. The trail continues to climb via switchbacks that show off the excellent trail-

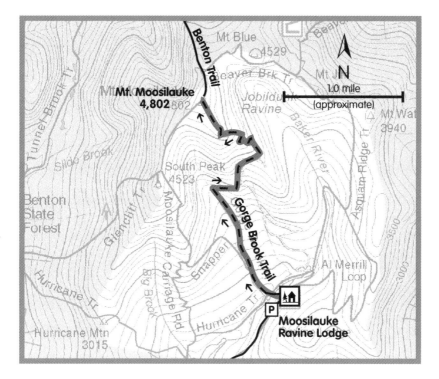

MOUNT MOOSILAUKE

building skills of the Dartmouth Outing Club. As the trees get shorter, the views get better and better and begin to include Franconia Ridge to the northeast and other mountains to the south and east. You reach the plateau below the summit after making one last right-hand switchback. The trail teases as you hike in and out of the trees with the bare summit in view. Shortly before reaching the summit, you break out of the trees for good and are surrounded by a meadow of rocks, grasses, and sedges, with blueberries, cranberries, and three-toothed cinquefoil adding splashes of color.

The alpine summit of Mount Moosilauke is somewhat separated from the rest of the White Mountains to the east, giving you a unique view of the national forest from Kinsman Ridge to Franconia Ridge to the Presidential Range. Immediately to the west is the low, flat Connecticut River valley. Rising up to the west of the river are the Green Mountains of Vermont, and on clear days you can see all the way to New York's Adirondack Park. Scattered about the summit are the foundations of various structures that are part of the mountain's history. The most notable building was a hotel built in 1860 called the Prospect House and later known as the Tip Top House and Summit House. During the winter of 1869–1870, Joshua Huntington and Amos Clough became the first people to spend a winter on one of the summits in the White Mountains. They used Prospect House as a base to study the weather, and in February of 1870 measured winds in excess of 100 MPH—the strongest winds ever recorded at that time. They remained on the mountain from January 1 through February 26 and their success inspired them to begin the weather observatory on Mount Washington the following winter.

To finish your hike, you can either return via the Gorge Brook Trail or make a loop using the Carriage Road (Appalachian Trail) and Snapper Trail. While the Gorge Brook Trail is a much more scenic hike than the wide, rock-filled Carriage Road (it really looks like a road), the lure of hiking the Appalachian Trail down the narrow ridge connecting Mount Moosilauke with its south summit is hard to pass up. To complete this optional loop, which only adds 0.1 mile to the hike, follow the Carriage Road south from the summit, making sure to turn left at its junction with the Glencliff Trail. When you reach the Snapper Trail, turn left again and then take a right onto the Gorge Brook Trail when you reach Gorge Brook.

Directions

From I-93 take Exit 32, following NH 112 west for 2.9 miles and turn left on NH 118. In 7.0 miles, turn right on Ravine Lodge Road. Park at the end of Ravine Lodge Road, 1.6 miles from NH 118.

glacial cirques: remnants of the ice age

ONE OF THE MORE prominent geologic features of the Presidential Range is the glacial cirque, an amphitheatre-shaped basin carved out of the side of a mountain by a glacier during the last ice age. A perfectly formed cirque is semicircular in shape with high, steep walls on the side. The bottom of the cirque is usually flat or concave and often contains a small lake known as a tarn. Tuckerman Ravine is the best known cirque in the White Mountains. Hermit Lake is an example of a glacial tarn. A hike up Mount Washington via the Boott Spur and Lion Head Trails is a great way to see Tuckerman Ravine and try to visualize a glacier at work (see trip #29).

There are, of course, other cirques in the White Mountains. Cirques in the Presidentials are Madison Gulf, Jefferson Ravine, King Ravine, Huntington Ravine, the Gulf of Slides, and the Great Gulf, the largest cirque in the White Mountains. A few cirques exist outside of the Presidential Range, the most conspicuous being Jobildunk Ravine on Mount Moosilauke. In the White Mountains cirques often are found on northern and eastern slopes where a large accumulation of ice and snow remained year-round. Over the course of centuries, gravity caused this ice and snow to flow downhill, taking along rocks and soil. Eventually, these alpine glaciers carved out the basins we call cirques.

The U shape of cirques easily distinguishes them from ravines and valleys carved by streams and rivers, which have a V shape. A great place to see the difference between these two types of ravines is the Air Line Trail on Mount Adams. Once above treeline you are standing on a ridge with the U-shaped King Ravine to the west and a V-shaped valley to the east (home to the Valley Way Trail). It is easy to see King Ravine as a glacial cirque in this comparison.

Mount Jefferson via Caps Ridge

> **Rating: Strenuous**
>
> Distance: **5.0 miles round-trip**
>
> Elevation Gain: **2,700 feet**
>
> Estimated Time: **4.5 hours**
>
> Maps: **AMC White Mountain Map #1, USGS Mount Washington Quadrangle**
>
> **A quick ascent to rocky ridges, alpine vegetation, and spectacular views of Mount Washington and the Northern Presidentials.**

THIS HIKE OFFERS SPECTACULAR VIEWS from the summit of 5,716-foot-tall Mount Jefferson with only 2,700 feet of elevation gain—the Caps Ridge Trail has the highest trailhead in the White Mountains at 3,008 feet. While this is a substantial elevation gain for a day hike, it is considerably less than other hikes to peaks in the Northern Presidentials, which usually require 3,500 to 4,200 feet of elevation gain. The Caps Ridge Trail is a great way to quickly reach the alpine zone, but just because this hike has less elevation gain than other hikes, do not make the assumption that this trip is easy. It includes steep scrambles that can be dangerous in wet or icy conditions and frightening to people with a fear of heights in any weather. A considerable amount of exposure to the elements also is a part of this trip. Caution should be taken if thunderstorms look possible, or if rain, snow, or high winds are forecast. That said, the above-treeline hiking on the Ridge of the Caps is inspiring, and the views from the summit of Mount Jefferson are spectacular.

From the summit of Mount Jefferson, view of Mount Adams in the distance.

Due to the high elevation of the trailhead, the Caps Ridge Trail begins in the spruce-fir forest that is common at higher elevations, between 2,500 and 4,000 feet, in the White Mountains. As you begin your hike, you will traverse wooden puncheons through wet terrain that is characterized by a forest floor covered in sphagnum moss. The footing becomes difficult as the trail is covered with rocks and tree roots. The tree roots become less of a problem as the trail begins its steep climb, but the rocks will be with you all the way to the summit. Along the trail you will be treated to a variety of ferns, mosses, and heaths, including the ghostly white Indian pipe—a waxy, translucent saprophytic plant that takes its nourishment from decayed organic matter.

One mile from the parking area, the trail reaches its first viewpoint, a granite outcrop to the right of the trail. This outlook is a worthwhile destination in and of itself with excellent views of the summit of Jefferson, the Ridge of the Caps, Mount Clay, and the Southern Presidentials. Shortly after this outlook, the Link enters

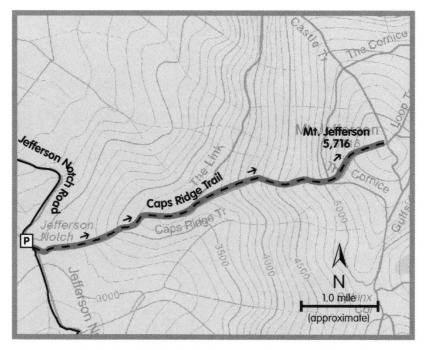

MOUNT JEFFERSON VIA CAPS RIDGE

from the left, providing a route to the Castle Trail, which traverses the northwest ridge of Mount Jefferson. Continuing straight on the Caps Ridge Trail, it becomes much steeper as the trees get shorter. Views to the west become increasingly interesting as you can see all the way to Mount Lafayette in Franconia. Just prior to the lower Cap, you encounter the first, steep scramble over rock ledge. After reaching the lower Cap at 1.5 miles, the trail remains above treeline for the rest of the hike.

The 0.4 mile between the lower Cap and upper Cap is also steep and difficult with scrambles over steep ledges. This difficult place to hike is also a difficult place for plants to survive. At this point the only trees you will encounter are short, scrubby balsam fir known as krummholz. They rarely reach four feet in height but can be over 100 years old—natural bonsai. As you continue to climb, even the krummholz finds it hard to survive, and the environment becomes an alpine world of sedges, lichens, and tough herbaceous wildflowers such as three-toothed cinquefoil and diapensia. At 2.1 miles the Cornice enters from the left and in 20 yards leads to the right, providing a link to the Gulfside Trail and Mount Washington. Continue straight and follow the Caps Ridge Trail for the final 0.4 mile to the summit.

The summit is a pile of glacially broken boulders that sits atop a small depression surrounded by three other boulder piles. The views are spectacular in all directions, with the view of Mount Washington across the Great Gulf headwall seeming particularly dramatic. The Great Gulf is the largest glacial cirque in the Whites, and its headwall is about 1,700 feet tall. While taking in the views, look for ravens playing on the thermals of air, warm columns of air that rise from the valley floor. In fall, hawks, eagles, and even monarch butterflies ride these same thermals in search of an efficient flight to their wintering grounds.

This is an up-and-back trip, so to complete your hike just retrace your route back down the Caps Ridge Trail.

Directions

From the westernmost intersection of NH 16 and US 2 in Gorham, New Hampshire, drive west on US 2 for 9.25 miles and turn left on Valley Road in Jefferson. After 1.25 miles (the last 0.2 of which is gravel), turn left onto Jefferson Notch Road. This gravel road is rough in places, but is suitable for low-slung two-wheel-drive vehicles. The parking area is on the left, 5.2 miles south of Valley Road. From the south, the parking area is 3.4 miles north of Base Road, which is the road running from NH 302 near Bretton Woods to the Cog Railway.

Mount Webster and Mount Jackson

> **Rating: Strenuous**
>
> Distance: **6.5 miles round-trip**
>
> Elevation Gain: **2,500 feet**
>
> Estimated Time: **4.5 hours**
>
> Maps: **AMC White Mountain Map #3, USGS Crawford Notch Quadrangle**
>
> **A hike high above Crawford Notch with excellent views and a visit to the upper reaches of Silver Cascade.**

MOUNT JACKSON, at 4,052 feet, is the southernmost 4,000-footer on Mount Washington's great southern ridge. While part of the ridge that makes up the Presidential Range, Mount Jackson was not named after President Andrew Jackson but Charles Thomas Jackson, state geologist of New Hampshire in the early nineteenth century. Its rocky summit rises above the spruce-fir forest of the Presidential Range–Dry River Wilderness to provide 360-degree views. Mount Webster, named after American statesman Daniel Webster, is a craggy outlook at the top of the dramatic cliffs on the east side of Crawford Notch. This hike leaves from Crawford Notch and loops over both peaks via the Webster-Jackson and Webster Cliff Trails.

This trip begins on the Webster-Jackson Trail, which leaves the east side of US 302—across the street and about 100 yards north from the small parking area on the west side of the road. Just to the south of the trailhead is the rocky outcropping known as Elephant Head, which marks the "gate" of the notch. In one of his early travel essays, *Sketches from Memory*, Nathaniel Hawthorne described his

Looking toward Crawford Notch from Mount Webster.

passage through the notch in 1835 in the standard poetic style of the time. "It is indeed a wondrous path. A demon, it might be fancied, or one of the Titans, was traveling up the valley, elbowing the heights carelessly aside as he passed, till at length a great mountain took its stand directly across his intended road. He tarries not for such an obstacle, but rending it asunder, a thousand feet from peak to base, discloses its treasures of hidden minerals, its sunless waters, all the secrets of the mountain's inmost heart, with a mighty fracture of rugged precipices on each side. This is the Notch of the White Hills." Dramatic words for a dramatic place. Today we just say that a glacier carved the notch during the last ice age.

The hike up the Webster-Jackson Trail ascends the steep eastern side of the notch, seeking out the "rugged precipices" for the views they afford. Soon after leaving US 302, a spur path leads right for 0.2 mile to the top of Elephant Head, which overlooks Crawford Notch. Continuing on the Webster-Jackson Trail, the hiking alternates between moderate climbing and relatively flat walking until at 0.6 mile, where a short path marked "view" leads to Bugle Cliff and its excellent views of the notch. From here the trail begins to climb

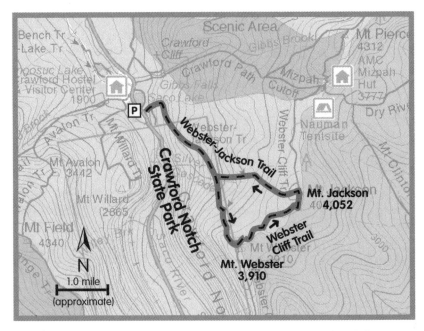

MOUNT WEBSTER AND MOUNT JACKSON

steeply. At 1.4 miles the Webster-Jackson Trail splits into two routes. The left route leads to Mount Jackson and will be the way you return. Take the right fork, which soon crosses Silver Cascade Brook just below a large pool and impressive 40-foot waterfall that drops over a wide, moss-covered rock slab.

After the falls the trail climbs steeply through a dark forest of balsam fir, red spruce, and paper birch, and reaches the ridge between Jackson and Webster, 2.4 miles from US 302. Turn right here on the Webster Cliff Trail for a short 0.1-mile walk to the summit of Mount Webster. From the summit of Mount Webster, cliffs drop very steeply down to the floor of Crawford Notch, 2,500 feet below. Excellent views can be seen of the Willey Range, Mount Hancock, Mount Carrigain, and the Presidentials.

To reach Mount Jackson, return to the junction of the Webster-Jackson Trail and the Webster Cliff Trail. At the trail junction continue straight (east) on the Webster Cliff Trail. The 1.4 miles between the two summits makes for an interesting hike past small bogs and through forests of short balsam fir growing through a bed of sphagnum moss. (An excellent example of an alpine bog can be found on the Webster

Cliff Trail between Mount Jackson and Mizpah Hut.) Just before reaching the summit, you will encounter one very steep section with a scramble over bare rock. This extra effort is worth it, though, as you are rewarded suddenly with excellent views in all directions. The views into the Presidential Range–Dry River Wilderness and up to Mount Washington are especially spectacular.

To complete your hike, turn left at the summit to follow the Jackson branch of the Webster-Jackson Trail. The trail descends steeply for most of the 1.2 miles down to its junction with the Webster branch of the trail. From this junction continue straight for the final 1.4 miles of the hike.

Directions

The parking area is on US 302 in Crawford Notch, about 0.3 mile south of the AMC Crawford Hostel. The hostel is 8.5 miles south of the intersection of US 3 and US 302 in Twin Mountain, and 21.0 miles north of the intersection of NH 16 and US 302 in Glen.

Mount Chocorua

Rating: Strenuous

Distance: 7.5 miles round-trip

Elevation Gain: 2,600 feet

Estimated Time: 6 hours

Maps: AMC White Mountain Map #3, USGS Mount Chocorua Quadrangle

A scenic loop hike to one of the most photographed mountains in New England.

MOUNT CHOCORUA (pronounced Chu-CORE-ooh-a) is a popular peak at the eastern end of the Sandwich Range, south of the Kancamagus Highway. Often photographed from the shores of Chocorua Lake in Tamworth, this peak is the first large mountain seen by travelers approaching the White Mountains from the south on NH 16. You can reach the 3,500-foot-high summit from just about any direction, but any hike of Chocorua involves significant elevation gain. It is worth the climb, though, as the bare summit dome of Chocorua provides excellent 360-degree views. This trip makes a loop up over the summit via the Brook and Liberty Trails on the southwest side of the mountain. These trails are a good alternative to the more popular Piper Trail on NH 16, and the very crowded Champney Falls Trail on the Kancamagus Highway.

This loop is completed in a clockwise direction and begins on the Brook Trail, which is found by walking past the gate at the end of Paugus Road. Follow the dirt road for about 100 yards, turn right at the fork, and follow signs for the Brook Trail. Just before a bridge over Claybank Brook, the Brook Trail leads into the woods on the right and parallels the brook. As is common throughout the northern hardwood forests of the White Mountains, the cool micro-

Reflections in Chocorua Lake.

climate of the brook provides the perfect habitat for eastern hemlock. The trail climbs gradually, passing the Bickford Trail at 0.9 mile and crossing the brook at 2.5 miles. After crossing the brook, you pass through a forest of beech and birch that was heavily damaged during the 1998 ice storm. From here to the summit the trail climbs steeply, reaching the first open ledges after 3.0 miles with views opening up to the south and west. The trail makes several difficult rock scrambles (be very careful in wet or icy conditions), and at 3.4 miles the Liberty Trail enters from the right.

At the junction with the Liberty Trail, turn left to complete the last 0.2 mile of climbing to the summit, making sure to stay to the right at a junction with the Piper Trail. Though well below treeline, the summit of Chocorua is completely exposed and can be a dangerous place to be in a thunderstorm. Of course, this exposure is what makes the views from the summit so spectacular, taking in Lake Winnipesaukee, the Sandwich Range Wilderness, the mountains that rise above the Pemigewasset Valley, and Mount Washington.

To complete this trip, follow the Brook Trail back down from the summit, turning left at its junction with the Piper Trail. Turn left

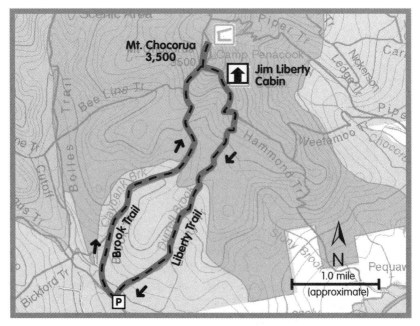

MOUNT CHOCORUA

again onto the Liberty Trail, 0.2 mile below the summit. The Liberty Trail makes a very steep descent over bare rock ledges at first, but soon you will find the hike down very easy. At 0.3 mile below the Brook Trail you will pass the Jim Liberty Cabin, and at 0.9 mile you pass a trail junction with the Hammond Trail (stay to the right). When you cross Durrell Brook it is only 1.1 miles to the parking area on Paugus Road.

Directions

From the intersection of NH 16 and NH 113 in Chocorua, New Hampshire, drive west on NH 113. In 2.9 miles turn right on NH 113A. In another 3.3 miles turn right on Fowlers Mill Road. In another 1.2 miles turn left on Paugus Road, following the sign for the Liberty and Brook Trails. The parking area for both trails is at the end of Paugus Road, 0.7 mile from Fowlers Mill Road.

the legend of chocorua

AS CELEBRATED AS THE VIEWS from Chocorua's summit are the stories of its namesake, an Abenaki Indian named Chocorua, the great-great-grandson of Chief Passaconaway. In the mid-seventeenth century Passaconaway had urged his Penacook tribe to seek a peaceful coexistence with white settlers; however, by the time of Chocorua in the early 1700s, most of the Penacook and other Abenaki tribes had been killed or driven from New England to Quebec. The first published account of Chocorua was written by Henry Wadsworth Longfellow in 1825. His poem, *Jeckoyva*, described the tragic tale of a Penacook hunter falling to his death from the summit of Mount Chocorua. A few years later, painter Thomas Cole climbed Mount Chocorua and wrote a tale in which white settlers killed Chocorua on the mountain's summit.

The most popular legend comes from a story written in 1830 by Lydia Maria Child. In Child's account, Chocorua lived peacefully among the white settlers of the area. When visiting other members of the Penacook tribe who had fled to Quebec, Chocorua left his son with a local white family, the Campbells. While away, his son accidentally swallowed fox poison and died. When hearing of his son's death, Chocorua killed Cornelius Campbell's wife and children. Campbell and several other men then chased Chocorua to the summit of the mountain, and the trapped Chocorua leapt from the mountain to his death, uttering a curse upon the white men that was blamed for years for the mysterious death of cattle in nearby towns. While probably very little of this story is true, Mount Chocorua does bear the name of a Penacook chief as do several other peaks in the Sandwich Range: Paugus, Passaconaway, Wonalancet, and Kancamagus.

Trip #23

Mahoosucs Adventure:
Goose Eye and Mount Carlo

Rating: Strenuous

Distance: 7.7 miles round-trip

Elevation Gain: 2,700 feet

Estimated Time: 6 hours

**Maps: AMC White Mountain Map #6, USGS
Shelburne and Success Pond Quadrangles**

**A rugged hike to spectacular views in the
wild and woolly Mahoosuc Range.**

STRADDLING THE MAINE–NEW HAMPSHIRE BORDER northeast of Gorham, the Mahoosucs are a rugged range of peaks that run southwest to northeast. While only one peak breaks the 4,000-foot barrier (Old Speck at 4,170 feet), the remote and rocky nature of the range makes the hiking both challenging and rewarding. The Appalachian Trail runs the entire length of the Mahoosucs, crossing all of the major summits as well as through Mahoosuc Notch, a 1.0-mile stretch of house-sized boulders that is often described as the most difficult mile on the entire Appalachian Trail. This hike up Mount Carlo and Goose Eye Mountain avoids the notch, but nonetheless contains some rough hiking over steep sections of exposed rocks. The effort is worth it, though, as the views from the bald summit of Goose Eye Mountain are some of the best in the White Mountains.

This trip leaves Success Pond Road on the Goose Eye and Carlo Col Trails, which follow an old logging road. After about 100 yards, turn left on to the Goose Eye Trail, which immediately descends the steep road bank and crosses a stream. The trail soon

Hiking the Appalachian Trail below Goose Eye Mountain.

turns right, heading over muddy ground through a second- or third-growth forest of spruce, fir, and birch. There is not much elevation gain as the trail crosses two fairly wide streams that can be difficult to cross in high water. Soon after the second large stream crossing, the Goose Eye Trail joins a logging road for about 100 yards before leaving the road, passing through a set of cairns on the right.

After leaving the road, you will notice the trail begins to climb, gradually at first. The forest is in various stages of growth, as most of the northwestern slopes of the Mahoosucs are owned by paper and forest management companies who manage the land for wood products. The trail gets steeper as you enter a forest of hardwoods filled

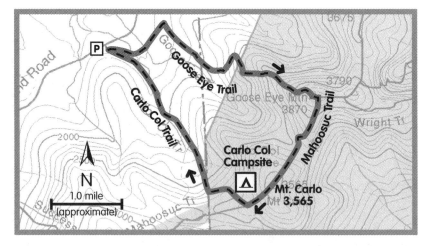

GOOSE EYE AND MOUNT CARLO

with the typical wildflowers of the area—trout lilies, mayflowers, early yellow violets, red trilliums—as well as forest birds such as ovenbirds, hermit thrushes, and ruffed grouse. As the trail angles up and around the northwestern side of Goose Eye Mountain, the footing gets rougher and the climbing steeper. As you climb, you will enter the familiar spruce-fir-paper birch forest that is common at higher elevations in New England.

You get a short break from the steep climbing as you attain the ridgeline and catch a glimpse of the rocky, pointed summit of Goose Eye through the trees. Of course, the trail soon gets steep again as you climb the summit cone, with the last 300 yards being very steep with some scrambling over bare rock. Shortly before reaching the summit, you emerge above the treeline into a world of krummholz. Sheep laurel, Labrador tea, mountain cranberries, and diapensia grow through a mat of sphagnum moss and reindeer lichens. After 3.2 miles and 2,250 feet of elevation gain, you attain the summit and are treated to excellent views in all directions, with the Presidential Range to the southwest and the wild undeveloped Northern Forest to the north and east. You can also see the Appalachian Trail as it winds its way across the treeless ridge to the north.

From the summit, follow the Goose Eye Trail 0.1 mile to the Mahoosuc Trail (Appalachian Trail) and turn right to head toward Mount Carlo. The Mahoosuc Trail immediately makes a steep and difficult descent over rocky ledges to a flat area below the summit containing an alpine bog. After the bog the trail continues a steep descent to the col between Goose Eye and Mount Carlo, then begins a steep climb through spruce-fir forest. The trail passes through another boggy area and makes a series of small climbs and descents before reaching the actual summit of Mount Carlo, about 1.5 miles from Goose Eye. Despite some small trees on and around the summit, good views can be seen in all directions.

Continue south on the Mahoosuc Trail for a 0.4-mile descent to the Carlo Col Trail and turn right. The Carlo Col Trail descends steeply to the Carlo Col Campsite, 0.3 mile below the Mahoosuc Trail. (This is the first reliable source of water since the stream crossings on the Goose Eye Trail.) After leaving the campsite, the Carlo Col Trail continues a steep descent following the banks of a stream, crossing it often, and sometimes following the stream course itself—just keep your eyes open for trail blazes and a worn footpath. After leaving the stream, the trail descends more moderately, crossing several small brooks. As the trail begins to level out, it follows a large brook (on the left) for about 0.3 mile. The trail then crosses the brook, turns right, and follows an old woods road for the final 0.8 mile, ending back at the parking area on Success Pond Road.

Directions

From the western junction of NH 16 and US 2 in Gorham, New Hampshire, follow NH 16 north for 4.5 miles and turn right onto the Cleveland Bridge. In another 0.7 mile, continue straight through a set of lights. After the lights, the road bears right, crosses a set of railroad tracks, and then bears to the left and becomes Hutchins Street. At 1.3 miles beyond the traffic light, turn right onto Success Pond Road, a dirt logging road often marked only by a sign saying "OHRV Parking, 1 mile." The Goose Eye and Carlo Col Trails will be on the right, 7.8 miles from Hutchins Street. Take care driving on Success Pond Road as it is an active logging road. Always yield to working logging vehicles for your own safety. The road is usually passable for most vehicles, except in early spring when it can be deeply rutted and missing some culverts.

the appalachian trail

An unmistakable white blaze marks the Appalachian Trail along this stretch of trail in New Hampshire.

MANY OF THE HIKES in this book use the Appalachian Trail (AT) for at least part of the trip, as it tends to follow the major ridges through the White Mountains. The AT is more than a path through the White Mountains—it is a 2,167-mile trail from Springer Mountain in northern Georgia to Katahdin in Maine. It supports a community of its own during the warmer months of the year as thousands of hikers attempt to complete the entire length of the trail. The AMC maintains approximately 122 miles of the AT in New Hampshire and Maine. Other hiking clubs also maintain the trail, with much of the trail work being completed by volunteers.

The AT was the vision of Benton MacKaye, who in 1921 wrote an article for the *Journal of American Architects* titled

"An Appalachian Trail, A Project in Regional Planning."
MacKaye believed that an increasingly urban America was
in need of wilderness camps that would provide workers a
respite from their jobs in factories and offices. He envisioned
the Appalachian Trail as a footpath from Mount Mitchell in
North Carolina to Mount Washington in New Hampshire. Along
the way would be farms, work camps, and study camps, where
hikers could spend time communing with nature and other
hikers. Within a couple of years his idea took root and eager
volunteers blazed the AT's first miles. Now a National Scenic
Trail administered by the National Park Service and extending
from Georgia to Maine, the AT has become a national treasure.

In 1948 Earl Shaffer became the first person to complete
an end-to-end hike of the trail. Known as thru-hikers, people
attempting to hike the entire length of the trail in one season
are now a common sight. About 2,500 people a year attempt
a thru-hike, most of them starting in Georgia and walking
north. Other hikers complete the trail over the course of
several years and are known as section hikers. Only about
one in ten complete a thru-hike, with physical and/or mental fatigue causing most people to pack it up and head
home. It takes most thru-hikers five or six months to complete the trail, averaging 12.0 to 15.0 miles a day. The trail
passes near towns every few days, allowing hikers the
chance to resupply at local stores or at the post office,
where friends back home mail carefully planned boxes of
food. Whether a hiker completes a thru-hike or not, he or
she is guaranteed to be rewarded with awe-inspiring views;
quiet, thought-provoking moments; and new friendships.

While you can now read books or take classes on how to
complete a hike on the Appalachian Trail, the act of actually
following the trail is rather simple. The AT is marked by rec-
tangular, white-paint blazes (two inches wide and six inches
tall) on trees and rocks from its beginnings in Georgia to the
summit of Katahdin. The hiking itself varies considerably,
from flat valley walks in thick oak-hickory forests to the long
above-treeline trek across the Presidentials. Passing over the

Smokies, the Blue Ridge Mountains, and the Green Mountains before hitting the Whites and western Maine, the Appalachian Trail explores the most rugged, scenic terrain in the eastern United States.

As of the summer of 2000, only about 20.0 miles of the trail remained unprotected, but Congress had already appropriated all the money sought to complete its protection. To learn more about how to protect the trail or how to hike it, contact the Appalachian Trail Conference (ATC) at: 799 Washington Street, P.O. Box 807, Harpers Ferry, WV 25425-0807; 304-535-6331. Plenty of good information is also available on the ATC's website, www.atconf.org.

Mount Liberty

> Rating: **Strenuous**
>
> Distance: **8.0 miles up and back**
>
> Elevation Gain: **3,150 feet**
>
> Estimated Time: **6 hours**
>
> Maps: **AMC White Mountain Map #2,
> USGS Lincoln Quadrangle**
>
> **A climb to excellent views on the bald
> summit of Mount Liberty.**

MOUNT LIBERTY LIES at the southern end of Franconia Ridge. While this hike begins near the crowded Flume Gorge Visitor Center, it is quiet forests, big trees, and the sound of your own breathing that will soon surround you. You will be climbing more than 3,000 feet in elevation over rocky trails on your way to Mount Liberty's rocky summit, which barely rises above the surrounding boreal forest to reveal views in every direction. The Liberty Spring Trail is part of the Appalachian Trail and draws its share of visitors; if you are hiking on a summer or holiday weekend, try to get an early start. Mount Liberty is also one of New Hampshire's 4,000-footers, topping out at 4,459 feet.

Start your hike on the Whitehouse Trail, which leaves the parking area just north of the Flume Gorge Visitor Center. This part of the hike is a relatively flat walk that parallels the Franconia Notch Parkway on its way to the Liberty Spring Trail. (An alternative approach is to hike the Franconia Notch Bicycle Path from the visitor center or the Basin parking area to the Liberty Spring trailhead.) At about 0.6 mile turn left as the Whitehouse Trail merges with the bike path along the shores of the West Branch of the Pemigewasset

View into Pemigewasset from Mount Liberty.

River. After crossing two bridges, you will reach the Liberty Spring Trail at 0.8 mile on your right.

The Liberty Spring Trail is part of the Appalachian Trail and takes you quickly away from the highway and bike path. You are now hiking in the northern hardwood forest of Franconia Notch State Park. This part of the White Mountains has not seen logging in a very long time, so you will find big trees here: sugar maple, American beech, and yellow birch. You also will find smaller trees and large decaying trunks on the forest floor, indicating a healthy, mixed-age forest capable of supporting a diverse combination of plant and animal species. Painted and red trilliums, partridgeberry, and rose twisted stalk are just some of the wildflowers you will find here. The trail climbs moderately at first, following switchbacks as it makes its way up the lower slopes of Mount Liberty. At 0.6 mile stay to the left at the Liberty Spring Trail's junction with the Flume Slide Trail.

After the trail junction, the Liberty Spring Trail straightens out and continues to climb moderately. At 1.1 miles the trail crosses a brook and soon begins to climb steeply on a rock-strewn footpath.

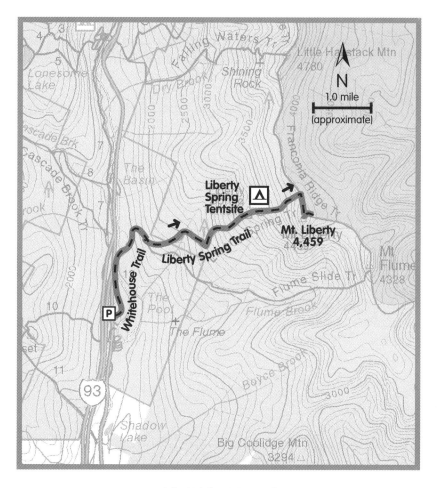

MOUNT LIBERTY

Trail maintainers have created hundreds of rock stairs from here to the ridgeline. These stairs are not obvious at first, appearing to be rocks in the trail, but look closely and you will notice that each rock is strategically placed to give hikers a place to step. This heavily used trail would have eroded into the Pemigewasset by now without this excellent trail maintenance. As you are climbing steeply, you will quickly leave the hardwoods behind and enter a forest of dark green fir and spruce, occasionally joined by the white of a paper birch. Flocks of chickadees and nuthatches may fill the canopy, occasionally joined by kinglets and warblers.

About fifteen to twenty minutes after passing the border of a Forest Protection Area, the trail reaches the Liberty Spring Tentsite (2.6 miles from the bike path). The last sure water source on this hike is on a spur path to the right of the tent site. The AMC maintains ten tent platforms, which are an excellent place to spend the night if you are in the backpacking mood (a small fee is collected by the caretaker). A ledge with restricted views to the west is just beyond the spring. From the tent site, continue up on the Liberty Spring Trail for 0.3 mile of steep climbing to Franconia Ridge. Franconia Ridge is well-known for its alpine, knife-edge traverse between Mounts Lincoln and Lafayette. In contrast, this part of the ridge, while still narrow, is covered by balsam fir. It nonetheless has an exciting character all its own, a secluded cloud forest resting below the harsh alpine world of the summits.

Turn right on the Franconia Ridge Trail for the final 0.3 mile to the summit, which lies 3.2 miles from the bike path. The 360-degree views extend from the Presidential Range in the east to Vermont in the west. What is most inspiring is the view into the 45,000 acres of the Pemigewasset Wilderness Area—the largest National Forest Wilderness Area east of the Mississippi River. Once devastated by clearcuts and forest fires, it is now completely forested and home to moose and bears. This is an out-and-back trip, so to complete your hike, return via the Franconia Ridge, Liberty Spring, and Whitehouse Trails. If you got an early start and are feeling strong, it is possible to make a loop over Mount Flume and return via the Flume Slide Trail. Be aware that there is a 500-foot drop in elevation between the peaks, followed by a 400-foot climb up Mount Flume. More importantly, the Flume Slide Trail descends a very steep rockslide on the western slope of Mount Flume and can be extremely hard on weary knees and very slippery and dangerous in wet weather. This optional loop will add 4.4 miles and four hours to your hiking day.

Directions

Start this hike on the Whitehouse Trail. Parking for this trail is on US 3, 0.2 mile north of the Flume Gorge Visitor Center in Franconia Notch State Park. To get on US 3, you can take either Exit 33 on I-93 or Exit 1 on the Franconia Notch Parkway.

the boreal forest

THE BOREAL FOREST is the northern most forest ecosystem in the world as it circles the globe across northern North America, Europe, and Asia. It is characterized by a dominance of evergreen trees, usually white spruce and balsam fir or jack pine. Other species such as hemlock, white pine, and red pine are also found here, and birch, poplar, and aspen populate disturbed sites. In the Southern Appalachians, red

An early snow coats the boreal forest on New Hampshire's Mount Lafayette, Franconia Ridge, White Mountains.

spruce is more common than white spruce, and Fraser fir replaces balsam fir. In the White Mountains, the boreal forest contains predominantly red spruce and balsam fir and can generally be found above 2,500 to 3,000 feet.

The boreal forest is a dark place, often preventing the growth of an understory of smaller trees or shrubs. Thin acidic soil, a product of recent glaciation and a slow rate of decomposition, also prevents many plants from taking root.

Some common plants that do manage to grow beneath the canopy of evergreens include partridgeberry, bunchberry, wood sorrel, and star flower. The most common mammals in the boreal forest are the red squirrel, porcupine, beaver, snowshoe hare, and moose. The moose is so readily identified with the boreal forest that it is sometimes called the "spruce-moose" forest. Other mammals that live in the boreal forest are fishers, pine martens, and lynx. It is believed that lynx no longer live in the White Mountains and it is rare to see fishers and pine martens. The boreal forest is also home to spruce grouse, gray jays, boreal chickadees, and finches like crossbills, pine grosbeaks, and pine siskins. Spring brings colorful migrant warblers like Blackburnian, bay-breasted, yellow-rumped, and Cape May.

Spruce and fir trees are remarkably adapted to survive the long winters of the high latitudes. Their conical, Christmas tree shape sheds the heavy snows of winter so that their branches are not damaged. The short growing season makes it inefficient to grow new leaves every year, so the trees' needles stay on year-round and go dormant during the winter. The needles are protected by a thick wax on the outside and a sugary fluid on the inside, which acts much like an antifreeze and prevents frost damage. The way needles are arranged on the tree has been shown to prevent wind chill and evaporation, and actually helps keep the trees warmer in winter. The needles can quickly begin photosynthesizing in the spring when temperatures rise.

At about 4,000 feet in the White Mountains, balsam fir is usually the only tree found in the boreal forest. The balsam fir is well-adapted to survive at higher elevations where the soil is thin and devoid of nutrients. Eventually, even balsam fir cannot survive standing up and the forest becomes stunted. This waist-high natural "bonsai" forest known as the krummholz is still dominated by balsam fir, but might also contain prostrate black spruce. Since the krummholz is not worth much as a wood product, this forest has never been cut and many of the small trees are more than 100 years old.

Trip #25

North and South Baldface

> Rating: **Strenuous**
>
> Distance: **9.7 miles round–trip**
>
> Elevation Gain: **3,600 feet**
>
> Estimated Time: **7 hours**
>
> Maps: **AMC White Mountain Map #5, USGS Wild River and Chatham Quadrangles**
>
> **A spectacular day hike with more than 3.0 miles of hiking above treeline.**

WHILE BOTH NORTH AND SOUTH Baldface top out at less than 4,000 feet, this hike near Evans Notch contains a long stretch of hiking over open ledges. It is somewhat removed from the traditional hiking centers in the White Mountains and thus receives far less foot traffic than trails in the Presidential Range, Pemigewasset Wilderness Area, and Franconia Notch. It does attract some hikers, though, because the views over the Wild River valley to the Carter Range and Mount Washington are spectacular. This is a difficult hike with substantial exposure that creates dangerous conditions in bad weather. One crossing of Charles Brook can be treacherous in high water. In good weather, however, this is one of the best loop hikes in New England.

Begin your hike on the Baldface Circle Trail, which leaves the west side of ME 113 across from the parking lot just north of the AMC Cold River Camp. The scent of pine immediately overtakes you as you enter a mixed forest of white pine, spruce, and various hardwoods. The trail parallels a stone wall for a while as it climbs gradually and then passes through a cool, dark grove of hemlock as you near Charles Brook. At 0.7 mile you reach a fork in the trail known as Circle Junction. A side trail leads left 0.1 mile to Emerald Pool, a deep

Mount Washington as seen from the Baldface Circle Trail.

swimming hole that sits below a rocky gorge and a steep bank topped by hemlock trees. This is a great place to cool down at the end of your hike. For now, follow the Baldface Circle Trail to the left, heading toward South Baldface. The trail soon begins to climb moderately through a northern hardwood forest that becomes increasingly dominated by American beech trees. The trail gets steeper shortly before it reaches the South Baldface Shelter at 2.5 miles.

After the shelter, you will climb very steeply over rock ledges as you begin to reap the rewards of this trip with good views to the east and south. This is the most difficult section of the hike with many steep scrambles over exposed rock. In wet or icy conditions this is a dangerous undertaking. This portion of the trail is marked by paint blazes on rock, as it is impossible to build cairns on the steep rock face. Vegetation is restricted to small shrubs such as pin cherry, blueberries, and rhodora. At 3.0 miles you reach the east ridge of South Baldface and the hiking becomes much easier, although it is still a steep climb the rest of the way to the summit— 3.7 miles from ME 113. The 360-degree views from this 3,570-foot

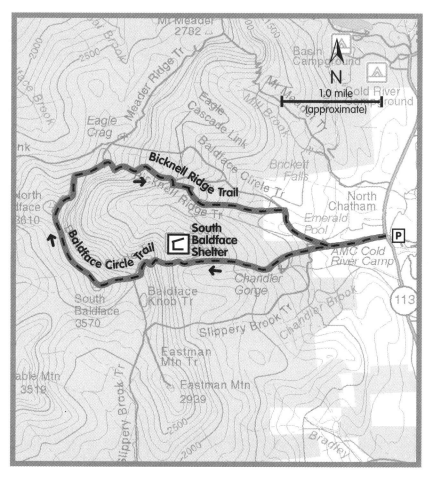

NORTH AND SOUTH BALDFACE

peak are spectacular and include Mount Washington, the Mahoosucs, and the Caribou–Speckled Mountain Wilderness.

The trail turns to the northwest to make the traverse of the ridge between the two Baldface summits. The trail descends back into the trees for a short distance, but you will spend most of your time hiking in the open for the 1.2 miles between the two peaks. About 200 feet of steep climbing is needed in order to reach the summit of North Baldface, but it is much less difficult than the climb up South Baldface. The summit of North Baldface has more of the excellent views you saw while on the south peak. The Carter Range is about 7.0 miles to the west, separated from the Baldface Range by the thick forests of the Wild River valley (the Spruce Brook Campsite and Perkins Notch Shelter make excellent backpacking destinations for those who want to explore the wilderness along the Wild River). The nearby peaks in the Evans Notch area are Mount Meader, Royce Mountain, Caribou Mountain (see trip #16), and Speckled Mountain.

The trail leaves North Baldface heading northeast as it descends steeply through spruce and fir before breaking out into the open again. Warm air rising above the open ridges of the Baldfaces makes this a great place to watch for hawks and geese during the fall migration. It is also a good spot for sampling wild blueberries in late summer. The trail travels in and out of the trees until its junction with the Bicknell Ridge Trail (5.8 miles from ME 113) in a flat area thickly populated with sheep laurel, blueberries, and mountain cranberries. At this point you can either stay on the Baldface Circle Trail or turn right onto the Bicknell Ridge Trail. We suggest taking the Bicknell Ridge Trail, which stays out in the open a little longer.

Bicknell Ridge is a rocky outcropping of schist flecked with shiny mica and lined with veins of quartz and basalt dikes. It also provides an excellent view of North and South Baldface and the circular ridge connecting the two. The trail makes a steep descent, finally entering the forest for good as the trees change from conifers to hardwoods. Shortly before its lower junction with the Baldface Circle Trail, the trail crosses Charles Brook (in high water cross about 20 yards upstream). Once you are back at the Baldface Circle Trail, turn right. You will soon cross Charles Brook again. This crossing can be very difficult in high water—try downstream this time. Shortly after crossing the brook, you complete the loop and have a flat 0.7-mile walk back to the car.

Directions

From the junction of ME 113 and US 302 in Fryeburg, Maine, head north on ME 113. Park in the lot on the right side of ME 113, which is 17.1 miles north of Fryeburg and just past the AMC Cold River Camp. The trail is across the road from the parking area.

North Moat and Red Ridge

> Rating: **Strenuous**
>
> Distance: **10.0 miles round-trip**
>
> Elevation Gain: **2,900 feet**
>
> Estimated Time: **8 hours**
>
> Maps: **AMC White Mountain Map #5,**
> **USGS North Conway West Quadrangle**
>
> **Open ridge walking, great views, and close to North Conway.**

"THE MOATS" are three peaks that sit atop the long ridge rising to the west of North Conway. They are modest peaks with only one, North Moat, rising above 3,000 feet in elevation. However, many open ledges along the ridge provide spectacular views of the surrounding peaks and countryside. These mountains have been climbed for as long as any in the White Mountains, as local settlers cleared trails up the ridge in order to pick berries. Even today, if you make this hike in late July or early August, you will be able to supplement your trail food with handfuls of wild blueberries. This trip makes a loop up Red Ridge and over the summit of North Moat. It also passes Diana's Baths, an excellent place to take a swim at the end of a long hike.

This hike begins and ends from a new parking area on the west side of West Side Road in North Conway, about 0.2 mile north of the old parking area. You start on a new section of the Moat Mountain Trail that passes through a beautiful forest of eastern hemlock and white pine for about 0.5 mile. At this point turn right on a dirt road that leads quickly to Diana's Baths, a series of attractive pools and cascades on Lucy Brook. The Moat Mountain Trail continues past Diana's Baths and is practically flat as it parallels Lucy

Brook. At 1.1 miles turn left onto the Red Ridge Trail, which crosses the brook and heads south over relatively flat terrain.

At 1.9 miles from West Side Road the Red Ridge Trail passes the Red Ridge Link Trail. It then crosses a dirt fire road at 2.6 miles (this road is good for biking, see trip #41). Take special care to practice Leave No Trace techniques here, as much of the first 2.6 miles of this hike is on private property. After crossing the fire road, the trail finally begins to gain some elevation, climbing moderately next to Moat Brook and crossing it at 3.1 miles (follow the yellow arrows). You now start to climb steeply up Red Ridge, which juts out to the northeast from the main Moat Mountain Ridge, between North and Middle Moat. You are soon rewarded with good views to the east.

These views are just the beginning. The Red Ridge Trail continues to climb steeply in and out of the trees over rock ledges populated with pine, spruce, blueberries, and sheep laurel. The views keep improving and soon you are looking east and south over Conway and Conway Lake and north to Mount Washington. The climb moderates somewhat as you crest the ridge, re-enter the trees, and reach the main ridge of Moat Mountain, 4.7 miles from West Side Road. At this point the Red Ridge Trail ends at the Moat Mountain Trail. Just a few yards to the left of this junction are some large boulders with more great views. To continue on to North Moat, turn right on the Moat Mountain Trail.

From the trail junction, the Moat Mountain Trail drops back into the trees before climbing 600 feet to the summit of North Moat. A couple of very steep sections are a part of the hike—you will be glad to be going up instead of down. The summit of North Moat has spectacular 360-degree views. To the south the entire Sandwich Range, including Mount Chocorua, seems close enough to touch. Hancock and Carrigain in the Pemigewasset Wilderness Area can be seen to the west, and the Presidentials rise above everything else in the north. Like most of the bare ridges in the Whites, the Moats are a great place to watch for hawks during the fall migration; although on a hot summer day, you are likely to see turkey vultures circling above the summit and over the forests to the west.

From North Moat, follow the Moat Mountain Trail down the mountain's steep northeast ridge. Trees are sparse for much of this descent, which means good views even on the way down. About 1.5 miles below the summit, you enter the forest for good in a thick

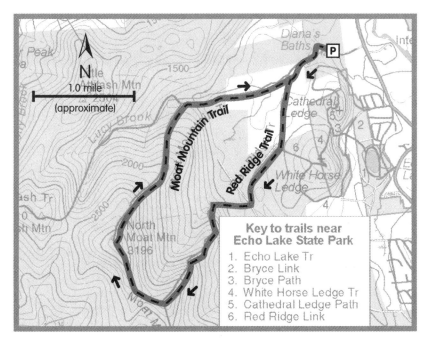

NORTH MOAT AND RED RIDGE

stand of tall red spruce. In another 0.4 mile the trail flattens out, runs into Lucy Brook, and makes a sharp right turn, following the south bank of the stream. By now the forest has changed to the northern hardwoods common at lower elevations. About 1.3 miles from the end of the hike, the trail crosses the brook and soon passes its junction with the Red Ridge Trail. From here it is 1.1 miles back to the parking area on West Side Road. Don't forget to stop and cool off in Diana's Baths on the way out.

Directions

From the intersection of NH 16 and River Road in North Conway (the light near the Eastern Slope Inn), head west on River Road, which soon turns into West Side Road. The parking area is on the left, about 2.5 miles from NH 16.

Mount Hight and Carter Dome

> Rating: **Strenuous**
>
> Distance: **10.2 miles round–trip**
>
> Elevation Gain: **3,600 feet**
>
> Estimated Time: **8 hours**
>
> Maps: **AMC White Mountain Map #5,
> USGS Carter Dome Quadrangle**
>
> **A strenuous all–day hike to Carter Dome
> and the spectacular views from Mount
> Hight.**

AT 4,832 FEET CARTER DOME is the "official" 4,000-footer of this trip, but it is Carter Dome's bald northeastern shoulder, Mount Hight, that has the dramatic close-up views of Mount Washington and the Northern Presidentials. This hike begins on the Nineteen-Mile Brook Trail and then loops up and over Mount Hight and Carter Dome via the Carter Dome and Carter-Moriah Trails. On the trip down from Carter Dome, you can visit a boulder field known as 'the Rampart' and the AMC Carter Notch Hut (a cozy place to spend the night) before heading back down the Nineteen-Mile Brook Trail. The only exposure to the weather on this trip is near the summit of Mount Hight, making it easy to find shelter during unexpected stormy weather. However, this is a long trip with substantial elevation gain that should be attempted only by those in good physical condition.

Starting from the trailhead on NH 16, the Nineteen-Mile Brook Trail is a gentle beginning to a strenuous day. For the first 1.9 miles of this hike, you will ascend gradually and parallel Nineteen-Mile Brook, which drains the west sides of Carter Dome and Wildcat Mountain. These are big mountains and the stream carries a lot

A view of AMC Carter Notch Hut below Carter Dome.

of water over boulders and under fallen trees. Refreshing swimming holes abound. The cool, moist microclimate around the brook creates the ideal conditions for hemlock trees, which grow thickly in a forest dominated by beech and maple only 100 yards or so away from the brook.

After 1.9 miles turn left on the Carter Dome Trail, which climbs moderately next to a small stream. This trail follows the route of an old road that once led to a fire tower that stood on the summit of Carter Dome. At 2.4 and 2.7 miles from NH 16 you cross the stream and then ascend the mountain via a set of well-graded switchbacks. By the time you reach the trail junction known as Zeta Pass at 3.8 miles, you are in a typical White Mountain, high-elevation boreal forest of balsam fir. Zeta Pass is the broad, flat col between Mount Hight and South Carter. To the left the Carter-Moriah Trail leads north toward South Carter and Mount Moriah. To the right the Carter-Moriah Trail shares the footpath with the Carter Dome Trail. In both directions the trail is a part of the Appalachian Trail. Turn right to make your way toward Mount Hight.

In 0.2 mile from Zeta Pass turn left on the Carter-Moriah Trail, which makes a steep climb over rocky terrain to the summit of Mount Hight. The bald summit of Mount Hight is small, but has spectacular views in all directions, especially toward the Northern Presidentials to the west and the Baldface Range to the east. Looking toward the Baldface Range across the undisturbed forest of the Wild River valley, it is hard to believe that only 100 years ago logging rail-roads climbed along every brook on the east side of the Carter Range. From 1890 to 1903 this entire valley was logged and the timber was sent to mills in Hastings, Maine, which processed 40,000 to 60,000 board feet of lumber a day. Forest fires destroyed what was left of the forest in 1903, and the town of Hastings disap-peared soon after.

From Mount Hight, the Carter-Moriah Trail drops down into a forest of fir before climbing the ridge between Mount Hight and Carter Dome. At 0.4 mile from Mount Hight the trail is joined once again by the Carter Dome Trail and soon passes the Black Angel Trail, which provides access to the Wild River valley. In another 0.4 mile you reach the summit of Carter Dome, which at 4,832 feet is 157 feet taller than Mount Hight. While you now have the satisfaction of climbing New Hampshire's ninth tallest mountain, the spruce-fir forest at the summit provides limited views at best. To continue your hike, follow the Carter-Moriah Trail south for a steep descent into Carter Notch.

In the 1.2 miles you hike from Carter Dome to Carter Notch, you will lose 1,500 feet of elevation. While very steep, the descent is not difficult unless you have sensitive knees. About 1.0 mile below the summit, a short spur path (marked "view") on the left leads to an excellent outlook on a ledge next to Pulpit Rock. From the ledge are good views of Wildcat Mountain and Carter Notch. The AMC Carter Notch Hut is also visible next to the Carter Lakes and the

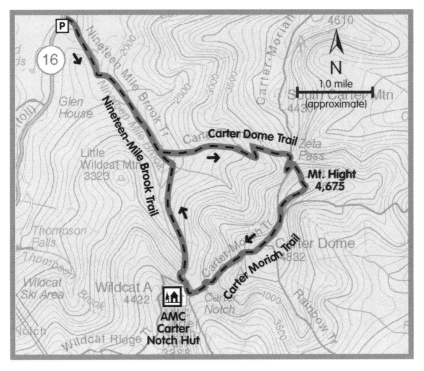

MOUNT HIGHT AND CARTER DOME

Rampart. From Pulpit Rock, it is about twenty minutes of steep climbing down to the Nineteen-Mile Brook Trail and the western-most of the two Carter Lakes. If you need to fill up on water (or candy bars), turn left for a short walk to Carter Notch Hut. (If you have plenty of energy, you might want to head out behind the hut and explore the Rampart, up to the summit of Wildcat, and out into the Wild River valley.) If you forgo the hut stop, turn right for a 3.8-mile hike back to the trailhead.

Directions

From the intersection of NH 16 and US 2 in Gorham, follow NH 16 south for about 7.0 miles. The parking area for the Nineteen-Mile Brook Trail will be on your left. From the south, the trailhead is 4.0 miles north of the AMC Pinkham Notch Visitor Center.

Franconia Ridge

> **Rating:** **Strenuous**
>
> **Distance:** **8.9 miles round-trip**
>
> **Elevation Gain:** **4,000 feet**
>
> **Estimated Time:** **8 hours**
>
> **Maps:** **AMC White Mountain Map #2,**
> **USGS Franconia Quadrangle**
>
> **This spectacular loop over Mount Lafayette and Mount Lincoln includes the longest above-treeline hike in the White Mountains outside of the Presidential Range.**

THIS TRIP IS EASILY NEAR the top of the list of best hikes in New England. Of course, Franconia Ridge also can be a very busy place during any weekend with good weather; however, early risers and weekday hikers stand a good chance to have at least part of the ridge all to themselves. The reward for climbing 4,000 feet in a day is getting to spend several hours above treeline, soaking in views from well above the surrounding mountains and forests. Below treeline is exciting as well, as you pass several waterfalls and hike through all of the major forest types found in the White Mountains. You will also pass the AMC Greenleaf Hut, which at 4,220 feet is the highest hut outside of the Presidentials and offers an excellent base for those who would prefer to make this a two-day trip.

CAUTION: Franconia Ridge is extremely exposed to the weather. Its knife-edge ridgeline is susceptible to lightning strikes and very strong winds. Check the weather forecast before undertaking this hike, and realize that, even in good weather, the summits can experience suddenly dangerous weather conditions. Plan ahead and pack appropriate clothing and equipment. (See Safety and Etiquette on page 36.)

Franconia Ridge as seen from the summit of Mount Lafayette.

This trip makes a loop by utilizing four trails: the Old Bridle Path, the Greenleaf Trail, the Franconia Ridge Trail, and the Falling Waters Trail. The loop can be hiked in either direction. By following the Falling Waters Trail first, you attack the steepest climbing on the way up and get to Franconia Ridge a little quicker. This is the preferred route for those who tend to get sore knees on steep descents. However, this description follows the Old Bridle Path up Mount Lafayette at the beginning, saving the waterfalls (and their feet-soaking pools) for the end of the trip. The Old Bridle Path leaves from a parking area on the east side of the Franconia Notch Parkway. (You can also park at Lafayette Campground on the west side of the parkway and walk through the tunnel under the highway to the trailhead.)

The hike begins in a typical northern hardwood forest, soon passing the Falling Waters Trail on the right at Walker Brook. The hiking is easy as you climb at a moderate grade for about 1.0 mile. The trail gets steeper and at 1.6 miles makes a sharp left turn at an obstructed view of Mount Lincoln through what is now a spruce-fir forest. In the spring, hobblebush, trilliums, rose twisted stalk, and star flowers add splashes of white, red, and pink to an otherwise green and brown forest. At 1.9 miles you walk out of the forest onto open ledges, which have excellent views of Mount Lafayette and Mount Lincoln. In good weather you may be able to see very small figures making their way across the top of the ridge between the peaks. That is your destination and you should be there in about two more hours.

After making your way across the ledges, you once again enter the boreal forest and make a steep climb up to Greenleaf Hut (2.9 miles), which sits above Eagle Lake, a small but scenic pond surrounded by a bog filled with interesting flora such as sundew, mountain cranberries, and pitcher-plants. Eagle Lake itself is colored yellow by blooming water lilies in June and July. Greenleaf Hut is a good place to fill up on potable water and chocolate bars. If you think you want to spend the night and experience the pleasure of eating a home-cooked meal at 4,200 feet, be sure to make reservations well ahead of time. The hut marks the end of the Old Bridle Path. To continue this trip, follow the Greenleaf Trail down to Eagle Lake and then 1.1 miles up to the summit of Mount Lafayette.

Much of the hike up Mount Lafayette from the hut is above treeline and the views to the west are excellent. However, the true visual prize is the view from the summit, where you stare across the vast, roadless forests and peaks of the Pemigewasset Wilderness Area. You also will find the stone foundation of an old shelter, which once gave refuge to early visitors to Mount Lafayette who climbed the summit via horseback on both the Old Bridle Path and the Greenleaf Trail beginning in the 1850s. Originally called Great Haystack, Mount Lafayette was named after the French general the Marquis de Lafayette during his visit to New Hampshire in the 1820s.

From the summit, take a right and follow the Franconia Ridge Trail south. Except for one brief section between Lafayette and Lincoln, your entire hike on the Franconia Ridge Trail will be above the trees in one of the few true alpine environments in the eastern United States. Just above treeline you will find the short, twisted, bonsai-like balsam fir known as krummholz. Soon, even these little trees disappear and you will find only alpine plants such as diapensia, mountain aven, deer's-hair sedge, and bear- berry willows. You reach the excellent views from the summit of Mount Lincoln about 1.0 mile from Mount Lafayette. About 300 feet of elevation gain is between the two summits, but after climbing

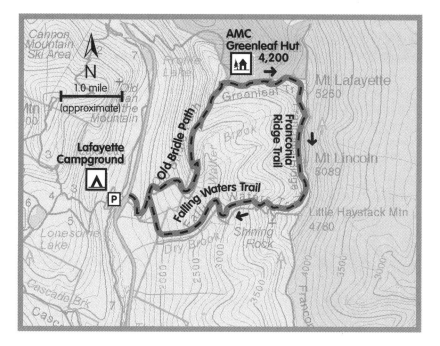

FRANCONIA RIDGE

3,600 feet to the summit of Mount Lafayette, you won't even notice the climb up Mount Lincoln.

From Mount Lincoln, continue south on the Franconia Ridge Trail. The knife-edge nature of the trail between Mount Lincoln and Little Haystack Mountain is perhaps the most exciting section of this hike; the mountain drops off steeply on both sides of the trail, giving you the feeling of being on top of the world. The hike to Little Haystack is all above treeline with one short section of climbing. From the summit of Little Haystack (5.7 miles), the Franconia Ridge Trail continues south to Mount Liberty, but to complete this hike, turn right onto the Falling Waters Trail and begin a very steep descent.

From Little Haystack, the Falling Waters Trail drops 3,000 feet in just 3.2 miles. It is a steep trail, but there is no scrambling. The trail enters the boreal forest almost immediately after leaving the ridge, and at 1.4 miles below the ridge it reaches a short spur trail that leads 100 yards to Shining Rock, which has excellent views of Franconia Notch, Cannon Mountain, and Kinsman Ridge.

The Falling Waters Trail continues its steep descent and reaches Dry Brook 1.6 miles below the Franconia Ridge. You soon begin to encounter the waterfalls that give this trail its name. First you will see two 25-foot cascades that face each other and fall together to form the pool above Cloudland Falls. From the top of Cloudland Falls—one of the most beautiful waterfalls in the White Mountains—you get an impressive view to Mount Moosilauke. The trail continues its steep descent and passes Swiftwater Falls and finally Stairs Falls where it begins to flatten out.

With 0.7 mile left to go, you will cross Dry Brook and have a relatively easy hike the rest of the way. After crossing Walker Brook on a wooden bridge, turn left onto the Old Bridle Path for the final 0.2 mile of the loop.

Directions

From the Franconia Notch Parkway (I-93), follow signs to Lafayette Campground, 7.6 miles north of NH 112. Park in the hiker parking area at the Lafayette Campground in Franconia Notch State Park. The exit for the campground is on the southbound side of the parkway, but hiker parking is also on the northbound side. The Old Bridle Path leaves the parking area on the northbound side of the highway.

the alpine zone

ALPINE HABITAT IS RARE in the eastern United States, occurring on separate mountain peaks in the Adirondacks, Mount Mansfield in Vermont, and Katahdin in Maine. The White Mountains have the most extensive areas of alpine habitat in the east (eight square miles), most of it occurring

Mountain aven

on Mount Washington, the Presidential Range, and the Franconia Range. Generally occurring above 4,500 feet in the White Mountains, the alpine zone is a world without trees that provides hikers with the spectacular views they spend hours of effort trying to achieve. More importantly, this

treeless habitat is an environment that contains a unique mix of plants and animals, some of which are found nowhere else in the world. Immersing yourself in the miniature world of diapensia and alpine azalea, plants more commonly found in the Arctic, can be a fascinating experience.

The alpine habitat in the White Mountains has a growing season of only 60 to 70 days, making it impossible for annuals to grow, which is why you will find only perennials growing above treeline. Plants include not only herbaceous (non-woody) plants like mountain sandwort, but also dwarf shrubs and trees, ferns and mosses, lichens, sedges, grasses, and rushes. Each species employs different strategies for survival, but they all hug the ground in order to survive the cold and strong winds (which regularly reach hurricane force) that are a fact of life above treeline. The fight for survival is so difficult for these plants that a misplaced step by a hiker can kill a plant that took decades to grow. When above treeline, please make an effort to stay on the trail or on the rocks.

Several different alpine communities are within the alpine zone, each with its own habitat characteristics and species composition. Diapensia communities consist of hummock-shaped mats of white and yellow flowered diapensia scattered among bare patches of rocks and, sometimes, mats of pink alpine azalea and Lapland rosebay. Bigelow's edge communities consist mostly of Bigelow's edge and look like grassy meadows. Other communities include the dwarf shrub and heath, snowbank, alpine bog, and streamside communities. In snowbank, streamside, or bog communities you may find the beautiful yellow mountain aven, which lives only in the

White Mountains and a few islands in Nova Scotia. The rarest plant in New England is the federally endangered dwarf cinquefoil, which has small yellow flowers (1/4 inch across), and is found only on Mount Washington and in the Franconia Range.

New England's alpine communities are a remnant from the tundra environments that recolonized the area after the last ice age. As the climate warmed and trees began spreading northward, the arctic plants that thrived in the tundra were pushed farther north and higher up the mountains until approximately 10,000 years ago when the distribution of plant species reached its current makeup in New Hampshire.

The harsh conditions in the alpine zone support far less animal life than the comfy confines of the forests below. Birds you might encounter include ravens, dark-eyed juncos, white-throated sparrows, yellow-rumped and blackpoll warblers, American pipits, and the increasingly rare Bicknell's thrush. Mammals like moose, fox, and coyote are rare visitors to the alpine zone. You are likely to encounter snowshoe hares near the treeline and even woodchucks high up on the slopes of Mount Washington. Cold-blooded amphibians and reptiles cannot survive for long above treeline, although in the summer you might find red efts and American toads at higher elevations. We have even seen wood frogs in the stream next to the AMC Madison Hut.

If you would like a great reference to the alpine zone of the White Mountains, check out the *AMC Field Guide to the New England Alpine Summits* by Nancy G. Slack and Allison W. Bell.

Trip #29

Mount Washington
via Boott Spur

Rating: Very Strenuous

Distance: 9.5 miles round-trip

Elevation Gain: 4,300 feet

Estimated Time: 8 hours

**Maps: AMC White Mountain Map #1,
USGS Mount Washington Quadrangle**

**A climb up New England's tallest peak, with
plenty above-treeline hiking and awesome
views.**

AT 6,288 FEET, Mount Washington is the highest point in New England, and its weather is considered the worst in the world. It is easily one of New Hampshire's most popular attractions, with an auto road and cog railway bringing up visitors who are unwilling or unable to use one of the various hiking trails that approach the summit from every direction. This hike uses the Boott Spur Trail for the ascent, taking you away from the almost certain crowds on the Tuckerman Ravine Trail. Views are spectacular of the glacial cirque known as Tuckerman Ravine from the Boott Spur Trail and the Lion Head Trail on the way down.

CAUTION: This is a very strenuous hike, gaining 4,300 feet in elevation over sometimes rough terrain. Attempt this hike only if you are in excellent physical shape, well-equipped for a day above treeline, and the weather forecast looks favorable; people die almost every year on Mount Washington due to falls, hypothermia, avalanches, and rockslides. All of the above-treeline portion of this hike is extremely exposed to the weather and is susceptible to lightning strikes and very strong winds. Check the

A hiker on Mount Washington's Tuckerman Ravine Trail on an icy, late-summer day.

weather forecast before undertaking this hike and realize that, even in good weather, this area can experience suddenly dangerous weather conditions. Be prepared to seek shelter or turn around if the weather changes for the worse.

This hike begins behind the AMC Pinkham Notch Visitor Center on the Tuckerman Ravine Trail. The trail is wide and rocky and climbs moderately, reaching the Cutler River and Crystal Cascade in just 0.3 mile. At 0.4 mile turn left onto the Boott Spur Trail where the Tuckerman Ravine Trail makes a sharp right. The Boott Spur Trail climbs very steeply at times, reaching an outlook with views of Wildcat Mountain and the Carter Range about forty-five minutes above Pinkham. At 1.4 mile a short spur path leads left to a good view of Huntington Ravine, Lion Head, and Boott Spur. The trail continues to climb steeply through spruce and fir, and at 2.1 miles another side trail leads right to Harvard Rock, which has excellent views of Tuckerman Ravine. Shortly after Harvard Rock, the trail climbs above treeline, makes a brief southward turn, and levels out (catch your breath here) before turning right at a large boulder known as Split Rock and resuming its steep climb.

At 2.6 miles the trail reaches the Boott Spur Link, which leads 0.6 mile down to the Hermit Lake Shelters in Tuckerman Ravine. From this junction it is another 0.7 mile and 800 feet up to the end of the Boott Spur Trail. Along the way you will have spectacular views into Tuckerman Ravine, at times being more than 1,500 feet above the floor of the ravine. During your rest breaks, look at the alpine flora next to the trail. Depending on the time of year, you may see berries of various colors—red, blue, white, and black. The red ones are mountain cranberries, also known as lingonberries. Blueberries are either dwarf alpine blueberries or bog bilberries. The white ones are creeping snowberries and the black are black crowberries. All of these plants are common in arctic and subarctic environments in eastern North America.

The Boott Spur Trail ends at the Davis Path, 3.4 miles from Pinkham Notch. The summit of Boott Spur is the large jumble of rocks to the left. While 5,500 feet tall, from here Boott Spur looks like just a resting spot on the way to Mount Washington, which looks close enough to touch. Looks can be deceiving, however, as you are still 2.0 miles and 900 feet below the summit. To reach the summit turn right onto the Davis Path. At 0.6 mile from the Boott Spur Trail the Davis Path passes the Lawn Cutoff (if you are too tired to continue to the summit, follow the Lawn Cutoff to Tuckerman Junction and take the Tuckerman Ravine Trail back to Pinkham Notch). It soon crosses the Camel Trail and Tuckerman Crossover on its way to the Crawford Path, 1.4 miles below Boott Spur. Turn right onto the Crawford Path for the final 0.6 mile to the summit.

The summit of Mount Washington is a bustling place, with hikers mixing with tourists who either rode the Cog Railway or drove their cars up the Mount Washington Auto Road. A snack bar is open during the summer months, complete with restrooms and cafeteria-style seating. A building also houses the Mount Washington Observatory (www.mountwashington.org) and its scientists who observe the weather and subarctic environment on Mount Washington year-round. The views from the summit are, of course, spectacular in every direction, although Mount Washington averages only 65 clear days a year. The craggy peaks and cirques of the nearby Northern Presidentials provide the most dramatic scenery. To the west the

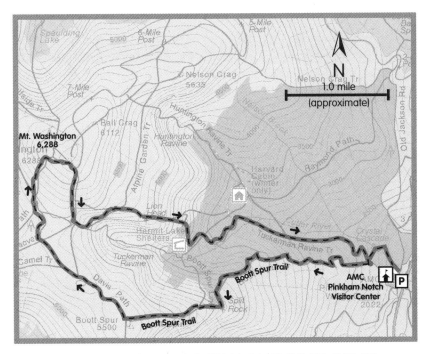

MOUNT WASHINGTON VIA BOOTT SPUR

Southern Presidentials gradually slope down toward Crawford Notch. On clear, smog-free days you can see the sun reflecting off the Atlantic Ocean, about 80.0 miles to the southeast.

To return to Pinkham Notch find the Tuckerman Ravine Trail, which leaves the Auto Road just below the lower parking lot on the summit. Follow the trail from boulder to boulder as it makes a steep descent from the summit cone. You will begin to understand why Mount Washington is nicknamed "the rock pile." At 0.4 mile below the summit turn left onto the Lion Head Trail, which continues the steep descent over lichen-covered boulders. At 0.9 mile below the summit you cross the Alpine Garden Trail, which leads across an alpine plateau well-known for its early-summer wildflower displays. Soon you reach the Lion Head, a craggy overhang with spectacular views into Tuckerman Ravine.

From Lion Head the Lion Head Trail continues a steep, rocky descent to the Hermit Lake Shelters and the Tuckerman Ravine Trail, which you reach 2.0 miles below the summit. By the time you reach the shelters (Hermit Lake is a short walk to the right up the Tuckerman Ravine Trail), you have completed the above-tree-line portion of your hike. Turn left on the Tuckerman Ravine Trail for 2.3 miles of hiking over rocks with sore feet and tired legs during your moderate descent back to Pinkham Notch.

Directions

This hike begins behind the AMC Pinkham Notch Visitor Center on the Tuckerman Ravine Trail. The visitor center is about 12.0 miles north of US 302 in Glen and 11.0 miles south of US 2 in Gorham.

mount washington: tallest, stormiest, deadliest

MOUNT WASHINGTON, originally called Agiochook by the local Abenaki people, is the tallest mountain in the north-

A glimpse over the trees of Mount Washington.

east, rising 6,288 feet above sea level. The first recorded climb of the mountain was by Darby Field in 1642. Field moved to New Hampshire from England to escape religious persecution. He left his home in Durham with several Native Americans as guides and made his way to the Mount Washington area by following the coast to Saco, Maine, where he followed the Saco River north and west. Once he was near the mountain, local Native Americans showed him the route to the summit, where he went in search of jewels. What he found was "terrible freesing weather" and views all the way to the Atlantic Ocean. His route to the summit is still debated with some historians believing he attained the summit via Boott Spur, first going up either the Ellis River or the Rocky Branch. However, there are those who believe he ascended via the southern Presidentials. In any event, Field convinced a few others to climb the mountain later that year, but it was not until the 1720s that reports of other people climbing the mountain began to appear.

As the highest peak north of the Smokies and east of the Rockies, Mount Washington now draws several hundred thousand visitors a year who arrive at the summit by foot, car, or cog railroad. Awaiting those visitors are incredible views and a collection of structures that house a visitor center and cafeteria, the Mount Washington Observatory, and various TV and radio antennas. Nicknamed "the rock pile," the summit cone is strewn with acres and acres of boulders and talus created by the freezing and thawing of ice over thousands of years.

Mount Washington is famous for having the "worst weather in the world," and for being the deadliest mountain in the eastern United States. The mountain lies in an area of North America that is at the confluence of three major storm tracks. This confluence, combined with the mountain's height and north-south orientation, creates optimal conditions for extended periods of extremely high winds. The highest wind speed ever recorded on the planet was 231 MPH on Mount Washington on April 12, 1934. Stronger wind gusts have most likely occurred elsewhere that were not recorded, but this does not diminish the fact that Mount Washington's weather can be deadly as it is consistently cold, wet, and windy with low visibility.

In the winter the average high temperature on the summit is 15 degrees and the wind regularly reaches hurricane strength. When it's not snowing, the summit is often covered in a thick fog that freezes on contact, creating a layer of rime ice on rocks, buildings, and plants. In the summer the temperature rarely rises above the low fifties, and rain, fog, and high winds are common. It snows on the summit every month of the year. To learn more about the weather on Mount Washington, visit the Mount Washington Observatory on the summit or at their Weather Discovery Center, 2936 White Mountain Highway, NH 16 in North Conway. You can also visit the observatory online at www.mountwashington.org.

It is usually the weather that causes problems for visitors to the mountain. With mountains twice as high regularly hiked in shorts and T-shirts in the western United States, it is easy for people to get lulled into thinking that Mount Washington must not be a dangerous place. Winter, of course, has proven to be the deadliest season on the mountain, but people have died of hypothermia in all seasons on Mount Washington; they are not prepared for windy, wet weather that can come unexpectedly and chill to the bone. More than 120 people have died here since it became a regular tourist destination in the late 1840s. Several have died within just a few hundred yards of the summit buildings or one of the huts, and some have merely disappeared, presumably getting lost and dying of exposure. *Not Without Peril* by Nicholas Howe is an excellent read for those interested in the more compelling stories of those who have lost their lives on Mount Washington. Don't fall victim to Mount Washington's weather. Plan ahead and pack appropriate clothing and equipment. (See Safety and Etiquette on page 36.)

Trip #30

Hut to Hut
Presidential Traverse

Rating: **Very Strenuous**

Distance: **23.2 miles one-way without summits, 25.5 miles including all summits**

Elevation Gain: **6,500 feet without summits, 9,600 feet including all summits**

Estimated Time: **3-4 days**

Maps: **AMC White Mountain Map #1, USGS Mount Washington, Carter Dome, Stairs Mountain, and Crawford Notch Quadrangles**

Three days of spectacular views on the largest piece of alpine real estate in the eastern United States.

HIKING THE PRESIDENTIAL RANGE from end to end is one of the United States' classic treks. Of course, numerous trails can be used to accomplish this trip, although the main route between Madison Hut and Mizpah Spring Hut via Lakes of the Clouds Hut is fairly standard. What is great about this trip is you can visit as many of the major summits as you want, bagging up to eight 4,000-footers. Even if you choose to skip the summits, you will have an incredible hike above treeline, peering into glacial cirques, taking in views that stretch from horizon to horizon, and encountering alpine plant species that are more common on the tundra of northern Canada than in New England. Some people (very fit people) can complete this hike in a day, but most people take three or four days in order to enjoy a unique experience. By staying at AMC huts, you can lighten your load and have an easier time of it while scaling the heights.

AMC Lakes of the Clouds Hut near Mount Monroe.

CAUTION: A large portion of this hike, from Madison Spring Hut (reached on Day 1) to the summit of Mount Pierce (Day 3) is extremely exposed to the weather. The entire Mount Washington area is susceptible to lightning strikes and very strong winds. It can snow any month of the year, but any kind of wet weather above treeline can create the potential for hypothermia, especially when it is windy. Bring extra clothing no matter what the forecast, and study the maps ahead of time in case you need to make an emergency trip below treeline to escape unsafe weather. Check the weather forecast before each day's hike (a forecast is posted at each hut at 8:00 A.M.) and realize that, even in good weather, you may experience suddenly dangerous weather conditions.

This is a one-way hike that starts in the Pinkham Notch area and concludes in Crawford Notch. If you are hiking in a group, you can spot cars at either end. If not, the AMC runs a hiker shuttle daily during the summer. To reserve a spot on the shuttle and at the huts call 603-466-2727. Space fills up quickly, especially in July and August, so try to reserve your space as far in advance as possible.

This hike begins with an approach of Madison Hut from Madison Gulf. The headwall of Madison Gulf is very steep and dangerous in bad weather. If someone in your group has a fear of heights or if there is an unfavorable weather forecast, you should consider hiking the Valley Way Trail as an alternative. The Valley Way begins at the Appalachia parking area on US 2 west of Gorham and remains safely below treeline for most of its 3.8 miles to the hut.

Day 1–NH 16 to Madison Hut. *5.9 miles, 3,600-foot elevation gain, 5 hours*

From the parking area on NH 16, begin your hike on the Great Gulf Trail, which parallels the Peabody River for much of the way between the parking area and the Madison Gulf Trail. The Peabody River drains the Great Gulf, which is the largest glacial cirque in the White Mountains. At 1.8 miles you will pass the Osgood Trail, an alternate route to Mount Madison. At 2.7 miles the Osgood Cutoff continues straight and you will need to turn left to remain on the Great Gulf Trail, which crosses Parapet Brook and soon reaches the Madison Gulf Trail. Turn right onto the Madison Gulf Trail, which soon has you climbing steeply through a dense boreal forest. The next 3.0 miles will be the most difficult of your trip.

The Madison Gulf Trail lies within the Great Gulf Wilderness Area, 5,552 acres of roadless wilderness. The trail is well marked, but makes numerous stream crossings where care must be taken to remain on the trail by following the blue-paint blazes. In high water some of these stream crossings can be difficult, but they are usually passable. Two miles from the Great Gulf Trail, you will reach Sylvan Cascade, an attractive waterfall that falls 30 feet over a moss-covered wall of rock. Sylvan Cascade marks the entrance to Madison Gulf, an attractive glacial cirque. After a moderate climb across the floor of the gulf, you begin the very steep climb up the headwall. Make no mistake about it: this is one of the most difficult sections of trail in the White Mountains, with steep scrambles over rocky ledges that can be slippery and dangerous when wet. Expect to spend a lot of time on the headwall, particularly if you have a heavy pack.

As you climb the headwall, you will begin to have good views to the south and east, but you do not emerge from treeline until you crest the ridge and reach the Parapet Trail 5.5 miles after leaving the parking area. Turn left on the Parapet Trail for a short walk to Star Lake, a small alpine lake that sits in the col between Mount Madison and Mount Adams. Star Lake seems a world apart from the thick forests you just spent the day hiking through. Its shallow waters reflect the treeless, rock-strewn upper slopes of Mount Adams and Mount Madison, while alpine plants like cotton grass, mountain aven, and pale laurel grow in the thin soils filling the spaces between boulders covered with map and target lichens. At Star Lake turn right onto the Star Lake Trail for a short, mostly flat walk to Madison Hut.

Optional Mount Madison Summit Hike. *0.5 mile, 550-foot elevation gain, 35 minutes*
Once at Madison Hut it is easy to add the 5,366-foot summit of Mount Madison to your list of 4,000-footers. Just take the Osgood Trail from the hut to the summit. It is a steep hike from boulder to boulder. The summit has great views in all directions, especially to the north and east where the towns of Gorham and Berlin give way to the wild expanse of the Northern Forest.

Day 2–Madison Hut to Lakes of the Clouds Hut. *6.9 miles, 2,050-foot elevation gain, 4 hours, 40 minutes (not including summits)*
After getting your fill of an expertly cooked AMC hut breakfast, start your day on the Gulfside Trail. Your entire day will be spent above treeline on what may be the most beautiful stretch of hiking in the White Mountains. In just 0.3 mile you reach the Air Line Trail, which coincides with the Gulfside Trail for about 100 yards before branching to the left and heading to the summit of Mount Adams—the second highest mountain in the Northeast. To bypass the summit continue straight on the Gulfside Trail, which rises moderately on the way to Thunderstorm Junction, 0.9 mile from the hut. Along the way you will have spectacular views into King Ravine on the right.

Optional Mount Adams Summit Hike. *0.9 mile, 650-foot elevation gain, 55 minutes.*
From the Gulfside Trail turn left onto the Air Line Trail, which reaches the conical summit of Mount Adams about 0.6 mile above the Gulfside Trail. At 5,799 feet you are standing on the highest mountain in the Northeast without a road, and the views are truly spectacular. On

a clear day, Mount Washington looks close enough to touch. To continue your hike toward Lakes of the Clouds, take Lowe's Path west to Thunderstorm Junction, where you turn left onto the Gulfside Trail.

From Thunderstorm Junction, continue straight on the Gulfside Trail, enjoying an easy hike amongst the boulders and alpine flora of the Presidentials. Shortly after Thunderstorm Junction, the Israel Ridge Path joins the Gulfside Trail. At 1.5 miles from Madison Hut the Israel Ridge Path turns right. Continue straight on the Gulfside Trail and you will soon see Jefferson Ravine to the left. At 2.2 miles from the hut you reach Edmands Col, and in another 0.2 mile you reach the Mount Jefferson Loop. If the weather is good and your legs are up for it, turn right here to add Mount Jefferson to your day, otherwise continue straight on the Gulfside Trail.

Optional Mount Jefferson Summit Hike. *0.7 mile, 600-foot elevation gain, 40 minutes*
To reach the summit of Mount Jefferson just turn right onto the Mount Jefferson Loop Trail, which reaches the 5,716-foot summit of Mount Jefferson in 0.4 mile. More great views—you will come to expect them by this point in the hike. From the summit follow the Mount Jefferson Loop Trail southeast for a 0.3-mile descent back to the Gulfside Trail. Turn right to continue to Lakes of the Clouds Hut.

After Mount Jefferson, the Gulfside Trail descends Sphinx Col before beginning the climb around Mount Clay on its way to Mount Washington. At 3.8 miles from Madison Hut you will reach the Mount Clay Loop. Turn left onto the Mount Clay Loop (if you are low on water, continue straight on the Gulfside Trail, where in 0.2 mile a side trail leads to Greenough Spring). About 0.5 mile above the Gulfside Trail, you reach the summit of Mount Clay, which has spectacular views of the Northern Presidentials and the Great Gulf. You can easily imagine a glacier carving out the gulf, being joined by glaciers flowing from Jefferson Ravine and Madison Gulf. Continuing south from the summit, the Mount Clay Loop Trail rejoins the Gulfside Trail in another 0.7 mile.

Turn left on the Gulfside Trail and follow it for a few hundred yards to its junction with the Westside Trail. To reach Lakes of the Clouds Hut turn right onto the Westside Trail and follow it for 0.9 mile to the Crawford Path. Turn right onto the Crawford Path for the final 0.9 mile to the hut.

Optional Mount Washington Summit Hike. *1.6 miles, 800-foot elevation gain, 1 hour, 15 minutes*
Instead of turning right onto the Westside Trail, continue straight on the Gulfside Trail, which begins a steady climb up the northwest summit ridge of Mount Washington. As you climb from boulder to lichen-encrusted boulder, you will understand why Mount Washington is nicknamed "the rock pile." At 1.0 mile above the Westside Trail turn right onto the Crawford Path for the final 0.2 mile to the summit. The views from Mount Washington, the tallest mountain in the Northeast, are of course spectacular. On its summit you also are treated to the highest snack bar in the Northeast. From the summit follow the Crawford Path 1.5 miles to Lakes of the Clouds Hut.

Optional Mount Monroe Summit Hike. *0.8 mile, 350-foot elevation gain, 30 minutes*
Mount Monroe is so close to Lakes of the Clouds Hut that an after dinner summit hike is almost irresistible. From the hut follow the Crawford Path for about 100 yards where you should turn right onto the Mount Monroe Loop Trail. A short, steep climb gets you to the summit (5,372 feet) in about twenty minutes.

Day 3–Lakes of the Clouds Hut to Mizpah Spring Hut. *4.8 miles, 350-foot elevation gain, 3 hours*
You have the option of finishing your trip on Day 3 by hiking the Crawford Path from Lakes of the Clouds Hut for 7.0 miles down to Crawford Notch. However, you can extend your stay in the mountains by spending the night at Mizpah Spring Hut and spending Day 4 bagging a few more peaks. Either way, from Lakes of the Clouds Hut take a right on the Crawford Path, which skirts around the summit of Mount Monroe and passes through an area rich in alpine flowers like pale laurel, mountain aven, diapensia, and alpine azalea. This area is also one of only two places on the planet (Franconia Range is the other) where the tiny dwarf cinquefoil lives. Take care to stay on the trail, as all of these plants are extremely fragile. With the Dry River valley below you on the left, you will have about 2.0 miles of hiking before reaching the Mount Eisenhower Trail. Shortly beyond this trail, you reach the Mount Eisenhower Loop Trail, which leads right to the summit of Mount Eisenhower.

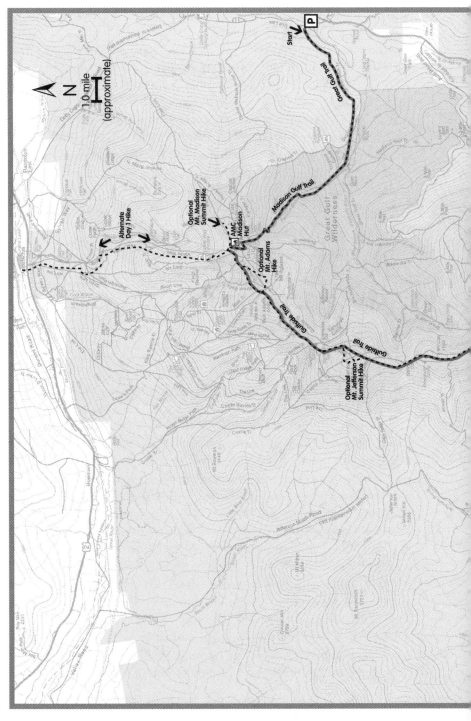

P
Start
Great Gulf Trail

N
1.0 mile
(approximate)

Madison Gulf Trail

Great Gulf Wilderness

Optional
Mt. Madison
Summit Hike

Alternate
Day J Hike

AMC
Madison
Hut

Optional
Mt. Adams
Hike

Gulfside Trail

Gulfside Trail

Optional
Mt. Jefferson
Summit Hike

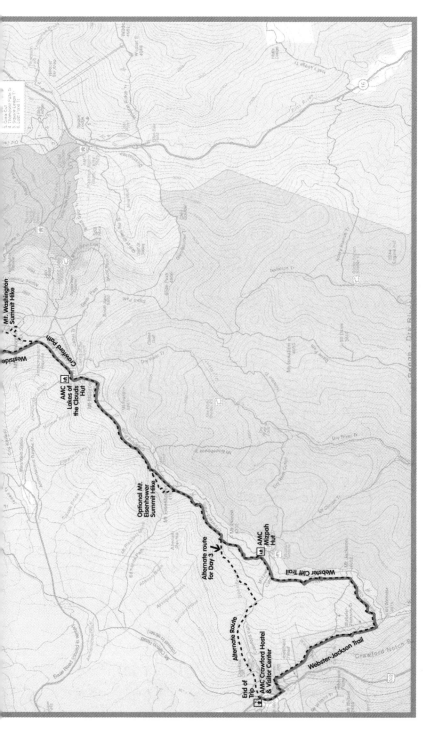

HUT TO HUT PRESIDENTIAL TRAVERSE

Mt. Washington
Summit Hike

Westside

Crawford Path

AMC
Lakes of
the Clouds
Hut

Optional Mt.
Eisenhower
Summit Hike

Alternate route
for Day 3

AMC
Mizpah
Hut

Webster Cliff Trail

Alternate Route

End of
Trip

AMC Crawford Hostel
& Visitor Center

Webster-Jackson Trail

Crawford Notch

Optional Mount Eisenhower Summit Hike. *0.8 miles, 300-foot elevation gain, 35 minutes*

Turn right off the Crawford Path onto the Mount Eisenhower Loop Trail and make the short, steep climb to the bald summit of Mount Eisenhower (4,760 feet), which takes about thirty minutes. To return to the Crawford Path, continue over the summit on the Mount Eisenhower Loop Trail, which reaches the Crawford Path in 0.4 mile.

Continuing on the Crawford Path, you will make a moderate descent to the col between Mount Eisenhower and Mount Pierce, where you will find a small stream if you are in need of water. The trail then climbs moderately to the Webster Cliff Trail, 3.9 miles from Lakes of the Clouds Hut. If you are opting to skip Mizpah Spring Hut and Day 4 of this trip, continue straight on the Crawford Path for the final 2.9 miles to Crawford Notch. Otherwise, turn left onto the Webster Cliff Trail and follow it for the short 0.1-mile climb to the summit of Mount Pierce (4,312 feet), which has good views back toward Mount Washington. From the summit of Mount Pierce, follow the Webster Cliff Trail for a steep, 0.8-mile climb down to Mizpah Spring Hut.

Day 4–Mizpah Spring Hut to Crawford Notch via Mount Jackson and Mount Webster. *5.6 miles, 500-foot elevation gain, 4 hours*

Day 4 is divided fairly evenly between a wooded ridge walk to Mount Jackson and Mount Webster, and a steep climb down through the woods to your final destination, Crawford Notch. From the hut follow the Webster Cliff Trail to the left for a walk through high-elevation forest on your way to Mount Jackson. This is a good place to watch for spruce grouse, an increasingly rare bird in New Hampshire that can survive only in spruce-fir forests. Once you find them, they are easy to watch as they are very tame—tame enough to earn them the nickname "fool's hen" because they are so easy to catch.

You reach the summit of Mount Jackson 1.7 miles after leaving Mizpah Spring Hut. Mount Jackson (4,052 feet) provides dramatic views of the Presidentials as seen across the expanse of the Presidential Range–Dry River Wilderness. From the summit walk south on the Webster Cliff Trail for a 1.4-mile ridge walk to Mount Webster (3,910 feet). Mount Webster sits atop a cliff with impressive views that look straight down into Crawford Notch. To complete your hike, walk back toward Mount Jackson on the Webster Cliff Trail for 0.1 mile and turn left onto the Webster-Jackson Trail. At this point you have nowhere to go but down, and this trail takes you 2.4 miles and 2,050 feet down to the floor of Crawford Notch. About 1.0 mile below Mount Webster you will need to turn left after a beautiful waterfall on Silver Cascade Brook. At the end of the trail turn right on US 302 for a short walk to Crawford Notch Depot Visitor Center where you can catch the hiker shuttle.

Directions

This hike begins on the Great Gulf Trail, which starts on the west side of NH 16, 6.7 miles south of US 2 in Gorham and 16.2 miles north of US 302 in Glen. The trail ends in Crawford Notch at the parking area for the Webster-Jackson Trail, about 0.3 mile south of the AMC Crawford Hostel. The hostel is 8.5 miles south of the intersection of US 3 and US 302 in Twin Mountain, and 21.0 miles north of the intersection of NH 16 and US 302 in Glen.

amc huts: spending the night in the backcountry

A GREAT WAY to spend the night in the backcountry of the White Mountains is to stay at one of eight AMC huts. The huts are spaced roughly one day's hike apart along the Appalachian Trail and provide hikers with the opportunity to travel lightly while still spending a night in the woods (or above the trees). A stay at a hut includes an all-you-can-eat dinner and break- fast prepared and served by enthusiastic members of the hut "croo." Each hut accommodates between 30 and 90 guests who sleep in bunkrooms. Toilets and running water are a luxury that most of the huts provide.

Each of the huts sits near great mountain views and interesting mountain habitat. For example, Lonesome Lake Hut, with its spectacular views of Franconia Ridge, also gives visitors a chance to study plants and animals that live in and around a nearby bog. Madison and Lakes of the Clouds Huts are both above treeline and provide a unique opportunity to spend quality time studying rare alpine vegetation and take in spectacular sunsets. During the summer each hut has its own resident naturalist who leads nature talks and walks and can answer visitors' questions about the surrounding environ- ment. Kids can participate in the AMC Junior Naturalist pro- gram by completing the nature activities in the *Junior Naturalist Activity Book*. The activity book is a fun way for kids to learn about natural history, minimum-impact hiking, and safety in the outdoors.

All of the huts are open from early June through mid- September. Some huts have an extended self-service season in spring and fall, while two huts, Zealand Falls Hut and Carter Notch Hut, are open year-round. Reservations are highly recommended as bunk space is often sold out. For more information or to make reservations, you can call the AMC at 603-466-2727, 9 A.M. to 5 P.M., Monday through Saturday, or visit their website, www.outdoors.org.

Fall foliage

5
mountain biking

MOUNTAIN BIKING is a relatively new sport in the White Mountains. As a result, few trails are maintained specifically for use by bikes, but the Forest Service does recognize the popularity of mountain biking and has begun to manage some areas with bikes in mind. The majority of bike trips in the White Mountains use a combination of dirt roads, old logging roads, snowmobile trails, and single-track, creating a trail system that is highly diverse. For the most part, mountain biking in the White Mountains is confined to the lower elevations, which means you will not find the spectacular views that you might encounter on a hike in the Presidentials. However, a bike ride in the White Mountains can take you through beautiful northern hardwood forests, past rushing trout streams and waterfalls, or to remote mountain ponds that are home to moose and other wildlife.

Trip Times

The times listed for the bike rides in this chapter are fairly conservative and based on what we feel it would take a rider in average physical condition to complete the trip. We do assume that you have

Mountain biking on the Lincoln Woods Trail.

been riding a bike recently and that your heart and leg muscles are in riding shape. Infrequent bikers may need more time. Those who ride consistently from week to week will probably need less time. You should add extra time when trails are wet or when rain is expected.

Trip Ratings

We list two ratings for each trip: aerobic level and technical difficulty. Aerobic level is based on changes in elevation and the number of miles. Trips with few ups and downs are generally listed as *easy*, though longer mileage trips on gently rolling terrain may be listed as moderate. *Moderate* trips usually contain a fair amount of elevation gain, which is broken up into shorter sections of climbing. On a *strenuous* trip expect significant elevation gain via either steep climbs or long, drawn out climbs of 2.0 or more miles. Technically, an easy trip usually means that most of the riding is on a dirt road with an easily rideable surface. Moderate trips include single-track (a narrow trail usually used for hiking) or double-track (usually an old logging road or snowmobile trail) trails that have a varying amount of roots and rocks requiring some maneuvering on the part of the bike-rider. Most intermediate riders can handle these trails. A trip rated as technically *difficult* usually involves a consistently difficult ride over roots and rocks, often on steep terrain. All but the best riders will end up walking sections of these trails.

Set a Good Example

Among some hiking circles mountain biking is still seen as a reckless sport, eroding trails and endangering walkers. In the White Mountains, most bike trips are on logging roads where erosion by bicycles is not a problem. Hikers rarely use these roads, so the incidence of hiker-biker conflict is low. However, some of these trips, like the Sawyer River Trail or the Tunnel Brook Trail, use hiking trails. In fact, biking is allowed on any trail in the White Mountain National Forest (except for a few posted high-traffic areas) that is not in federally designated wilderness. For this reason, it is important that all mountain bikers use good judgment when riding in order to protect the environment and to allow others to enjoy their wilderness experience. To practice responsible riding, follow the "rules of the trail" as suggested by the International Mountain Biking Association (www.imba.com):

- Ride on open trails only. Respect trail and road closures (ask if uncertain); avoid trespassing on private land; and obtain permits or other authorization as may be required. Federal and state wilderness areas are closed to cycling. Remember: the way you ride will influence trail management decisions and policies.

- Leave No Trace. Be sensitive to the dirt beneath you. Recognize different types of soils and trail construction and practice low-impact cycling. Wet and muddy trails are more vulnerable to damage. When the trailbed is soft, consider other riding options. This also means staying on existing trails and not creating new ones. Do not cut switchbacks. Be sure to pack out at least as much as you pack in. (Also follow the Leave No Trace guidelines set forth in this book's introduction.)

- Control your bicycle. Inattention for even a second can cause problems. Obey all bicycle speed regulations and recommendations.

- Always yield the trail. Let your fellow trail users know you are coming. A friendly greeting or bell is considerate and works well; do not startle others. Show your respect when passing by, slowing to a walking pace or even stopping. Anticipate other trail users around corners or in blind spots. Yielding means slow down, establish communication, be prepared to stop if necessary, and pass safely.

- Never scare animals. Animals are startled by an unannounced approach, a sudden movement, or a loud noise. This can be dangerous for you, others, and the animals. Give animals extra room and time to adjust to you. When passing horses use special care and follow directions from the horseback riders (ask if uncertain). Running cattle and disturbing wildlife is a serious offense. Leave gates as you found them or as marked.

- Plan ahead. Know your equipment, your ability, and the area in which you are riding—and prepare accordingly. Be self-sufficient at all times; keep your equipment in good repair; and carry necessary supplies for changes in weather or other conditions. A well-executed trip is a satisfaction to you and not a burden to others. Always wear a helmet and appropriate safety gear.

Most trail erosion in the White Mountains occurs during spring and after heavy rains. Try to avoid riding on single-track trails at these times. In the Whites trails are pretty muddy from the time the snow melts until at least mid-June. We usually wait until mid-July to avoid the mud and the hordes of black flies.

Safety and Comfort

Since bike trips in the White Mountains are usually completed at lower elevations, the above-treeline, weather-related risks associated with hiking are not generally a problem. Of course, rain and wet leaves can make descending on rocky trails a more dangerous proposition, and long rides on a cold, rainy day can create hypothermic conditions. Most mountain biking accidents occur on technical trails, where riders get going too fast for their abilities. For a safe and comfortable mountain-biking experience keep your bike under control at all times and consider the following tips:

- Select a trip that is appropriate for everyone in the group. Match the ride to the abilities of the least capable person in the group.

- Plan to be back at the trailhead before dark. Determine a turn around time and stick to it even if you have not reached your goal for the day.

- Check the weather forecast. Avoid riding during or immediately after heavy rains. Give yourself more time to stop in the rain, as wet brakes do not work as well as dry ones.

- Bring a pack or pannier with the following items:

    Water—two or more quarts per person depending on the weather and length of the trip
    Food—Even for a short, one-hour trip, it is a good idea to bring some high-energy snacks like nuts, dried fruit, or snack bars. Bring a lunch for longer trips.

    Map and compass
    Extra clothing—rain gear, sweater, hat
    Flashlight
    Sunscreen

> First-aid kit
> Pocketknife
> Basic bike-maintenance tools and a spare inner tube and/or tire-repair kit

- Wear appropriate footwear and clothing. Consider wearing hiking boots, since having to push or carry your bike over rough trails is a real possibility. Legwear should be tight fitting: loose pants can get stuck on pedals and in the gears of a bike, causing nasty accidents. Bring rain gear even in sunny weather, since unexpected rain, fog, and wind is possible at any time in the White Mountains. Avoid wearing cotton clothing, which absorbs sweat and rain, making for cold, damp riding. Polypropylene, fleece, silk, and wool are all good materials for keeping moisture away from your body and keeping you warm in wet or cold conditions.

Maps

Many of the logging roads that these trips follow are not shown on the AMC series of White Mountain maps, although these maps are still excellent for determining your position if you have good map and compass skills. You should consider purchasing two other maps if you plan to do a lot of mountain biking in the White Mountains. The first is a mountain-bike map printed and sold by the White Mountain National Forest. This map covers the western portion of the national forest and includes trip descriptions for 30 bike rides (several of which are in this chapter). You can buy it at any Forest Service visitor center or district office. Another great map is the *Mountain Bike Map of the Mount Washington Valley*, which as its name implies covers many of the biking trails in the Mount Washington valley area, including those near Bear Notch Road. AMC cartographer Larry Garland created the graphics for this map. The trips were chosen and described by one of the more knowledgeable mountain bikers in the area, Peter Minnich at Red Jersey Cyclery in Glen. You can buy this map at most bike shops in the Mount Washington area.

The trips in this chapter range from an easy, flat ride along the banks of the Pemigewasset River, to the thigh-burning, suspension-testing ordeals of Province Pond or Tunnel Brook. If you were to ride all of these trips, you would experience New Hampshire's forests at their best: fresh mountain air, waterfalls and wildlife, and secluded mountain ponds reflecting rounded and craggy peaks. During your rides you might encounter deer, moose, coyote, and bears—you will definitely see signs of their presence. You will also enjoy the thrills of careening down a trail or road as fast as you can safely stand it. All in all, mountain biking in the White Mountains is as diverse and rewarding as any other outdoor adventure.

Bartlett Experimental Forest

Aerobic Level: **Easy**

Technical Difficulty: **Easy on gravel roads;
Moderate on single-track**

Distance: **4.8 miles round-trip**

Elevation Gain: **400 feet**

Estimated Time: **1 hour**

Maps: **AMC White Mountain Map #3,
USGS Bartlett Quadrangle**

**A smooth ride through beautiful forest
followed by a fun and bumpy stretch of
single-track.**

THE BARTLETT EXPERIMENTAL FOREST is a 2,600-acre tract in
the White Mountain National Forest used by Forest Service scientists to study various aspects of forest ecology and the effects of
forest management on the forest and the wildlife that lives there.
Established in 1931, this experimental forest was chosen because
its elevation, soils, climate, and tree composition was typical of
northern New England and New York (for more info, visit the
Forest Service's Bartlett Experimental Forest website at
www.fs.fed.us/ne/home/ research/forests/bartlett). For the mountain biker, this area provides a few miles of smooth gravel roads
as well as some fun single-track. A little bit of elevation gain is on
this trip, but for the most part it is an aerobically easy ride. Experienced riders will find the single-track to be a fun test of their
abilities; beginner and intermediate riders will also enjoy it,
although they may need to walk a few short difficult sections.

Begin your trip by riding up the gravel road, heading away
from Bear Notch Road. (While you are on this side of Bear Notch

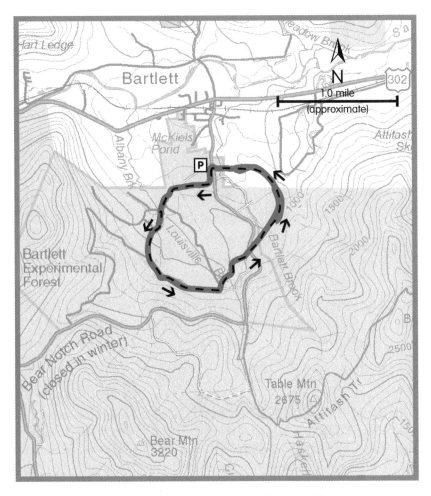

BARTLETT EXPERIMENTAL FOREST

Road, feel free to explore the gravel roads, but please stay off of the single-track, as it has recently been posted as off-limits to bikes.) At **0.7 mile** bear right at a fork in the road and ride past a large water tank on the left. You then cross Albany Brook, which cascades over a long and picturesque stretch of rock ledges culminating in a deep swimming hole. A mix of hardwoods and hemlock shades the banks of the brook. At **1.0 mile** turn left onto another dirt road. At **1.5 miles** you will reach a fork in the road, stay to the left. At **2.4 miles** continue straight as a road comes in from the left. Up until this point you have climbed about 300 feet in elevation over a series of gentle ups and downs.

At **2.5 miles** you will cross a stream on a wooden bridge and then enjoy a nice downhill cruise through a beautiful northern hardwood forest. At **3.1 miles** turn right onto Bear Notch Road and follow it for about 0.1 mile before turning left back into the woods onto the Reservoir Brook Trail. This is the single-track portion of the ride, as the trail is narrow with occasional rocks and roots. At **3.4 miles** you make the first of two stream crossings, both of which can be difficult to ride due to the steep banks. After the second stream, you enter an old clearcut with some obstructed mountain views before making a moderate descent over rough trail to another stream crossing and a trail junction at **3.6 miles**.

At this junction turn right for a short, steep climb to another trail junction at **3.7 miles**, where you should turn left. You now make a sometimes steep and technical descent on a narrow and windy trail. At **4.0 miles** continue straight at a trail junction as the trail eases in steepness and difficulty. At **4.3 miles** stay to the right at a trail junction and continue the downhill ride over a wider trail. The trail levels off at **4.7 miles**, where you should turn left, cross the stream, and take the left fork up the steep hill. At **4.8 miles** you return to Bear Notch Road; turn left for a short ride back to the starting point, which will be on your right at **4.9 miles**.

Directions

From the intersection of US 302 and Bear Notch Road in Bartlett, head south on Bear Notch Road for 0.8 mile and turn right onto a gravel road. Park in the pullout on the left.

Trip # 32

Conway Recreation Trail

Aerobic Level: **Easy**

Technical Difficulty: **Easy**

Distance: **6.0 miles up and back**

Elevation Gain: **200 feet**

Estimated Time: **1 hour 30 minutes**

Maps: **AMC White Mountain Map #5, USGS North Conway East and Conway Quadrangles**

An easy ride through tall pines next to the Saco River.

CLOSE TO CENTER CONWAY, the Conway Recreation Trail is a great ride for those in need of an early morning leg-stretcher. It is also a fun and easy ride for kids, with the trail paralleling the Saco River for about half of the trip. You also can visit an old mineral spring, where water from under the ground still bubbles up through the pool. This trail, which is located in Conway's Smith-Eastman Recreation Area, is a popular place for runners and walkers, so you will want to watch your speed on tight corners in order to avoid unexpected collisions. Some of the trails on this ride are adjacent to private property; please make an extra effort to adhere to Leave No Trace rules in order to ensure these trails will remain open to bike-riders in the future.

From the parking area follow the trail to the right and cross the narrow footbridge (you will need to walk across). With the Saco River on your left, you will be riding over a thick bed of pine nee-dles, which provide a soft ride except for the occasional tree root. As you breathe in the scent of pine and listen to the rushing waters of the Saco, you will soon understand why this level trail is a favorite with the locals. The Saco is also a popular river for paddlers, as it

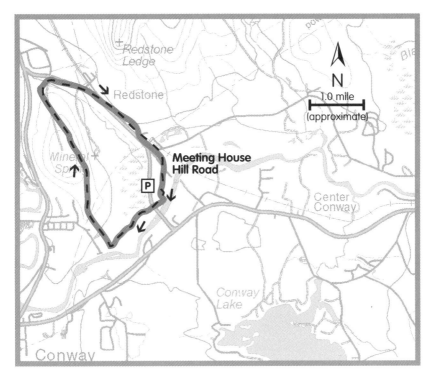

CONWAY RECREATION TRAIL

contains long stretches of easy paddling and sandy beaches. At **0.4 mile** the trail drops down to river level in order to pass under a bridge carrying US 302. At this point you will experience the sands of the Saco firsthand. Beginner riders may need to walk their bikes for a few yards to get through this section.

After the bridge the trail climbs back up to the level ground above the river and continues its ride through the pines. At **0.75 mile** stay left where a side trail comes in from the right. At **0.9 mile** turn right, following the arrow. The trail leaves the river, but riders who enjoy riding on a twisting, rolling trail will find the change enjoyable. Yellow "caution" signs precede the few rocks, roots, and water bars that add a slight challenge to the ride, but beginner riders should have no problem tackling these relatively minor obstacles. You will see a few unmarked, narrow side trails on this stretch of trail; just stay on the obviously well-traveled, wide path.

At **2.2 miles** you enter a grassy field. An old building at the edge of the field on the left houses a pool that collects water from a mineral spring. The water from this spring was bottled during the late 1800s and sold to tourists visiting the White Mountains. Water continues to bubble up through the pool, but like any water source in the White Mountains, filter or chemically treat the water before drinking it. To continue the trip, ride through the field. As the trail enters the woods a side trail leads to the right. Stay to the left on what becomes a wide dirt road that passes through a mixed forest of pine, oak, maple, and birch. At **2.9 miles** you pass under some power lines, and at **3.0 miles** you reach US 302 and the end of the Conway Recreation Trail.

To complete your trip, you have two options. The first is to turn around and return the way you came. The second option is to make a loop of this trip by turning right on US 302, left on East Conway Road, and then right on Meeting House Hill Road. However, the return ride through the woods is much more worthwhile.

Directions

From the intersection of NH 16 and US 302 in Conway, New Hampshire, head west on US 302. In 1.5 miles, turn left onto East Conway Road. Take your first right onto Meeting House Hill Road and follow it 0.4 mile until it ends in the parking lot for Conway's Smith-Eastman Recreation Area.

Lincoln Woods

> **Aerobic Level: Easy**
>
> **Technical Difficulty: Easy except for crossing the
> Pemigewasset River**
>
> **Distance: 6.4 miles round–trip**
>
> **Elevation Gain: 300 feet**
>
> **Estimated Time: 1 hour 30 minutes**
>
> **Maps: AMC White Mountain Map #2, USGS Mount
> Osceola Quadrangle**
>
> **An easy ride along the rushing waters of
> the Pemigewasset River.**

THIS IS AN EXCELLENT CHOICE for families and people just getting used to riding bikes over rocks and through mud. Experienced
riders in the mood for an easy ride next to one of the most beautiful
rivers in the White Mountains will also enjoy this trip. This trip
begins at the Lincoln Woods parking area on the Kancamagus Highway just east of Lincoln, New Hampshire. It follows an old woods
road up the east side of the Pemigewasset River; crosses the river
over a series of large boulders; and returns via the Lincoln Woods
Trail above the west bank of the river. It is also possible to make a
side trip to Franconia Falls, where you can swim in the cold waters
of Franconia Brook. (Please note that the Forest Service now limits
the number of visitors it allows at the falls, so check with the ranger
station at the Lincoln Woods parking area about obtaining a Franconia
Falls visitor permit. A permit is not required to ride on the Lincoln
Woods Trail.)

Beginning from the Lincoln Woods parking area, ride north
on the old road that begins just beyond the Forest Service information building. The road surface is good gravel, with only a few larger

East Branch of the Pemigewasset River.

rocks to avoid. At **0.2 mile** a spur path leads 0.1 mile to a clearing filled with raspberries and aspen that provides obstructed views

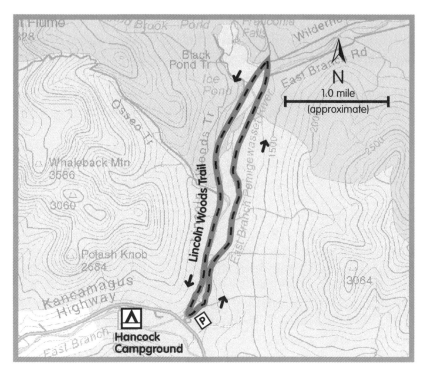

LINCOLN WOODS

toward the Bonds. At **0.6 mile** the Pine Island Trail leaves to the left. Continue straight on the road, which makes a short climb before resuming a relatively level grade. After crossing a stream and passing another side trail at **1.1 miles**, the road begins a moderate climb and at **2.5 miles** reaches an overlook high above the Pemigewasset River. From here you get a good look at the rushing waters of the Pemigewasset, where it is wide and filled with granite boulders. The banks are lined with sugar maple, yellow birch, and white pine, and in fall the foliage is truly spectacular. Good views also can be seen of Owl's Head, Mount Flume, and Whaleback Mountain.

At **2.7 miles** you reach the ranger headquarters for the Franconia Brook Campsites, which have replaced the tent sites that used to be on the western side of the river. Twenty-four campsites spread out on both sides of the road and outhouses are on the left. At **2.9 miles** you reach a gate that marks the boundary of the Pemigewasset Wilderness Area (bikes are not allowed in the wilderness area). The road turns left and descends a hill; to reach the river, turn right at the bottom of the hill. Here you are faced with the task of crossing the Pemigewasset. The Forest Service has placed a series of large boulders across the river at a wide spot in order to make the crossing easier. You still need to be able to carry your bike while balancing on these boulders. If this is too difficult (or the water level is too high), you can just return the way you came.

Once across the Pemigewasset, you will need to cross Franconia Brook, make a steep climb up the bank to the Lincoln Woods Trail, and turn left. (The Lincoln Woods Trail was formerly called the Wilderness Trail and remains the Wilderness Trail north of Franconia Brook.) At **3.4 miles** and immediately after recrossing Franconia Brook on a wooden bridge, a side trail leads 0.4 mile right to the falls, which form a natural granite waterslide that can provide hours of entertainment for hardy swimmers (or interested spectators). This side trail is not appropriate for bikes and, as we mentioned before, you must obtain a permit from the Forest Service to visit the falls.

The Lincoln Woods Trail follows the bed of an old logging railroad, making a gradual descent over partially buried railroad ties. This was one of the last logging railroads in operation in the White Mountains, finally closing down in the 1940s. At **3.8 miles** you pass the Black Pond Trail, and at **5.0 miles** you pass the Osseo Trail, which backpackers use to hike to Mount Flume and Franconia Ridge. The trip ends at **6.4 miles**, where you should turn left, cross the river on the large suspension bridge, and follow the trail up to the information center.

Directions

Take Exit 32 off of I-93 in Lincoln. Drive east on the Kancamagus Highway (NH 112) for 5.0 miles. The Lincoln Woods parking area will be on the left, immediately after crossing the East Branch of the Pemigewasset River.

fall foliage:
why leaves change

FALL IS ONE OF THE BUSIEST SEASONS in the White Mountains as millions of "leaf peepers" crowd the area's highways in search of witnessing the peak of one of nature's most beautiful displays of color. In the White Mountains peak fall colors usually occur anywhere from the last week of September to Columbus Day weekend. River valleys and mountain slopes below 3,000 feet are covered in northern hardwood forests, where beech, maple, birch, and other hardwoods provide dramatic colors—yellow, orange, gold, red, and purple. New England's climate tends to create conditions for what many people consider the best foliage displays in the world. Generous summer rainfall followed by a September of cool nights and sunny days are generally thought to provide the most brilliant colors. The state of New Hampshire makes foliage forecasts on their website at www.visitnh.gov/foliageframe.

During the summer months tree leaves are producing food for the tree in the form of chlorophyll, which is green in color. As summer nears an end, cold weather causes the tree to stop producing chlorophyll as it prepares to go dormant for the winter. As this chlorophyll breaks down, the colors of other chemicals in the leaves begin to show through. The decomposition of chlorophyll is hastened by cool weather and sunshine. Pigments such as carotene and xanthophyl are present in the leaves year-round, but their orange and yellow colors do not show up until chlorophyll production stops. Dry weather can increase the concentration of sugars in leaves, leading to the production of anthocyanin, which is responsible for the brilliant reds and purples found in red maple, sumac, red oak, and other trees. As winter nears, leaves that manage to stay on the trees eventually turn brown, a result of a waste product known as tannin.

Popular foliage driving tours focus on NH 112 (Kancama-gus Highway), US 302 through Crawford Notch, and US 2 north of the Presidentials. During peak foliage weekends, traffic on these routes can be very heavy, so your best bet is to get out of the car and out onto the trails. Any bike ride in this book will give you a good look at the foliage from within the forest, and getting above the trees can give you a good overall look. Easier fall foliage hikes include Square Ledge in Pinkham Notch (trip #1), the Roost in Evans Notch (trip #2), Mount Willard in Crawford Notch (trip #7), and Mount Pemigewasset in Franconia Notch (trip #9).

Trip #34

Chocorua–Tamworth Loop

Aerobic Level: **Moderate**

Technical Difficulty: **Easy**

Distance: **11.4 miles round–trip**

Elevation Gain: **600 feet**

Estimated Time: **1 hour 30 minutes**

Maps: **AMC White Mountain Map #3, USGS Mount Chocorua and Silver Lake Quadrangles**

An easy ride on gravel roads through the tranquil forests of Tamworth.

THIS IS THE ONLY RIDE in this book where you will be sharing the road with cars for the entire trip; however, these back roads in the town of Tamworth are little traveled and you will rarely, if ever, need to yield to motorized vehicles. The best views on this trip are actually from the parking lot, which has the classic view of Mount Chocorua as it rises above Chocorua Lake. Riding these roads that gently rise and fall through quiet northern hardwood forests is a great way to spend a summer or fall afternoon. Some climbs occur during this trip, but for the most part they are moderate and short and followed by relaxing downhills. Most of the ride travels through private property, so you will want to use the facilities in the parking area before getting under way. Please be respectful of private property.

Start your trip by riding over the bridge on Chocorua Lake Road, which becomes Fowler's Mill Road. As you leave the mountain views of the lake behind, you enter a different scenic New England: one of rolling dirt roads, stone fences, and tall white pine. At **0.6 mile** you reach an intersection with Loring Road. Stay to the right on Fowler's Mill Road, and then bear left at another fork at **0.9 mile**, following a sign for "Mountain Trails." From here you will climb

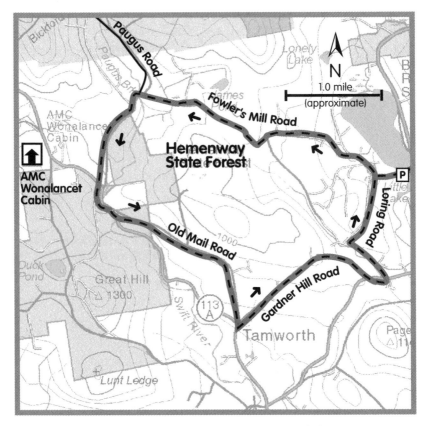

CHOCORUA–TAMWORTH LOOP

moderately until you reach another intersection at **1.8 miles**. Continue straight, staying on Fowler's Mill Road, which eventually begins a 1.0-mile-long descent at **2.3 miles**. At **3.3 miles** you pass Paugus Road on the left. After two stream crossings and a bumpy section of road, you reach NH 113A at **4.5 miles**.

Turn left onto the pavement of NH 113A and make a quick left onto Old Mail Road at **4.6 miles**. After making a steep but short climb, you will enjoy the packed dirt surface of Old Mail Road as it passes through the northern hardwoods of the Hemenway State Forest. At about **6.0 miles** you begin a gradual descent that takes you all the way to Gardner Hill Road at **6.8 miles**. Turn left onto the pavement of Gardner Hill Road (unmarked) and make a gradual climb until **7.6 miles**. You are then treated to another downhill ride that lasts until NH 113 at **8.6 miles** where you should turn left. Make a quick left onto Philbrick Neighborhood Road at **8.7 miles**.

Philbrick Neighborhood Road is a dirt road that sometimes gets a little bumpy, but takes you past a good view of Mount Chocorua on its way to Loring Road at **10.0 miles**. Turn right onto Loring Road, which is marked by a hard-to-spot, small, green sign (if you cross a wooden bridge, you've gone past it). At **10.8 miles** you come back to Fowler's Mill Road, where you should turn right for the ride back to the parking area at **11.4 miles**.

Directions

From the intersection of NH 16 and NH 113 in Tamworth, drive north on NH 16. Turn left in 1.6 miles onto Chocorua Lake Road and park in the lot on the left. This lot has a small picnic area on the lake as well as a portable toilet.

Ellsworth Pond Loop

Aerobic Level: Moderate

Technical Difficulty: Moderate to Difficult

Distance: 6.4 miles round-trip

Elevation Gain: 400 Feet

Estimated Time: 1 hour 30 minutes

Maps: AMC White Mountain Map #4, USGS Plymouth, Mount Kineo, Woodstock, and Rumney Quadrangles

A bumpy ride past bogs and streams and through the wild forests on the southern slopes of Mount Kineo.

HIKERS MOSTLY IGNORE THIS PART of the White Mountains, but mountain bikers know it well, as old logging roads and Forest Service roads wind their way through thick forests to ponds, bogs, and streams. This trip combines some riding on dirt and paved roads with the rough and rocky logging roads to the south of Mount Kineo in Ellsworth. Starting from downtown Ellsworth, this trip follows dirt roads past Ellsworth Pond before heading into the woods. Not much elevation is gained on this trip, but some very rough sections of trail will require less experienced riders to get off their bikes and push. Once emerging from the woods onto a dirt road, the trip finishes with a long and fast downhill on pavement. The rural New Hampshire scenery of Ellsworth and the quiet of its backwoods are the main ingredients for this excellent ride.

From the Ellsworth Town Hall, head north (away from Ellsworth Hill Road) on Ellsworth Pond Road, which descends through Ellsworth Village on a good dirt surface. At the bottom of the hill stay to the left at the fork. The road passes several houses

Mountain biking the Ellsworth Pond Loop.

and occasional mountain views, and you will notice the unmistakable scent of white pine as you ride. At **0.7 mile** the road crosses a

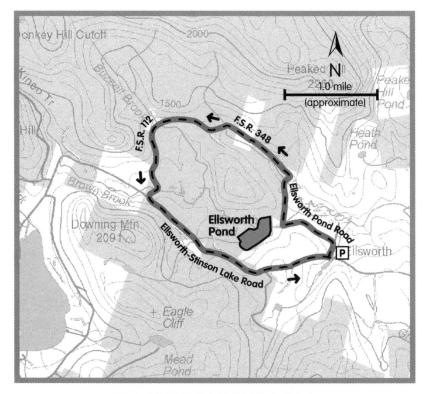

ELLSWORTH POND LOOP

picturesque stream that empties into Ellsworth Pond, which is soon
visible on the left. After crossing another stream, turn left at **1.3
miles** onto Forest Service Road 348. You almost immediately pass a
steel Forest Service gate and a snowmobile trail on the left. Continue
straight on the Forest Service road. Now the mountain biking begins as
you enter a typical New England second-growth northern hardwood
forest, complete with old stone walls marking former pastureland.
The rocky road is somewhat bumpy, but it is wide and level, making
it easy to keep up a good pace.

You pass a clearing at **1.7 miles** and at **2.25 miles** you enter
another clearing. In this second clearing turn left on a snowmobile
trail as it heads downhill and then crosses a stream on a wooden
bridge. The stream flows quickly over granite rocks and is lined with
paper birch, sugar maple, and hemlock. After the stream the trail
narrows and the riding gets tough, with large rocks and lots of mud

making it necessary to walk your bike from time to time. This is the most remote part of the trip, and the trail's location between several ponds and bogs make it an excellent place to find moose. After a moderate climb the trail begins to descend at **2.8 miles**. At **3.0 miles** stay left at a trail junction, following the yellow arrow downhill to a small clearing. After the clearing turn right onto Forest Service Road 112 and cross a stream, which has a cascade well worth visiting off to the right.

Once on Forest Service Road 112, the riding gets much easier as the road surface is smoother than the previous 0.75 mile. At **3.2 miles**, **3.5 miles**, and **3.8 miles** side roads lead to the right; continue straight at all three intersections. At **3.6 miles** the road passes a clearing and swings to the right. At **4.0 miles** you will need to make a stream crossing, which can be difficult in high water (try crossing downstream a few yards). At **4.1 miles** you will pass a Forest Service gate and emerge back into civilization on Ellsworth-Stinson Lake Road. (There is a parking lot here, so if the Ellsworth Town Hall lot is full, you can start your trip here instead.) Turn left onto the hardpacked dirt surface of Ellsworth-Stinson Lake Road and ride through the quiet northern hardwood forest over a series of gradual ups and downs. At **4.9 miles** a beaver dam on the left has created a pond with good views of Mount Kineo. At **5.9 miles** you crest a hill with a farmhouse on the left, and at **6.2 miles** you reach pavement and the final steep downhill back to the Ellsworth Town Hall, passing an interesting old cemetery on the left.

Directions

Take Exit 28 on I-93 and head west on NH 49. After 1.0 mile turn left on US 3 and then make a quick right onto Dan Web Road, following signs for Ellsworth and Stinson Lake. In a few hundred yards turn right onto Ellsworth Hill Road, follow it for 4.3 miles, and turn right onto Ellsworth Pond Road. Park immediately on your left in front of the Ellsworth Town Hall, across the road from St. John of the Mountains Chapel. Parking is available for only two cars here. If the lot is full, you can park 2.1 miles beyond Ellsworth Pond Road, where Ellsworth-Stinson Lake Road meets Forest Service Road 112 (mile 4.1 of the loop).

Moose Brook State Park

Aerobic Level: Moderate

Technical Difficulty: Moderate

Distance: 4.0 miles round-trip

Elevation Gain: 600 feet

Estimated Time: 1 hour 45 minutes

Maps: AMC White Mountain Map #6, USGS Berlin Quadrangle

A climb through moose country with a fun downhill return.

JUST WEST OF GORHAM, Moose Brook State Park offers comfortable camping facilities only a few miles from the hiking trails on the north side of the Presidential Range. The park also has its own set of woodland paths for families up for a leisurely few hours of forest exploration. Mountain bikers will find the short trip described here to be a fun diversion for a morning or afternoon. You will start this trip at the park headquarters and climb up to a beaver pond surrounded by a mish-mash of brushy vegetation, best described as moose food. On the way down, you will enjoy the experience of coasting downhill on narrow single-track that crosses streams and winds its way through a quiet northern hardwood forest. Some people will find stretches of the single-track to be somewhat challenging, as rocks, roots, mud, and sand conspire to force riders into a walk, but these sections are short. If you ride this trip while the park is open (Memorial Day through Columbus Day), stop by the park office to pick up a trail map.

From the parking lot ride over the bridge and stay to the left as the road forks and makes its way through the campground. You are now on Berry Farm Road, a gravel road that takes you all the way

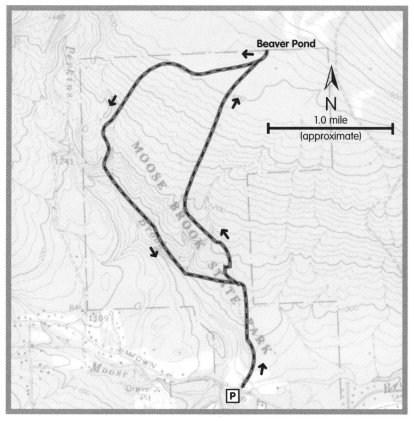

MOOSE BROOK STATE PARK

up to the beaver pond. Stay to the left again at another intersection with a campground road and begin a steady climb. The road is a good dirt surface, although rocks and water bars will sometimes make the ride a little bumpy. At **0.2 mile** and **0.5 mile** other trails lead off to the left. At both intersections continue straight on the road. The road continues to climb moderately and at **0.7 mile** you are rewarded with an excellent view of Mount Adams and Mount Madison from a small clearing with a picnic table. After the picnic table the road gets much rougher and a little steeper. At **1.0 mile** you will cross a small brook on a stone bridge (taking a look at the brook is a good excuse to take a breather).

The steady climb continues until you reach a trail junction at **1.5 miles**, where a trail leads to the left. This trail will be used for the descent, but continue straight on the road for now. The road levels off for the rest of the ride to the beaver pond, which is reached at **1.7 miles**. Some obstructed views can be seen across the pond to the west, but the main attraction is the large beaver lodge in the center of the pond. This lodge has been here for a while, as it has a crop of raspberries and alder growing on top of it. Alder also line the banks of the pond, which is surrounded by spruce and pine and the silver trunks of trees killed by the beaver pond. Moose tracks are usually evident in the mud on the road, which by now has narrowed to a wide snowmobile trail. Beyond the pond, the snowmobile trail continues to the northeast, but it enters private property and is not maintained for bike use.

For the return trip follow the road back down to the last trail junction, which should now be at **1.9 miles** on your odometer. Turn right onto this narrow single-track trail, which follows red trail blazes. Day hikers also use this trail, so be prepared to stop. The trail is level and brushy at first, but it soon begins its moderate descent through a northern hardwood forest filled with a good diversity of trees and standing snags, which provide good habitat for a variety of woodpeckers. This is the roughest section of the trip, due to a combination of rocks, roots, and sand, so you may need to walk at times. At **2.3 miles** you cross a small stream, and after the **3.0 mile** mark the trail widens and the riding gets easier. At **3.5 miles** you cross another stream and make a short climb back to Berry Farm Road at **3.7 miles**. Turn right onto Berry Farm Road and follow it back to the parking lot.

Directions

From the northern intersection of NH 16 and US 2 in Gorham, head west on US 2 for 1.2 miles and turn right onto Jimtown Road. In another 0.6 mile turn right into the parking area for Moose Brook State Park.

moose: an animal not soon forgotten

MOOSE ARE BY FAR THE LARGEST ANIMAL you will encounter in the White Mountains. The average adult moose stands six feet tall at the shoulder and weighs in at 1,000 pounds—five times larger than the average black bear. A moose sighting is always memorable, and if you spend enough time in New Hampshire's backcountry, you are bound to have your own moose tales to tell. Moose are readily identified with the boreal forest, often called the "spruce-moose" forest, but you can find moose just about anywhere in New Hampshire since they feed on the twigs and bark of both hardwoods and softwoods (moose means "twig-eater" in Algonquin). They also enjoy eating aquatic plants such as water lilies. It may be hard to believe that a moose can grow so large eating twigs and lilies, but they are definitely strict vegetarians, eating 40 to 60 pounds of food a day.

Only adult male moose, known as bulls, grow antlers, which can weigh as much as 60 pounds. Every year bull moose grow new antlers, which fall off in December after the fall mating season known as the rut. A bull's antlers are covered with a soft, blood-filled velvet during the spring and summer. About a month before the rut, the velvet dries up and falls off, leaving full grown, hard and bony antlers used to attract mates and to spar with competing males. These sparring matches can be violent, but they rarely result in serious injury. It is during the rut that bull moose are the most cantankerous and care should be taken to stay out of their way.

Moose usually mate in late September. Calves are born about 240 days later in late May or early June. They stand three feet tall at birth and weigh around 25 pounds. Twins are common and occur about 30 to 50 percent of the time.

A bull moose

Moose calves stay with their mothers through their first winter, but they are usually chased off to fend for themselves by the next spring when their mother is preparing to give birth again. Mother moose can be even more dangerous than a rutting bull, and they will charge a person if they feel their calves are being threatened—give moose cows and their calves a wide berth. A moose can seriously injure or kill a human. If a moose approaches you or if it shows irritation by folding its ears back, talk calmly to it (they have poor eyesight and might not realize you are a person) and slowly back away. If a moose charges you, run away. While you cannot outrun a moose, it should soon stop thinking of you as a threat and end its charge.

Four subspecies of moose can be found across northern North America, with Alaska and British Columbia having the largest populations. In the lower 48 states moose range from North Dakota east to Maine, as well as in the Northern Rockies south to Utah. In New Hampshire, moose were practically eliminated by over hunting by the mid-1800s. Their population began to rebound in the 1970s and today around 9,600 moose live in the state. You are most likely to see moose in edge habitats, where forests abut beaver swamps, ponds, clearcuts, and roadsides. If you fail to find a moose while hiking, biking, or paddling, take a drive at dawn or dusk along the Kancamagus Highway, up NH 16 north of Milan, or on US 3 north of Lancaster—just drive slowly and keep your eyes peeled. Moose enthusiasts should also check out the annual North Country Moose Festival held in Colebrook and Pittsburg, New Hampshire, and Canaan, Vermont, during the last week of August. You can get more information about the festival by contacting the North Country Chamber of Commerce in Colebrook at P.O. Box 1, Colebrook, NH 03576; 603-237-8939; www.northcountrychamber.org.

West Side of Loon Mountain

Aerobic Level: **Moderate**

Technical Difficulty: **Moderate**

Distance: **5.0 miles up and back**

Elevation Gain: **800 feet**

Estimated Time: **2 hours**

Maps: **AMC White Mountain Map #2, USGS Lincoln Quadrangle**

Sometimes bumpy but with good views and a long, exhilarating downhill.

THIS RIDE ON THE UNDEVELOPED, west side of Loon Mountain in Lincoln is short, but it packs in a lot of fun. Starting with an easy ride along the East Branch of the Pemigewasset River, you will eventually get your heart pumping as you climb 800 feet through northern hardwoods and over rushing streams. At the top of the ride you will find views toward Kinsman and Lafayette before turning around and making a fast descent over a wide and grassy logging road. The section between the river and the logging road contains some difficult riding over roots and rocks, which will challenge beginning mountain bikers who are not used to the bumps. However, riders who do not mind a few rocks, roots, and water bars will find this to be an enjoyable trip.

From the Lincoln town offices, head east on NH 112 for about 50 yards and turn right onto the second driveway for the Rivergreen Resort Hotel. At **0.2 mile** the road curves to the left and heads for the Pemigewasset River. After crossing the river turn right into a parking lot. Immediately after entering the parking lot, ride past the gate on the right, following a wide cross-country ski trail that goes down to the banks of the river. This flat and easy trail turns

Mountain biking on an old logging road near Loon Mountain.

to follow the river, giving you good views of the river as it washes over a seemingly endless procession of white boulders. At **0.7 mile** you will enter a clearing and see a trail on the left, which will be part of your return trip. Continue straight, following the river on the ski trail as it becomes rockier and muddier.

If the rocks are getting you down, a good rest spot and swimming hole are at about the **1.0-mile** mark, where you also pass into the national forest. From the river good views can be seen to the east of Big Coolidge and Whaleback Mountains. The trail soon begins to climb over rough trail filled with water bars. At **1.6 miles**

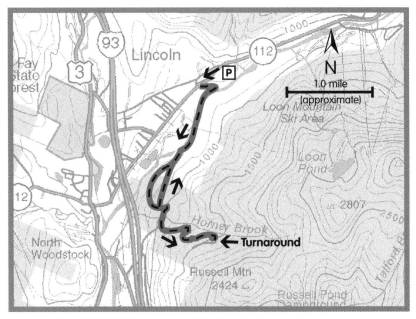

WEST SIDE OF LOON MOUNTAIN

turn right onto narrow single-track, which is marked by an old sign
that says "View." The rocks ease up a bit on the single-track, but you
still will find plenty of water bars to conquer. The trail passes
through a small clearing before entering the dark recesses of a hemlock grove at **1.8 miles**; a small, moss-covered cascade is on the
right. At **1.9 miles** you cross a small stream lined with birch, maple,
and fern.

Soon after crossing the stream, you will reach a trail junction; turn left following another sign that faintly says "View." You are
now on an old logging road that is wide and grassy with only a few
rocks. The trail climbs steeply via switchbacks as it makes its way up
to the view. Where the "View" *is* exactly is getting harder to determine, as trees fill in the clearcut that once provided the view. The
best view seems to be around **2.5 miles** from the beginning of the
trip, where you get a good look to the northwest toward Kinsman
and Franconia ridges. The logging road continues for another **0.5
mile** or so, but no more views can be seen once the trail leaves the
old clearcut.

Turning around at the viewpoint, enjoy the ride down the logging road where it is easy to pick up a lot of speed. This downhill is one of the highlights of the trip, as the trail is wide, the rocks are few, and the mountain views are right in front of you. At **3.0 miles** you will reach the intersection with a single-track; turn right. At **3.6 miles** you will reach an intersection with the ski trail from earlier in the trip. Instead of going straight and returning the way you came, turn right and follow a set of abandoned power lines. This trail has several ups and downs that provide some exciting riding, although it is rocky at times. At **4.3 miles** you reach a clearing; turn right onto the ski trail that parallels the Pemigewasset. When you reach pavement and the bridge over the river, turn left and follow the road back to your car.

Directions

Take Exit 32 on I-93 and head east on NH 112, the Kancamagus Highway. Park in the public lot adjacent to the Lincoln town offices, on the right 0.7 mile east of I-93.

Trip #38

Franconia Notch Bicycle Path

Aerobic Level: **Moderate**

Technical Difficulty: **Easy**

Distance: **18.4 miles out and back**

Elevation Gain: **600 feet**

Estimated Time: **2 hours 30 minutes**

Maps: **AMC White Mountain Map #2, USGS Franconia and Lincoln Quadrangles**

An easy ride on a paved bike path through Franconia Notch—one of the most scenic places in the White Mountains.

FRANCONIA NOTCH—home to Echo Lake, the Old Man of the Mountain, the Basin, and the Flume Gorge—is one of the main attractions of the White Mountains. The huge cliffs of Cannon Mountain and the high, alpine ridgeline of Mount Lafayette and Mount Lincoln create the walls of the notch, which were formed by glaciers during the last ice age. The bike path was created in the 1980s when the road through the notch was being redesigned as an interstate highway. The AMC and other environmental organizations advocated successfully to preserve the integrity of the notch and the road was built as the only segment of an interstate highway to be designed as a parkway. The wide, paved bike path is easy to ride and can be accessed from several parking areas. This trip describes the path from its northern end at a parking area on US 3, just north of the notch, to its southern terminus at the Flume Gorge Visitor Center. However, by spotting cars or planning shorter out-and-back trips it is easy to come up with your own variation of this trip.

From the Skookumchuck Trail parking area, ride south on the paved path. This is actually not part of the Franconia Notch

Franconia Notch Bicycle Path

Bicycle Path but the remnants of an older version of US 3. The path makes a gradual climb, parallel to the current US 3, up to the Lafayette Brook Overlook at **1.5 miles**. From the overlook excellent views can be seen to the west over the Connecticut River into Vermont, and to the east up to Mount Lafayette. On the other side of the bridge is a cul-de-sac and parking area. Be sure to follow the bike path to the right, where it drops down under I-93 before turning left and making a long but gradual climb. At **2.25 miles** you pass under NH 18 and reach Echo Lake and good views of Cannon Mountain and the cliffs on the eastern side of the notch. As you look at Cannon keep your eyes open for black bears, which are known to frequent the ski slopes in search of raspberries.

Cannon Mountain was one of the earliest downhill ski areas in the United States, and was home to the country's first aerial tramway built in 1938. This fact is memorialized at the ski museum, which you will pass at **2.7 miles**. The path continues through the notch, alternating between flat sections, gentle downhill sections, and short uphill sections. At **3.7 miles** you pass through the Old Man Viewing parking area where you will see a sign that says "Bike Walk;" you should get off of your bike and walk for the next 0.4 mile.

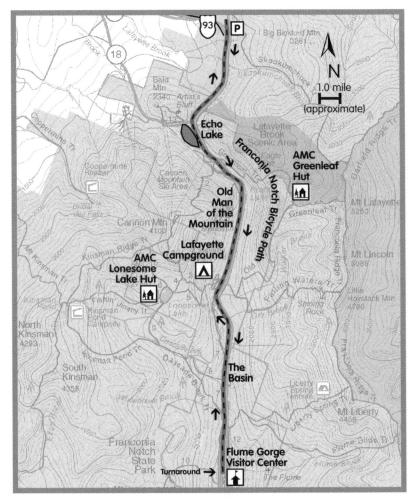

FRANCONIA NOTCH BICYCLE PATH

During your walk you pass the north end of Profile Lake and its view of the Old Man of the Mountain. Profile and Echo Lakes, as well as Franconia Notch itself, were all formed 12,000 to 15,000 years ago during the last ice age as a huge river of ice flowed through the notch—much as I-93 does today. In the second half of the nineteenth century the notch was home to two huge hotels: the Flume House and the Profile House, both of which accommodated visitors lured by the writings of Wordsworth and Thomas Starr King, as well as paintings by Thomas Cole.

After crossing under the highway the bike path reaches a parking area at **4.2 miles** with good views of the Old Man. After the parking area the path once again crosses under the highway and begins to parallel the Pemigewasset River. At **4.5 miles** you will pass a 300-ton boulder that recently fell from Cannon Cliffs, tumbling 0.5 mile down the mountain and knocking down 60-foot tall trees in its path. At **5.5 miles** you reach Lafayette Campground, which has bathroom facilities, fresh water, and a small store. Continuing past the campground, the bike path winds its way along the banks of the river, often crossing it on small wooden bridges. A gradual downhill continues from here to the end of the path. At **7.1 miles** you will reach a side path that leads to the Basin, a large 30-foot diameter pothole, that is well worth checking out. You will need to walk your bike on this short trail, as it is usually very crowded with sightseers. Formed by melting glacier ice as well as the rushing waters of the Pemigewasset, the Basin was visited by Henry David Thoreau during his first visit to Franconia Notch in 1846.

After the Basin the side trail brings you back to the bike path, which crosses under the highway one last time, passes through a parking area, and then continues its gradual descent along the banks of the Pemigewasset River. At **8.2 miles** you pass the Liberty Spring Trail (see trip #24) and ride over a bridge that spans the widening river. The deep shade of hemlock keeps you cool as you make a short but steep climb after the bridge. At **9.2 miles** you reach the end of the bike path and the Flume Gorge Visitor Center, which has restrooms, a restaurant, and a gift shop. The Flume Gorge is an impressive 800-foot-long gorge, with rock walls that are 70 to 90 feet tall and only 12 to 20 feet wide. It is a short hike to the gorge, but you will have to pay a $7 entrance fee at the visitor center. If you spotted a car at the visitor center, this is the end of your trip. If not, turn around and follow the bike path back through the notch to your car.

Directions

Take Exit 35 on I-93 following US 3 north. The Skookumchuck Trail parking area will be in 0.6 mile on the right. The bike path leaves from the south end of the parking lot.

Trip #39

Sawyer River

> Aerobic Level: **Easy**
>
> Technical Difficulty: **Moderate**
>
> Distance: **9.4 miles round-trip**
>
> Elevation Gain: **300 feet**
>
> Estimated Time: **2 to 3 hours**
>
> Maps: **AMC White Mountain Map #2, USGS Mount Carrigain Quadrangle**
>
> **A good mixture of single-track and gravel roads with excellent wildlife-watching opportunities.**

THIS TRIP EXPLORES the wildlife-rich forests to the east of Mount Carrigain. Several good views of the mountain can be seen from beaver ponds along the way, and three river crossings also make for good spots to sit and soak in the summer sun. The ride is fairly level; although one steep climb on a forest road will make you question the easy rating for a few moments, trust us—the climb is only 0.5 mile. You will be riding on hiking trails for portions of this trip, so be prepared to give hikers the right of way. You should also be prepared to yield to moose, as the Sawyer River Trail passes through a long stretch of boggy spruce forest. Since this trip begins with a crossing of the Swift River, you will not be able to ride it in spring when the river crossing is next to impossible (you can ride the loop portion of this trip by starting at the end of Sawyer River Road; see the map).

To start your trip follow the Sawyer River Trail for a short, rocky descent to the Swift River, where you will find a good swimming hole that can come in handy on the return trip. The trail parallels the river for a few yards before crossing it at **0.2 mile**. The trail is fairly level, but becomes difficult to ride at times because of a large amount

Swift River

of tree roots, rocks, and mud. At **0.5 mile** you pass the Nanamoco-muck Ski Trail, begin to descend gradually, and then reach the first of several wooden bridges at **0.7 mile**. The trail levels out and becomes very rough at **1.0 mile**, where you enter a 1.0-mile-long area of meandering streams, bogs, beaver ponds, spruce, and moose. You will get to see good views of Mount Carrigain. In addition to moose and beaver, this is also a good place to watch for warblers, fly-catchers, and forest raptors such as sharp-shinned and Cooper's hawks.

At **2.5 miles** you reach an intersection where the Sawyer River Trail goes straight, the Hancock Notch Trail goes left, and an unmarked forest road goes right. Turn right onto the forest road, which is Sawyer River Road. This is a wide, rolling forest road with a good surface for riding. At **2.9 miles** you will come to a clearing with good views and begin an enjoyable downhill run to the Sawyer River at **3.7 miles**. The wooden bridge over the river (or the large boulders in the river) is a good spot for a food and water break in the sun.

At **3.8 miles** make a sharp left onto Forest Road 86. Here is the hardest aerobic challenge of the trip, about 0.5 mile of moderately steep climbing. Fortunately, the packed dirt and gravel

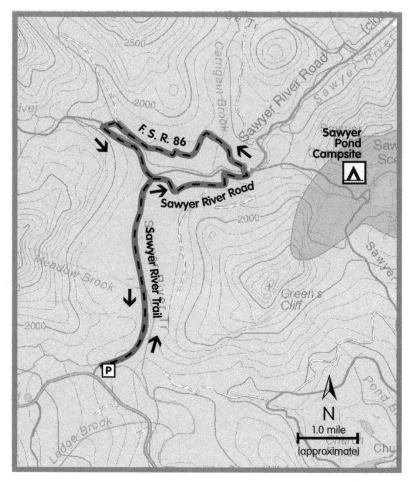

SAWYER RIVER

surface of the road gives you good traction with no obstacles other than gravity. At **4.3 miles** the road levels out for a fun ride through a scenic stretch of northern hardwood forest. At **5.9 miles** make a sharp left and cross a large brook on a wooden bridge. The road ends immediately after the bridge, and you are riding suddenly on narrow, overgrown single-track. You soon reach an unmarked trail junction; turn left. You probably will need to carry your bike over this boulder-strewn section of trail that leads to the Sawyer River at **6.1 miles**.

Carry your bike over the river and begin riding once again on level single-track, following the river as it flows downstream. Though you will not see any trail signs, you are now on the Hancock Notch Trail. The ride is good, though occasionally bumpy, all the way to the Sawyer River Trail at **6.9 miles**. Turn right and you are back on the section of the Sawyer River Trail that you rode during the beginning of the trip. You will reach the parking area in another **2.5 miles**, just beyond that enticing swimming hole on the Swift River.

Directions

From the intersection of NH 16 and NH 112 (Kancamagus Highway) in Conway, drive west on NH 112 for 18.7 miles. A small parking area is on the right for the Sawyer River Trail.

missing predators: wolves, mountain lions, and lynx

THE WHITE MOUNTAINS contain hundreds of thousands of acres of wilderness that are relatively healthy—rich forests teeming with wildlife such as otters, black bears, and moose. However, the ecological balance is drastically different now than before our forefathers settled New Hampshire and systematically extirpated the forest's largest predators. Most heavily persecuted were gray wolves and mountain lions, which were both feared as human-killers and blamed for the killing of livestock and for competing with people for game animals. While the smaller lynx were not as despised, they most likely have been extirpated from the White Mountains, due largely to habitat loss and trapping. The forest has, of course, found a new balance. Coyote have moved in from the west and taken over as top predators. People also are part of the mix, taking part in annual deer, moose, and bird hunts. Still, the lack of these historically present predators does create a sense that something is missing, that we have lost some of the region's wildness.

The Canada lynx, which resembles a large, long-haired tabby that weighs 20 to 40 pounds, was recently added to the federal list of threatened species by the U.S. Fish and Wildlife Service. Outside of Alaska and Canada, only Maine, Washington, and Montana have breeding populations of lynx. Of the large predators, the lynx survived for the longest in New Hampshire, with the last known lynx sighting reported in the state in 1993. Lynx are long distance travelers, often covering a few hundred miles, and most likely last bred in the state in the 1960s. Lynx have large, snowshoelike paws, which allow them to successfully hunt for their primary food:

snowshoe hares. With a breeding population in neighboring Maine, any lynx recovery efforts will most likely include the White Mountain National Forest.

Mountain lions, also known as pumas, cougars, catamounts, or panthers, are large cats that can grow to be eight feet long and weigh as much as 150 pounds. They are also the widest ranging predator in the New World, prowling the forests and deserts of both North and South America from western Canada to Patagonia. As a species mountain lions are not considered endangered, but the Florida panther and eastern subspecies are federally endangered. The eastern subspecies, which roamed all of New England until the early 1900s, is most likely extinct; however, mountain lion sightings in New England have persisted until the present, and some of these sightings have been confirmed by DNA analysis of the hair in lion droppings. The big debate: Are these lions that were illegally released into the wild by exotic pet owners, or are these animals remnants of the eastern subspecies that have somehow managed to reproduce successfully, unknown to scientists, for over 100 years?

The gray wolf is perhaps the most heavily persecuted animal on the planet. Feared and reviled throughout European history, wolves have been systematically hunted and eliminated from most of the United States. Wolves prey on small mammals such as mice and rabbits, as well as larger animals such as deer, moose, and musk ox. The last known wolf in New Hampshire was killed in 1887 and the closest viable populations that exist today are in Quebec. At least two wolves have been killed in Maine in recent years, although these animals most likely were lone wolves that came to Maine from Canada.

In the lower 48 states, the gray wolf is listed as a federally endangered species, with the largest and most stable population living in the forests of northern Minnesota. The recent successful reintroduction of wolves to

Yellowstone National Park has encouraged environmental groups and wolf lovers to push for the reintroduction of gray wolves to other parts of their historic range in North America. Biologists have identified the Northern Forest in Maine and New Hampshire as suitable habitat for wolf reintroduction, and the U.S. Fish and Wildlife Service is considering developing a reintroduction plan for the area. Who knows, maybe someday a night in the backcountry of the White Mountains will once again be accompanied by the sound of wolves howling.

Trip #40

Lower Nanamocomuck Ski Trail

Aerobic Level: **Moderate**

Technical Difficulty: **Moderate**

Distance: **8.4 miles up and back**

Elevation Gain: **800 feet**

Estimated Time: **2 hours 30 minutes**

Maps: **AMC White Mountain Map #3, USGS Bartlett and Mount Chocorua Quadrangles**

One of the more scenic backcountry rides in the White Mountains.

THE LOWER NANAMOCOMUCK SKI TRAIL winds its way along the scenic Swift River for several miles. This trip utilizes about 3.0 of those miles and includes a short hike to Rocky Gorge, where the waters of the Swift River are squeezed through a narrow chasm in the granite bedrock. This trail tends to collect a lot of water during the wet seasons, so you may encounter some muddy conditions; although the wettest part of the trail is skipped in this trip by beginning on a Forest Service road. The trail alternates between a relatively smooth, gentle footpath and a rough tree-root-ridden rut with frequent stream crossings. In spring the Swift River has some of the wildest and most dangerous whitewater in the White Mountains, but this ride also takes you past calm meandering oxbows, where big trees lean out over the water and heron wait patiently for their chance at a meal.

From the parking area on Bear Notch Road, ride north for **0.2 mile** and turn right onto Forest Service Road 209, a smooth gravel road. You make a long gradual climb on the service road

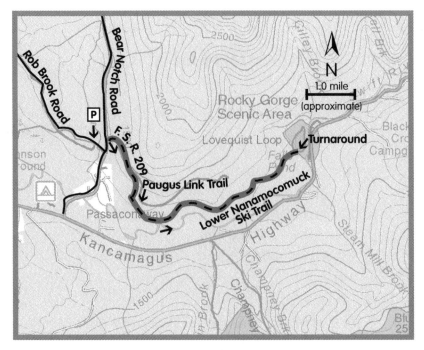

LOWER NANAMOCOMUCK SKI TRAIL

before descending to the Paugus Link Trail at **1.0 mile**. Keep an eye out for moose in here, as they often forage along the road. Turn right onto the Paugus Link Trail, which makes a rocky but passable descent on its way to the Nanamocomuck Ski Trail at **1.2 miles**; turn left onto the ski trail. The trail makes several short ascents and descents on its way to the banks of the Swift River, which will appear on your right at **1.6 miles**. The river curves gently with a slow current through a mixed forest of spruce, fir, pine, larch, and maple. This is one of the most enjoyable sections of mountain biking trail in the White Mountains.

The trail parallels the river and crosses a small stream on a wooden bridge at **2.0 miles**; stay to the right at a junction with the Paugus Ski Trail. The trail begins to get rougher as stream crossings and tree roots proliferate after the **2.5-mile** mark. Soon you enter a grove of hemlock trees, where the temperature drops a few degrees and the forest floor is covered with checkerberry plants, small evergreens with scarlet berries. If you crush the thick, shiny oval leaf of a checkerberry plant in your hands and inhale, you will know why it is also called wintergreen.

As the trail gets rougher, so does the river. The calm, lazy oxbows are replaced by rushing whitewater as the river drops steadily toward Rocky Gorge. At **3.6 miles** you make a very close approach to the river and will most likely pause to stare at the giant white pine that somehow survived the logging that took place in this area 100 years ago. A 0.1-mile stretch of trail here is very rough and will make some riders dismount and push their bikes. The ups and downs continue and you pass through a curious stand of red pine planted in neat rows just prior to reaching the Wenonah Trail at **4.2 miles**. This is the end of the bike riding part of this trip. From here, turn right and walk the 0.3 mile through a grove of tall spruce trees to the Rocky Gorge Scenic Area, which is next to the Kancamagus Highway and about 3.5 miles east of Bear Notch Road.

At Rocky Gorge the Swift River is forced through a cleft in the granite, about 20 feet wide, 100 yards long, and 30 feet tall. The water falls with incredible force through the gorge, constantly polishing the dark gray rock. From here the Swift River provides some of the most difficult, uninterrupted whitewater boating runs in New England. For a more mellow experience you can also hike the Lovequist Loop, an easy 1.0-mile walk around Falls Pond. To complete this trip, you can either ride back the way you came or take a right on the Kancamagus and follow it to Bear Notch Road and the Nanamocomuck trailhead. If you decide to ride the Kancamagus, be prepared for a road with a small shoulder and car drivers who may be paying more attention to the scenery than the road.

Directions

The Nanamocomuck Ski Trail parking area is on the west side of Bear Notch Road, 8.0 miles south of US 302 in Bartlett and 0.8 mile north of the Kancamagus Highway.

Trip #41

Mineral Site and Moat Mountain

Aerobic Level: Moderate

Technical Difficulty: Easy on gravel roads; Difficult on single-track (with an easy alternative)

Distance: 8.6 miles round-trip

Elevation Gain: 1,000 feet

Estimated Time: 2 to 3 hours

Maps: AMC White Mountain Map #5, USGS North Conway West Quadrangle

A fast downhill run over rocky single-track, followed by miles of riding on quiet forest roads.

GOOD VIEWS of Moat Mountain greet riders who make it to the end of this ride, which combines a swift descent on technical single-track with 7.0 miles of mellow forest roads. The single-track that begins this trip is difficult, but can be avoided by making this an up-and-back trip—see alternate trip description. Whether or not you skip the single-track, you will get a good workout, as about 1,000 feet of elevation gain is on this ride. Rock hounds can make a side trip to the Moat Mountain Smokey Quartz Area, and ambitious multi-sport athletes can combine this trip with a hike up North Moat Mountain via the strenuous Red Ridge Trail. Please note that while this trip is completely within the White Mountain National Forest, it abuts private land and many unofficial side trails lead to private houses; it is important to stay on the official Forest Service trails and roads. Mountain bikers have recently lost access to some trails in this area because of inappropriate behavior on private property.

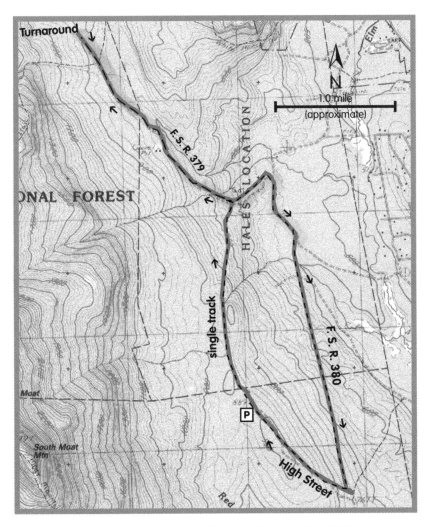

MINERAL SITE AND MOAT MOUNTAIN

From the parking area ride through the boulders onto the trail marked "Moat Mountain Mineral Site." At **0.1 mile** bear right onto a wide single-track trail that makes a moderate descent over rocks and roots. At **0.4 mile** cross a pair of streams with steep banks and follow the moderately technical trail over rolling terrain. At **0.7 mile** continue straight at a trail junction and at **1.0 mile** you reach the Moat Mountain Smoky Quartz Area, a part of the White Mountain National Forest set aside for visitors who want to look for quartz crystals. At the intersection with the mineral site trail, continue straight for a downhill ride to a clearcut with views of Cranmore Mountain and North Conway at **1.4 miles**. From just above the clearcut to an intersection with Forest Road 379 at **1.6 miles**, the trail makes a steep, difficult descent over loose rocks and gravel.

Turn left onto Forest Road 379 (unmarked), which soon crosses a stream in a grove of hemlock and makes a steady climb for about 0.5 mile. Technically, the ride is much easier, as the road has a good packed dirt and gravel surface. Just before the **2.4-mile** mark, you begin to get views of Moat Mountain as you enter an old clearcut. At **2.6 miles** the road gets rougher and you may need to walk your bike as you cross a stream filled with white, volleyball-sized boulders. Like all the streams on this side of Moat Mountain, this stream eventually flows to the Saco River.

After crossing another stream on a bridge, the road becomes a narrow single-track trail and crosses the Red Ridge Trail. If you are up for a strenuous hike up to incredible views, stash your bike here and turn left on the Red Ridge Trail (see trip #26). To complete this trip, continue straight at this intersection and enjoy the smooth surface of the single-track as it makes a few easy climbs and descents on its way to more views of Moat Mountain in a clearing at **3.5 miles**. Moat Mountain is actually a long ridge with three distinct peaks: North Moat, Middle Moat, and South Moat. North Moat, at 3,196 feet, is the tallest, but good views (and many blueberries) are available from many points along the ridge. While the trail does appear to continue beyond the clearing, it soon ends on posted private property.

Turn around and follow the single-track and then Forest Road 379 back for a well deserved, long downhill run. Ride past the mineral site trail you rode in on at **5.4 miles**, and ride around the Forest Service gate at **5.5 miles**. Continue the downhill ride until you reach a fork in the road at **6.1 miles**; bear right onto Forest Road 380 (unmarked). At first FR 380 rolls gently along through a fragrant forest of red and white pine and crosses a stream on a wooden bridge at **6.3 miles**. At **7.1 miles** you will begin an uphill ride that lasts for more than 1.0 mile, which will probably feel steeper than it is since you are at the end of the ride. At **7.9 miles** ride around the Forest Service gate and turn right onto the gravel road (High Street). At **8.3 miles** the road levels out and you can coast most of the way back to your car, which should be at the **8.7-mile** mark.

Alternate Trip

It is easy to avoid the difficult single-track portion of this trip if you are more in the mood for a relaxing ride through the woods on gravel roads. From the parking area just ride back down High Street until **0.8 mile**; turn left and pass the Forest Service gate onto Forest Road 380. From here just follow FR 380 to FR 379 and turn left, riding it to the end.

Directions

From the intersection of NH 16 and River Road in North Conway (near the Eastern Slope Inn), head west on River Road. After 1.0 mile turn left onto West Side Road. In another 5.4 miles turn right onto Passaconaway Road, and in another 1.2 miles bear right onto an unmarked gravel road known as High Street. In 1.8 miles bear left at a Forest Service gate (FR 380), following signs for the Moat Mountain Mineral site. Park at the end of the road in another 0.8 mile.

Trip #42

Bog Brook Eddy

> Aerobic Level: **Moderate**
>
> Technical Difficulty: **Difficult**
>
> Distance: **6.5 miles up and back**
>
> Elevation Gain: **1,000 feet**
>
> Estimated Time: **2 hours 30 minutes**
>
> Maps: **AMC White Mountain Map #2,**
>   **USGS Lincoln Quadrangle**
>
> **A somewhat technical ride to a high–**
> **elevation bog and good views of Franconia**
> **Ridge.**

LIKE MANY of the bike routes in the White Mountains that follow old logging roads, the Bog Brook Eddy trip is a rocky, uphill climb through a northern hardwood forest. However, this trail tops out at Bog Brook Eddy, a wide spot along Harvard Brook where the flow of water slows down enough to form an interesting bog filled with sphagnum, sheep laurel, and larch. The bog also creates enough of a clearing to get an excellent view of the surrounding mountains. Beginning just off US 3 in Lincoln, this is an up-and-back trip, but you will need to pay close attention to trail directions because the area is crisscrossed by numerous snowmobile trails.

From the parking area, ride past the chain-link fence, cross a wooden bridge, ride under I-93, and then turn left on the unnamed trail as it parallels the highway. The trail turns right and enters the woods at **0.2 mile**, where it begins a moderate climb through a second- or third-growth northern hardwood forest. Continue straight through two trail junctions at **0.3 mile**. The trail gets rougher as you climb and becomes very rough at **0.6 mile**, where a snowmobile trail enters from the left. All but the most experienced riders probably will need to walk the next hundred yards or so, as

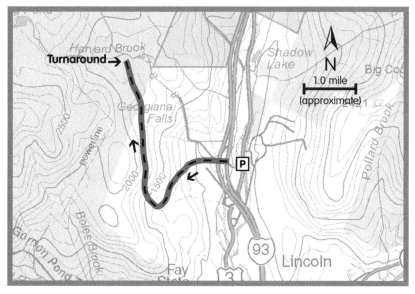

BOG BROOK EDDY

the loose boulders make it very difficult to make the steep climb. The trail eases to a moderate climb at about the **1.0-mile** mark, where another snowmobile trail leaves to the right. Water bars in this section add to the difficulty of the ride, although the Forest Service has recently completed some trail maintenance to make the water bars easier to ride over.

At **1.3 miles** the trail makes a sharp right and follows a northerly direction for the rest of the way up to the bog. The forest along this part of the trail is thick with large yellow birch and American beech. The leaves of these trees turn yellow and brown in the fall, giving the forest an amber glow during sunny fall days. At times this section of the trail is level and smooth, but it also makes some steep climbs over a rough, rocky roadbed. At **2.0 miles** a snowmobile trail enters from the right and it is an easy, level ride (except for those pesky water bars) until **2.5 miles**, where you cross a small stream over a smooth, wooden snowmobile bridge. After this stream crossing the trail climbs gradually for the next 0.4 mile, sometimes over rough trail.

At **3.0 miles** you enter a boreal forest and the trail levels out. The rocks disappear and you have an easy ride for the final 0.25 mile to Bog Brook Eddy. At Bog Brook Eddy, Harvard Brook widens out

A Bog Brook Eddy logging road

to fill a depression in this relatively flat area, 1,900 feet above sea level. Studying the mud next to the bog, you may spot the tracks of a coyote or bobcat, predators that might have recently visited this biologically diverse area in search of small birds, rodents, or amphibians. Except for the occasional larch, black spruce, or alder, the acidic soil of the bog prevents most trees from growing here. The benefit to the mountain biker is an open area with good views to Mount Pemigewasset, Franconia Ridge, and the Kinsmans.

The trail continues past the bog but ends in less than 1.0 mile, with little reward. To complete the trip, turn around at the bog and enjoy the downhill ride back to the parking area.

Directions

Take Exit 33 off of I-93 and head north on US 3. In 0.2 mile turn left onto Hanson Farm Road, opposite the Longhorn Restaurant. The parking area is on the left in 0.1 mile where the road ends.

Slippery Brook Road

Aerobic Level: **Strenuous**

Technical Difficulty: **Moderate**

Distance: **12.5 miles up and back**

Elevation Gain: **1,000 feet**

Estimated Time: **2 to 3 hours**

Maps: **AMC White Mountain Map #5, USGS Chatham Quadrangle**

Excellent forest scenery combined with moderate elevation gain and 6.0 miles of downhill riding.

SLIPPERY BROOK ROAD is a gravel Forest Service road for the first 4.0 miles of this trip, climbing steadily through northern hardwoods next to the rushing waters of Slippery Brook. At the 4.0-mile mark the road turns into double-track and climbs over moderately technical terrain before reaching a bridge over Slippery Brook. The return trip is pure mountain-biking fun, as you can test your speed-demon threshold while descending for most of the 6.2 miles back to the car. If you can slow down long enough you can make a side trip to Mountain Pond, a beautiful high-elevation pond surrounded by boreal forest that is home to moose and loons.

From the parking area, ride past the White Mountain National Forest sign and continue straight at the intersection with a gated forest road on the right. The packed dirt and gravel road is open to cars and trucks, but gets little use. It rises gradually, passing the East Branch Trail at **1.6 miles** where you begin to hear and see the rushing waters of Slippery Brook. The forest is a fairly mature northern hardwood forest. From here on, the road climbs at a moderate pace. At **2.6 miles** continue straight at an intersection with

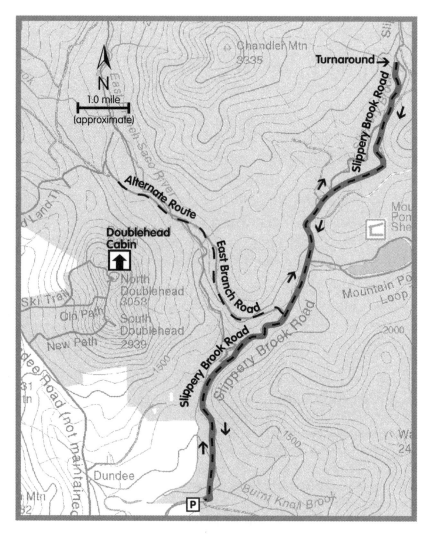

SLIPPERY BROOK ROAD

East Branch Road. (To add an additional 5.0 miles to your trip, you can turn left here, following East Branch Road over the East Branch of the Saco River to a beaver pond with nice mountain views. Be prepared for 2.0 miles of uphill on the way back.)

At **3.25 miles** you pass the parking area for the Mountain Pond Loop Trail. (If you feel like a short side trip, leave your bikes in the parking area, hike the 0.3 mile to the pond, and turn left at the fork. The trail makes a 2.7-mile loop around the pond, but a good lookout is on the right about 25 yards past the fork.) At **3.75 miles** you pass a beaver pond and an unmarked logging road on the right. At **4.0 miles** you reach the end of the gravel road and the Slippery Brook Trail. Ride past the gate onto grassy double-track.

The double-track alternates between level sections and moderate climbs. The riding is moderately technical at times due to rocks hiding in the grass and a series of several deep water bars. Occasional views can be seen as you pass through a few old log yards and recovering clearcuts. At around **5.6 miles** you will begin a very gradual downhill climb, passing an unmarked trail on the right at **6.0 miles** (stay to the left, following the yellow arrow). At **6.2 miles** the Slippery Brook Trail leaves to the right. Continue straight for the final few hundred yards to a bridge spanning Slippery Brook. This makes a good lunch spot and turnaround point (beyond the bridge, the trail is steep and overgrown and eventually ends in an old clearcut).

Just retrace your tire tracks for the return trip. The water bars seem a little easier on the way down and you have to watch out for those hidden rocks, but all in all the double-track descent is fun. Once you get back to the road, you will find you can ride as fast as you feel comfortable—just remember there can be cars on this road so be careful on the corners.

Directions

From the intersection of NH 16 and River Road in North Conway, drive north on NH 16 for 3.7 miles and turn right onto Town Hall Road. Continue straight at the stop sign in 0.1 mile. Bear left at a fork in the road 2.6 miles from NH 16. In another 0.8 mile park on the left across from the White Mountain National Forest sign.

the northern
hardwood forest

MOST HIKES IN THE WHITE MOUNTAINS begin in a northern hardwood forest—a forest made up predominantly of American beech, yellow birch, and sugar maple trees. It is the major forest type below 2,000 feet, and it can be found as high as 3,000 feet on south facing slopes with good soils. The northern hardwood forest is a transition forest that grows in a climate between the boreal forests to the north and the oak-hickory forests to the south. For this reason, you will often find species from these other forest types present in a northern hardwood forest such as white and red pine, red spruce, paper birch, eastern hemlock, and northern red oak. In the White Mountains the northern hardwood forest makes the transition to boreal forest as you gain elevation, usually between 2,500 and 3,000 feet.

The understory of this forest is populated by striped maple, a favorite food of moose, and hobblebush, with its broad round leaves and showy white flowers. Wildflowers include the pink lady's slipper, painted trilliums, and wood sorrel. White-tailed deer, red squirrels, porcupines, and snowshoe hares are common in a northern hardwood forest, as are the yellow-bellied sapsucker, red-eyed vireo, black-throated blue warblers, brown creeper, and the hermit thrush. Black bears also frequent this productive forest in search of beechnuts, acorns, and other tasty vegetarian fare. It is the red, yellow, and orange foliage of the northern hardwood forest that is responsible for northern New England's spectacular fall foliage displays.

Trip #44

Rob Brook Road

Aerobic Level: **Moderate**

Technical Difficulty: **Moderate**

Distance: **12.5 miles round-trip; 15.8 miles with optional single-track**

Elevation Gain: **200 feet; 500 feet with optional single-track**

Estimated Time: **3 to 4 hours**

Maps: **AMC White Mountain Map #3, USGS Mount Carrigain, Bartlett, Mount Chocorua, and Mount Tripyramid Quadrangles**

Easy woods riding on a gravel road with the option for some adventurous single-track.

ROB BROOK ROAD is a gated Forest Service road that provides excellent access to the forest south of Sawyer Pond, Green's Cliff, and Owl's Cliff. While riding this road's packed dirt and gravel surface you might encounter a logging vehicle or two, but usually the road is free of traffic, making it a great place for those seeking a long but fairly easy ride through quiet White Mountain scenery. This trip also includes an option for a few miles of exciting single-track up and around Birch Hill, as well as an option for a few miles of hiking to Sawyer Pond—one of the more scenic spots in the White Mountains (due to heavy hiker traffic, bikes are not allowed on the Sawyer Pond Trail). As a loop trip this ride ends up with 3.0 miles of riding on the Kancamagus Highway and Bear Notch Road. However, the crossing of the Swift River just prior to reaching the Kancamagus can be impossible in high water, necessitating a return trip on Rob Brook Road, that would make the trip 17.4 miles long.

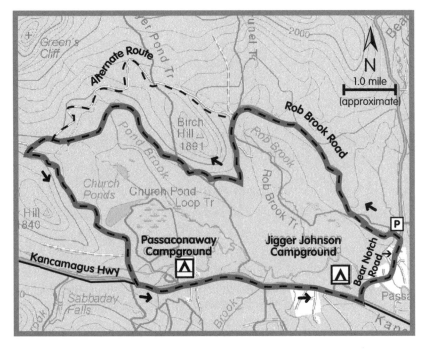

ROB BROOK ROAD

To begin your trip, pedal around the Forest Service gate onto Rob Brook Road. The road has an excellent riding surface for almost all of its 8.7 miles, occasionally climbing and descending gradually, with the downhills serendipitously feeling longer than the uphills. At **0.6 mile** you pass the first of several intersections with the Rob Brook Trail—just stick to the road at all of these intersections. The ride takes you through a mixed forest where there are signs of recent logging such as log yards and overgrown skidder roads. At **1.5 miles** and **1.8 miles** you will pass unmarked trails on the right, and at **2.1 miles** you will pass some large boulders and an unmarked trail on the left; continue straight. At **2.5 miles** you pass the Brunel Trail on the right and then a pair of unmarked trails, the second of which at **2.8 miles** is the beginning of the Birch Hill loop (see alternate description at the end of this trip).

The road continues its gently rolling nature as the forest becomes consistently populated by northern hardwoods with the occasional grove of hemlock. At **4.3 miles** you cross the Sawyer Pond Trail. (If you feel like taking a hike, stash your bike and turn right on the Sawyer Pond Trail; it is 2.8 miles up to the pond.) The road provides occasional views of Green's Cliff and the chance to see wildlife such as moose and white-tailed deer. In summer you are likely to encounter American toads and garter snakes soaking in the warmth of the sun on the road. You also will find wildflowers that tend to populate disturbed areas like roadsides and clearcuts. These flowers include nonnative invaders like black-eyed susans, daisies, and orange hawkweed, as well as native plants like milkweed, fireweed, and asters.

At **6.3 miles** the Birch Hill loop (unmarked) rejoins Rob Brook Road. At **6.6 miles** you pass an unmarked logging road in a clearing where a stream passes through a boggy area, providing more views of the cliffs as well as some bird-watching opportunities. At **8.2 miles** you come to an intersection where the main road bends to the right and up a hill, while a grassy logging road is straight ahead. Continue straight on this logging road, which immediately passes an intersection with the Church Pond Loop Trail and Nanamocomuck Ski Trail. Following a sign for the Kancamagus Highway you reach the Swift River at **8.7 miles**. The Swift River makes a great lunch spot and is a good place to cool off on a hot summer day. The river is usually easily crossed in summer, but in spring or after heavy rains you most likely will need to turn around and return via the way you just came (this is also a good idea if you prefer not to ride with the cars on the busy Kancamagus).

After crossing the river you will have a short stretch of single-track before reaching pavement at **8.8 miles**. Turn left onto the Kancamagus Highway, which has a narrow shoulder and occasionally heavy traffic. On your way to Bear Notch Road, you will pass several hiking trails and two campgrounds, as well as the Passaconaway Historic Site—the homestead of pioneer Russell Colbath built in the early 1800s. At **11.5 miles** turn left onto Bear Notch Road for the final 1.0-mile climb back to your car.

Alternate Trip

To add 3.3 miles of single-track adventure to this otherwise tame ride, turn right onto an unmarked jeep trail on the right immediately after crossing a small brook **2.8 miles** from Bear Notch Road. (This will be the second unmarked trail after you pass the Brunel Trail on the right.) This trail will take you around the north side of Birch Hill, climbing sometimes steeply over a rocky trail that is moderately technical most of the time. About **1.2 miles** after leaving Rob Brook Road you cross the Sawyer Pond Trail (no bikes) and continue to climb until you reach an old clearcut at **1.5 miles**. The forest is beginning to grow back, but some good views can still be seen up to Green's Cliff. After the clearcut continue straight at a trail junction where the trail re-enters the forest and begins its descent back to Rob Brook Road. The trail descends somewhat steeply over rocks, roots, and wooden snowmobile bridges for about 1.0 mile. The remainder of the loop is fairly level with a good riding surface until you reach Rob Brook Road. From here you can turn left to return to the car, or turn right to continue onto the Swift River and the Kancamagus Highway.

Directions

From the intersection of NH 16 and NH 112 (Kancamagus Highway) in Conway, drive west on NH 112 for 12.3 miles and turn right onto Bear Notch Road. Rob Brook Road will be on the left in 1.0 mile. Parking is allowed on the southbound side of the road. From Bartlett, Rob Brook Road is 8.0 miles south of US 302.

Trip #45

Wild River

Aerobic Level: **Moderate**

Technical Difficulty: **Moderate**

Distance: **16.8 miles up and back**

Elevation Gain: **800 feet**

Estimated Time: **3 hours**

Maps: **AMC White Mountain Map #5, USGS Wild River and Speckled Mountain (Maine) Quadrangles**

An easy ride on a dirt road next to the Wild River, followed by technical riding into the deep backcountry of the Wild River valley.

THE WILD RIVER begins in the roadless wilderness between the Carter and Baldface Ranges and flows for 17.0 miles through 100-year-old forests before emptying into the Androscoggin in Gilead, Maine. A logging railroad once followed almost the entire length of the river, as valuable old-growth spruce logs were harvested nonstop from the 1860s into the early 1900s. The trains are long gone and the railroad bed has been converted to the Wild River Road and the Wild River Trail. On this ride you will make use of both the road and the trail, which ride in close proximity to the river for most of their lengths. This trip begins at the eastern terminus of Wild River Road and finishes up at Spider Bridge, a good spot to take in the sounds of the river and the views of the nearby mountains. The packed dirt road makes for easy riding, but the Wild River Trail does have some challenging sections as you ride over loose fist-sized cobblestones. On the plus side, the 800 feet of elevation gain is spread out over 9.0 miles, so the ride is never steep.

From the parking lot turn right on Wild River Road, leaving ME 113 and Evans Notch behind. You are near the center of Hastings,

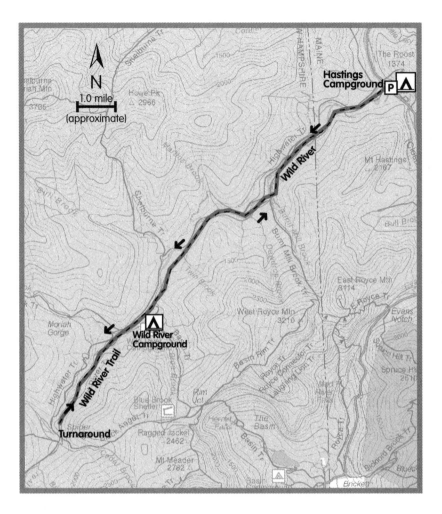

WILD RIVER

Maine, a logging town that in the late nineteenth century was home to a sawmill, general store, and several hundred people. At that time the Wild River valley was logged heavily. In its heyday the sawmill in Hastings processed 60,000 board-feet of lumber per day, but by 1903 the forest was played out. By 1918 the town was completely deserted and the buildings left behind to rot. Today the forest has reclaimed the landscape and all you will find of Hastings is an occasional stone cellar hole.

Back to the riding. The road follows the river on a good dirt surface and at a relatively level grade. At this point the river is fairly wide, swelled by the waters of numerous brooks that tumble down the slopes of the Carter-Moriah and Baldface Ranges. The old-growth spruce forest has been replaced by the diversity of a northern hardwood forest, providing good habitat for moose, bears, and beaver, which will be evident when you pass a beaver pond at **0.2 mile**. Continue straight at the intersections with dirt roads at **1.4 miles** and **3.2 miles**. The road crosses several brooks on its way to the Wild River Campground, with Dewdrop Brook at **3.1 miles** providing the best spot for a rest break as its waters cascade gently through a cool forest of tall hemlock. At **5.7 miles** the road ends as you enter the Wild River Campground, complete with toilets and potable water.

Ride through the campground to the cul-de-sac at the end of the road. In the back right corner of the cul-de-sac an unmarked trail heads into the forest. Follow this trail, crossing two small brooks on your way to the Wild River Trail, which starts out as a wide road covered with round rocks. The trail climbs moderately over these rocks, which at times makes for difficult riding. Once on the Wild River Trail, you will be sharing the path with hikers, so watch your speed and respect their wilderness experience. At **6.0 miles** you pass the Moriah Brook Trail on the right, and at around **6.7 miles** the trail climbs to the first good view of the river since leaving the road.

After the view the trail brings you back into the forest, continuing over cobblestones and climbing moderately. At **7.0 miles** you will cross a rocky streambed, and then a dry rocky streambed; if you do not own a bike with suspension, you will make a mental note to buy one. Fortunately, the forest and the river provide beautiful scenery as you ride above the south bank of the river through a grove of delicate paper birch. At **8.4 miles** you reach Spider Bridge and the end of the trip. Spider Bridge spans the Wild River above a particularly scenic section, where the rushing water cascades over large boulders and granite ledges. In fall the yellows and golds of birch and beech contrast brightly with the dark greens of red spruce and hemlock. The views of North Baldface and Mount Moriah complete the scene. To finish the trip, just return the way you came. However, if you are outfitted to spend the night, you can ride an additional 0.9 mile on the Wild River Trail to the Spruce Brook Shelter, a typical three-sided lean-to with space for eight to ten people.

Directions

From the intersection of US 2 and ME 113 in Gilead, Maine, head south on ME 113. In 3.0 miles turn right onto Wild River Road and park in the lot immediately on the right.

tracking: reading the signs of nature

ENCOUNTERING WILDLIFE on a hike, bike ride, or paddle is always an exciting experience, but many animals are rarely seen on a typical day trip in the White Mountains. Learning to read the signs that animals leave behind can open up a whole new world, where you not only discover which animals have passed through a particular place, but also what those animals were doing and eating, and how they interact with other animals. Dan Gardoqui, cofounder of White Pine Programs in Dover, New Hampshire, says, "Tracking is the process of observing and interpreting phenomena in the natural world. The process of tracking helps people feel more connected to the earth and find their roots in nature." Taking the time to see and understand the signs of such animals as bobcat, bears, or coyote is a fun and easy way to enhance any outing in the White Mountains. Tracking has, of course, been around for as long as humans have been hunting wildlife. Today tracking is also used for wildlife management, law enforcement, search and rescue, wildlife awareness, and recreation.

The actual art of tracking revolves around studying animal tracks and droppings, or scat, and other disturbances such as rubs, scrapes, digs, claw marks, and game trails. Common signs even the untrained eye can find in the White Mountains are moose tracks and scat along trails, and the claw marks of bears on the trunks of beech trees. With practice you can learn to spot where a moose spent the night, what a bear had for lunch, or the course a squirrel took in its attempt to outrun a bobcat. The easiest way to get started in tracking is to pick up a tracking field guide or how-to book like *A Field Guide to Animal Tracks* by Olaus Murie or *Tracking and the Art of Seeing* by Paul Rezendes.

Then just head out into the woods and poke around places like ponds, riverbanks, and wet, boggy places filled with shrubs like alder. With a little practice you will be finding animal signs on every trip you take into the mountains.

Luckily, the only way to get really good at tracking is to spend time outdoors studying nature's clues. Learning from an experienced tracker can also be a great way to accelerate your learning. In the White Mountains you can take classes through White Pine Programs of Dover, New Hampshire (www.whitepineprograms.org), or through the AMC (www.outdoors.org).

Trip #46

Livermore Road

> Aerobic Level: **Strenuous**
>
> Technical Difficulty: **Moderate**
>
> Distance: **10.0 miles up and back**
>
> Elevation Gain: **1,400 feet**
>
> Estimated Time: **3 hours**
>
> Maps: **AMC White Mountain Map #3, USGS Waterville Valley and Mount Tripyramid Quadrangles**
>
> **A steady but scenic climb through a beautiful forest next to the rushing waters of Avalanche Brook.**

LIVERMORE ROAD is an old logging road that is now used by hikers, mountain bikers, and cross-country skiers visiting the Waterville Valley area. Hikers use the road to access the trails that climb the three peaks of Mount Tripyramid. Skiers and bike-riders usually stay off the exceptionally steep trails on the mountain, but they do use the Livermore Road as a free alternative to the trail system of Waterville Valley. Livermore Road has an excellent riding surface until the 2.2-mile mark, where the rocks get a little bigger and the riding rougher. Stretches of the road climb steadily, making for some aerobically difficult riding at times as you gain 1,400 feet in elevation. The workout is worth it, though, as you ride through northern hardwoods, past big white pine, and next to rocky Avalanche Brook.

From the parking area Livermore Road heads into the mountains with a level, hard packed dirt surface. At **0.3 mile** you pass through a clearing at a junction with the Greeley Ponds Trail and the Deep Woods Path. The Greeley Ponds Trail is a technically challenging ride to the Greeley Ponds (also reached on foot via trip #8). The Deep Woods Path is part of the Waterville Valley Trail

Norway Rapids on Avalanche Brook

system. To ride on Waterville Valley trails you need to obtain a trail pass at their touring center. Continue straight on Livermore Road, which re-enters the woods and crosses the Mad River at **0.5 mile**. The road begins to climb gradually and passes several short side trails over the next 1.0 mile with descriptive names such as Boulder Path, Kettle Path, and Big Pines. Except for the big pines the forest is filled with northern hardwoods, making this a great trip to ride in fall.

At **1.1 miles** you pass through a small clearing with some views, and then at **1.8 miles** you reach a side trail that leads to Norway Rapids. The 0.1-mile hike to Norway Rapids is the best diversion on this trip. Norway Rapids is a long series of cascades where Avalanche Brook is squeezed through dark volcanic rock. Beyond the Norway Rapids Trail, Livermore Road continues its gradual climb until it reaches a trail junction at **2.2 miles**. At this junction another Waterville Valley trail enters from the right; stay to the left on Livermore Road as it narrows and begins to climb moderately over a rockier surface. For the next 0.5 mile you will hear the soothing sounds of Avalanche Brook, which is below the bank on your right. Water bars make the ride a little more interesting as you pass the south end of the Mount Tripyramid Trail at **2.6 miles** and the Avalanche Camp clearing (an old logging camp) at **3.1 miles**.

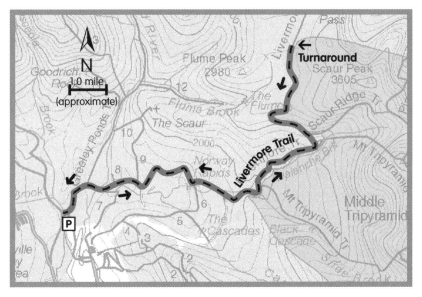

LIVERMORE ROAD

After the Avalanche Camp clearing you will breathe harder and hold on tighter, while the road gets steeper and rougher as a hairpin turn leads you past the north end of the Mount Tripyramid Trail at **3.6 miles**. At **3.8 miles** you pass the Scaur Ridge Trail and continue a steep, rocky climb with an occasional water bar. After crossing a brook at **4.8 miles** the gravel road ends in a clearing at **5.0 miles**. This is the end of the ride up, so after catching your breath, turn around and enjoy the long and exciting 5.0 miles of downhill back to the parking area. (Adventurous types with a good map and good technical skills can spot a car on the Kancamagus Highway across from Lily Pond; continue past this clearing for another 2.7 miles, riding through mud and past a gorge.)

Directions

Take Exit 28 from I-93 and head east on NH 49 toward Waterville Valley. After 10.2 miles turn left onto Tripoli Road. In 1.2 miles bear right, avoiding the entrance to Waterville Valley Ski Area. After another 0.5 mile turn right and cross the bridge. The parking area will be to the left.

Flat Mountain Pond

> Aerobic Level: **Moderate**
>
> Technical Difficulty: **Difficult**
>
> Distance: **16.4 miles up and back**
>
> Elevation Gain: **1,500 feet**
>
> Estimated Time: **5 hours**
>
> Maps: **AMC White Mountain Map #3, USGS Squam Mountain, Center Sandwich, and Mount Tripyramid Quadrangles**
>
> **A technical ride with good views along the edge of the Sandwich Range Wilderness Area.**

COUNTLESS WOODLAND streams and several views of the surrounding mountains are the highlights of this ride. This trip, which begins from Sandwich Notch Road, is the longest ride in the White Mountains that does not use logging roads, dirt roads, or pavement. The trade-off is a technical challenge, particularly on the second half of the trip when intermediate riders may need to push their bikes over several rough sections. However, much of the trail is free enough of obstacles to be ridden at a good pace. The trip follows the Guinea Pond and Flat Mountain Pond Trails, which use the bed of an old logging railroad for most of the route. As a result, the 1,500 feet of elevation gain is gradual; spread out more than 8.0 miles. The trip ends at Flat Mountain Pond, where a lean-to has space for 12 campers.

Ride past the Forest Service gate onto the Guinea Pond Trail, which starts out as a rough logging road that soon passes under a set of power lines. The trail follows the course of the old Beebe River logging railroad and rolls along gently, slowly making its way up through a mixed forest. The trail has its bumpy sections, but for the

Flat Mountain Pond, Sandwich Range Wilderness

most part it is an easy ride. At **1.2 miles** you pass a steel Forest Service gate and enter a boggy area with good views of the surrounding peaks. At **1.3 miles** turn right onto the single-track (unmarked) in order to avoid a ride through the bog. This rooty and rocky single-track can be tough to ride on at times. At **1.5 miles** you cross a series of three wooden bridges and then reach a trail junction at **1.6 miles**; turn right to stay on the Guinea Pond Trail and return to the old railbed. In another 30 yards, continue straight at intersections with the Mead Trail and the Black Mountain Pond Trail. The trail continues to climb gently over relatively easy terrain.

At **1.7 miles** you make the first of three quick stream crossings. After the third crossing a side trail leads left 0.2 mile to Guinea Pond, where the views of Sandwich Dome and the mountains to the north are definitely worth a look. At **2.4 miles** descend to a rough, washed-out section of trail and climb the steep opposite bank. At this point the trail forks—follow the yellow arrow and turn left onto very rough single-track, which will take you around an area flooded by a beaver pond. The beaver pond is filled with the bare, silver

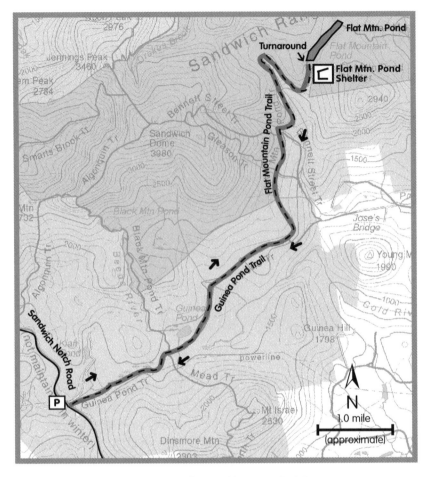

FLAT MOUNTAIN POND

trunks of dead trees and is surrounded by a typical northern hardwood forest with a mix of yellow birch, beech, and maple. At **2.7 miles** you rejoin the railroad bed and cross the Cold River at **2.9 miles**. Except for several stream crossings, where probably you will need to carry your bike, the trail makes for easy riding from here to the Flat Mountain Pond Trail at **4.2 miles**.

Continue straight toward Flat Mountain Pond on what is now called the Flat Mountain Pond Trail. The trail climbs more moderately on this half of the trip, but you will notice the rocks more than the climb. You soon reach the first rock water bar spanning the trail; water bars will plague you for the rest of the ride up to the pond. Expert riders can tackle most of them, but intermediate riders may need to stop occasionally to avoid a trip over the handlebars. At **4.8 miles** cross a stream and get ready to dodge many large rocks in the trail. At **5.1 miles** you will make a steep descent to a stream crossing with an all-but-impossible climb up the opposite steep and rocky bank.

At **5.2 miles** you will pass the Gleason Trail. If you peer down the Gleason Trail on the left you will notice a sign marking the Sandwich Range Wilderness Area, where bikes are prohibited. From now on the wilderness area borders the Flat Mountain Pond Trail on the left. At **5.6 miles** you ride over a series of railroad ties. Along the next stretch of trail you might encounter an actual piece of railroad track or even lumps of coal. At **5.7 miles** continue straight at an intersection with the Bennet Street Trail. At **5.8 miles** you cross another stream; the site of the "Great Horseshoe," the sharpest turn on any of the logging railroads in the White Mountains. The next 1.2 miles is probably the most technically challenging, as the trail is filled with cobblestones in many areas and you have to make several stream crossings. Remember that carrying or pushing your bike is an option.

At **7.0 miles** the trail crosses an area flooded by beaver. Take a look at the mountain views and the beaver lodge before trying to figure out how to get across. Usually, following a route over the beaver dam on the left is the driest alternative. After the beaver pond the climb eases and the trail becomes much easier to ride until a short, rough section at **8.0 miles**. At **8.2 miles** you reach a trail junction; leave the Flat Mountain Pond Trail and turn right onto a side trail that leads about 100 yards to the pond and a shelter. (Continuing on the Flat Mountain Pond Trail into the Sandwich Range Wilderness is an option for hikers only—bikes are not allowed.) Flat Mountain Pond is a long pond, about 23 acres in size, with good views of Flat Mountain and Whiteface. It is also a good place to look for frogs and newts. The forest surrounding the pond was the scene of the last large forest fire in the White Mountains. Started by a spark from a locomotive engine, the fire consumed over 3,500 acres and killed one firefighter in July of 1923.

A shelter is situated on a small rise south of the pond, a typical three-sided lean-to with space for 12 people. If you are not spending the night, just turn around and follow the Flat Mountain Pond and Guinea Pond Trails back to your car.

Directions

From the intersection of NH 113 and NH 109 in Center Sandwich, head west on NH 113 for a few hundred yards and turn right (north) onto Grove Street toward Sandwich Notch Road, following a sign for "Mead Base." In 0.5 mile take the left fork (straight) onto Diamond Ledge Road. In another 2.0 miles take the left fork onto Sandwich Notch Road Park at the Guinea Pond Trail, which will be on the right in another 3.0 miles. Alternately, from NH 49 near Waterville Valley, drive south on Sandwich Notch Road to the Guinea Pond Trail, which will be on your left in 5.1 miles.

federally designated wilderness

IN 1964 Congress passed the Wilderness Act, which protected 54 wilderness areas across the country and provided a process for creating additional wilderness areas in the future. In 1975 Congress passed the Eastern Wilderness Act that recognized both the need for and unique aspects of wilderness in the eastern part of the country. Unlike western wilderness, most eastern wilderness areas have a history of logging and other human uses and are in the process of recovering their natural wild character. As of 2000 there were 630 areas in the National Wilderness Preservation System, protecting approximately 104 million acres. Wilderness areas are generally roadless portions of national forests, parks, or wildlife refuges that are off-limits to motorized or mechanized vehicles (including mountain bikes), logging, and mining. On the 780,000-acre White Mountain National Forest there are currently five wilderness areas, comprising 114,932 acres:

- Great Gulf Wilderness — 5,552 acres

- Presidential Range–Dry River Wilderness — 27,380 acres

- Sandwich Range Wilderness — 25,000 acres

- Pemigewasset Wilderness — 45,000 acres

- Caribou–Speckled Mountain Wilderness — 12,000 acres

In addition to restrictions on vehicle use in White Mountain National Forest wilderness areas, the Forest Service has dismantled most of the shelters and cabins built in these areas before they were designated wilderness. Because of this, backpacking in the wilderness areas of the White Mountains is often a more rugged experience than in other parts of the national forest; it is also a more satisfying experience as few signs exist of human interference. When planning a hike or backpack into designated wilderness, you should be aware of the following restrictions:

- Hiking and camping groups may contain no more than ten people.

- No camping or wood or charcoal fires are allowed within 200 feet of any trail, except at designated campsites.

In addition to the designated wilderness areas, another 241,000 acres in the White Mountains are listed as Inventoried Roadless Areas. Currently, these areas are managed for multiple uses like the rest of the national forest, though only 45,000 acres are managed for regular timber harvest—primarily for backcountry recreation. It is possible that some of these roadless areas will be designated as wilderness in the future. To learn more about roadless areas in the national system, you can visit the U.S. Forest Service's "roadless" website at www.roadless.fs.fed.us.

Trip #48

Province Pond

> Aerobic Level: **Strenuous**
>
> Technical Difficulty: **All Levels of Difficulty**
>
> Distance: **13.7 miles round-trip**
>
> Elevation Gain: **1,600 feet**
>
> Estimated Time: **4 to 5 hours**
>
> Maps: **AMC White Mountain Map #5, USGS Chatham and North Conway East Quadrangles**
>
> **Exciting downhills, mountain views, and a visit to a remote pond make up for the long climbs on this challenging ride.**

THE 1,600 FEET of elevation gain will challenge most riders under-taking this difficult trip. The biggest mental challenge occurs during the final 500 feet of climbing, which sneaks up on you after you have spent most of your energy. So why attempt this ride? For one thing, it is in a little-traveled part of the White Mountains, so you can expect a high degree of solitude, especially on the Province Brook Trail. It also has some excellent scenic rewards from several spots, as well as good wildlife-watching opportunities at Province Pond. Of course, 1,600 feet of climbing leads to 1,600 feet of descent, much of it on fun but technical single-track. You will want to make sure your legs are in shape before pedaling to Province Pond, but, with this ride behind you, you will feel ready to tackle any mountain-biking trip the White Mountains have to offer.

The ride up Forest Road 450 is a long, steady climb on packed dirt and gravel. You will pass a few unmarked trails and gated forest roads on the way up—just continue straight on the main road at all of these intersections. At **2.4 miles** you reach the end of the road and the parking area for the Province Brook Trail.

Turn left onto the Province Brook Trail, which ascends moderately and becomes technically challenging. Intermediate riders should be able to tackle most of the rocks and roots, although it may be necessary to push from time to time. At **3.6 miles** you reach Province Pond, a shallow and marshy pond with silvery dead spruce standing in the water. Views of Twin Mountain and Mount Shaw provide the backdrop for a foreground of sheep laurel, cattails, and steeplebush. Kingfishers chatter and swallows gracefully maneuver in the air above the pond.

At **3.7 miles** a side trail leads left to a shelter (overnight camping is allowed). Follow the right fork, which leaves the pond and climbs steeply until **4.1 miles**. The northern hardwood forest here harbors a few big hemlock as well as moose, black bears, and white-tailed deer. Of course, you probably will not feel like studying the mud for tracks at this point because you stand perched at the beginning of 3.5 miles of downhill. The first 1.6 miles of this downhill is on rough but rideable double-track and a few water bars add a little extra challenge here and there. At **5.7 miles** you pass through a clearcut with excellent views of the Baldface Range. At this point the trail becomes a gravel logging road with a good riding surface.

At **6.3 miles** continue straight where a side road enters from the left. The road now parallels Langdon Brook, a rushing mountain stream that provides refreshing relief on a hot day. The downhill ride continues until you reach pavement at **7.7 miles**. Turn right here, following Robbins Hill Road between a church and a community center. In only 0.1 mile the road enters the woods, crosses a brook on a long wooden bridge, and becomes a rocky logging road. The trail climbs steadily and at **8.8 miles** reaches a clearcut with good views to the east. The climb continues over moderately technical terrain. At **9.2 miles** the rocks subside as you join a gravel logging road, and at **9.6 miles** you begin a much deserved 1.0-mile-long descent.

At **10.6 miles** turn right onto pavement, which is Green Hill Road. At this point the ride on pavement through the rolling countryside of rural New Hampshire is a welcome relief. At **13.7 miles** turn right on Forest Road 450 and you are back at your car.

Directions

From the intersection of NH 16 and River Road in North Conway, head north on NH 16 for 1.8 miles and turn right onto Hurricane Mountain

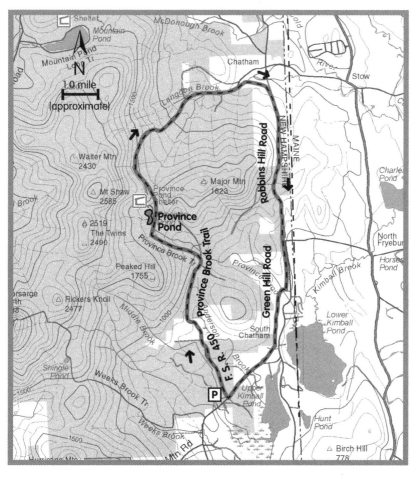

PROVINCE POND

Road. Follow Hurricane Mountain Road until it ends in 6.0 miles. Turn left onto Green Hill Road, following the sign for Chatham. Turn left onto Forest Road 450 in another 0.8 mile. Park in the small parking area on the left. Alternatively, from US 302 and ME 113 in Fryeburg, Maine, take ME 113 north. In 1.2 miles turn right, staying on ME 113. In another 0.9 mile turn left onto Green Hill Road. Forest Road 450 will be on the left in 3.3 miles.

Note: The parking area for this ride can accommodate only two or three cars. If necessary, you can find other places to park farther up Forest Road 450. The only drawback to doing this is more uphill to look forward to at the very end of your trip.

Beebe River Road

> Aerobic Level: **Moderate**
>
> Technical Difficulty: **Easy**
>
> Distance: **17.2 miles up and back**
>
> Elevation Gain: **1,100 feet**
>
> Estimated Time: **5 hours 30 minutes**
>
> Maps: **AMC White Mountain Map #4, USGS Plymouth and Squam Mountain Quadrangles**
>
> **A long ride with plenty of opportunities for riverside photo and snack stops.**

THE BEEBE RIVER ROAD winds along the Beebe River on the southern edge of the White Mountains, just north of Squam Lake. Cars are not allowed on this gravel road, although you may see an occasional logging truck since most of the land along this route is privately owned and currently being managed for timber production. Despite the signs of logging activity, this is still a beautiful trip that passes through a covered bridge and next to a horse farm on its way to the rushing waters of the Beebe River. Beginning at the old town hall in Campton, this trip includes about 2.0 miles of riding on pavement, although automobile traffic will not be a problem. The Beebe River Road makes a barely noticeable climb on its way to Sandwich Notch Road in the White Mountain National Forest. The return ride back down the Beebe River Road is about as easy as it gets. (It is also possible to ride a difficult 20.0-mile loop by combining the Beebe River and Sandwich Notch Roads with NH 49 and NH 175.)

From the old town hall turn left onto NH 175 and then turn right at the second right, which is Hog Back Road. It is a steep climb up the first 0.5 mile of this dirt road; past houses and through

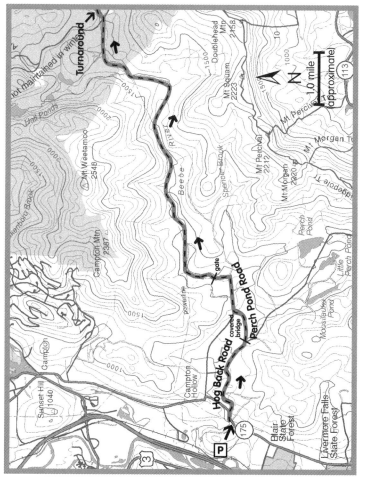

forest. At **1.0 mile** turn right onto Perch Pond Road and enjoy the easy riding on pavement. At **1.6 miles** the road turns to dirt after you turn left and cross the Beebe River on a covered bridge—a gateway to the pastoral scenery of a New England horse farm. In the distance you can see the Squam Mountains, a low ridge of peaks that rise above the northern shores of Squam Lake. At **2.0 miles** turn left onto pavement and make a very steep climb past houses and stone walls. The climb eases at **2.3 miles**; turn right. The road soon becomes dirt again as it passes Avery Road and a small family cemetery before descending to the Beebe River Road at **2.8 miles**.

Turn left onto the Beebe River Road, which is soon blocked by a metal gate. Walk your bike past the gate and leave civilization behind. Since the Beebe River Road is maintained for logging trucks, it is a wide road with a good gravel surface and moderate grades. Shortly after passing the gate, the road meets up with the river and stays close to it for the rest of the ride. At **3.2 miles** a great swimming hole is below a small cascade, complete with spots in the shade provided by white pine. At **5.1 miles** you pass a logging road and an old building foundation on the left. This foundation is most likely left over from the first half of the twentieth century when the Beebe River area was originally logged. In 1916 a logging railroad was built along the Beebe River. The first round of logging in this area provided logs for a high diversity of uses: lumber, pianos, textile bobbins, paper, and fuel. By 1942 the railroad was decommissioned as the forest was played out. Due to the recuperative powers of New Hampshire's forests, a second round of logging is now possible.

Near the **6.0-mile** mark, you enter a cool, dark hemlock grove and sounds of the river find their way up to you from below the road. At **6.4 miles** you pass a small waterfall that is worth visiting. At **7.0 miles** stay to the left as another logging road goes to the right and crosses the river. By now you should have noticed that a variety of wildlife travels along the river corridor. Signs of moose and coyote are common on the road and hawks often soar high above. Ruffed grouse forage amongst the hardwoods, feeding on acorns, beechnuts, and other seeds they find on the forest floor. Crow-sized pileated woodpeckers are common, as they seem to thrive on the second-growth forests of central New Hampshire.

At **7.7 miles** you pass a sign that signifies you are entering the national forest. The Beebe River Road ends **8.6 miles** from the old Campton town hall. Here, Sandwich Notch Road leads south to Sandwich and north to Waterville Valley. Before turning around for the return trip, walk across the bridge to the right on Sandwich Notch Road and check out the waterfall.

Directions

Take Exit 27 (Blair Bridge) off I-93. Head east on Blair Road, crossing US 3, and turn left on NH 175 after 0.8 mile. In another 0.6 mile, park on the left in the old Campton town hall parking lot.

Trip #50

Tunnel Brook

> Aerobic Level: **Strenuous**
>
> Technical Difficulty: **All Levels of Difficulty**
>
> Distance: **17.0 miles round-trip**
>
> Elevation Gain: **2,200 feet**
>
> Estimated Time: **5 hours**
>
> Maps: **AMC White Mountain Map #4, USGS Mount
> Moosilauke and East Haverhill Quadrangles**
>
> **A difficult but scenic ride through the rich
> wildlife habitat west of Mount Moosilauke.**

TUNNEL BROOK drains a series of ponds between Mount Moosilauke and Mount Clough that are popular with fly fishers, beaver,
and moose. This trip begins on North and South Road in Glencliff
and follows the Tunnel Brook Trail up to the ponds and excellent
views of the south peak of Mount Moosilauke. The trail is very rough
in spots and will challenge most riders—we ended up pushing our
bikes for at least 0.5 mile during this trip. At the end of the Tunnel
Brook Trail the technical part of the trip is over, but plenty of climbing is still to come, including a 5.0-mile climb near the end of the
ride. While this is a challenging adventure, it provides some of the
best scenery of any mountain-bike trip in the White Mountains.
Please note that hikers share the Tunnel Brook Trail.

From the parking area head south on North and South Road
for about **0.3 mile** and make a sharp left onto the Tunnel Brook
Trail, which actually parallels Slide Brook at this point. The trail is
easy double-track until it crosses a tributary brook at **0.5 mile**, just
below a cascade tumbling over rock tilted at a 60-degree angle. After
the stream crossing the trail becomes moderately technical single-
track and climbs gradually through a northern hardwood forest

Mud Pond, Mount Moosilauke

filled with large yellow birch and maple. The sounds of Slide Brook can be heard on your right. The trail continues its technical climb and you make more stream crossings at **0.9 mile** and **1.3 miles**. At **1.5 miles** you will pass a small human-made pond on the right. After crossing another streambed at **1.7 miles** the trail gets more difficult and climbs more steeply—pushing your bike is definitely an option.

The climb eases at **2.1 miles**, as paper birch and balsam fir begin to dominate the forest. Finally, at **2.3 miles** you get to enjoy a downhill ride to Mud Pond at **2.5 miles**. Mud Pond, surrounded by tall grasses, steeplebush, and alder, is home to beaver, black ducks, and amphibians such as green frogs and eastern spotted newts. From the trail you get an excellent view of the south peak of Mount Moosilauke, as well as a large rockslide about halfway up the mountain. This pond is just the first of a 1.0-mile-long series of ponds that you will ride by on your way to Tunnel Brook. Moose tracks are common in the mud on the trail, and you will see beaver dams and lodges along the way. Although it is a flat stretch of trail, plenty of rocks make the riding tough.

You pass the last pond (with good views of Mount Clough) at **3.3 miles**. After crossing a stream at **3.4 miles** you begin a difficult descent over a very rocky trail. At **3.9 miles** you cross three streambeds after which the ride gets much easier. At **4.6 miles** you reach the end of the Tunnel Brook Trail at Forest Road 147 (Tunnel Brook Road). Turn left and enjoy a long, fast downhill on a good packed dirt and gravel road all the way to the 7.0-mile mark. At **5.5 miles** you pass the Benton Trail, which climbs Mount Moosilauke (not suitable for mountain bikes). At **7.0 miles** follow the left fork in the road, but before you do, check out the view of Tunnel Brook from the bridge on the right fork. On a hot day, you may be lured into the deep swimming hole a few yards south of the bridge.

Following the left fork, you will begin climbing again and soon enter a residential area where the road rolls along over dirt and pavement. At **9.8 miles** turn left onto NH 116 at Boutin Corner, and turn left again at **10.1 miles** onto North and South Road (called Mountain Pond Road at this intersection). This is the beginning of a 5.0-mile climb to the height-of-land between NH 116 and your car. The road surface is easy to ride on, but the steady, moderate climb will have all but the strongest riders shifting into lower gears. At **12.0 miles** you get a reprieve with 0.3 mile of downhill. The road then continues its steady climb, passing Long Pond Road at **12.5 miles** (if you are up for a side trip, it is **0.6 mile** to a picnic area at the very scenic Long Pond). At **13.2 miles** you will reach a clearing on the right with good views of Long Pond and the cliffs of Black Mountain in the distance.

After the view of Long Pond the road continues to climb, but the ride is a little easier as several short downhill sections add relief. At **14.8 miles** you reach the height-of-land and begin an exhilarating descent. You deserve to go as fast as you can safely endure at this point, but be aware that cars do have access to this road. While you will probably be going too fast to notice, a brook begins to parallel the road at **15.3 miles**. You cross bridges at **15.7 miles** and **16.7 miles**, and you reach your car at the Blueberry Mountain Trail at **17.0 miles**.

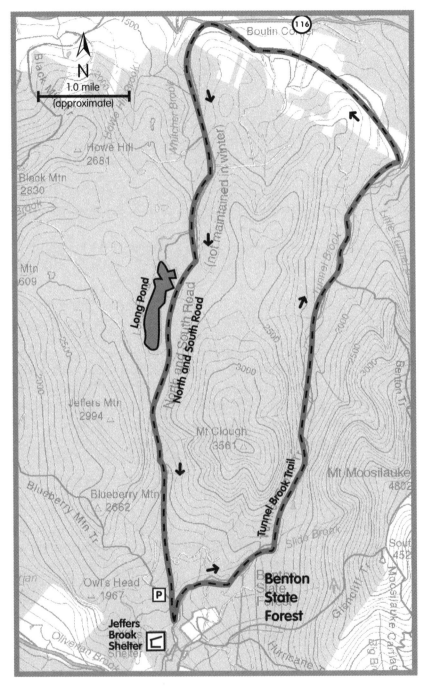

TUNNEL BROOK

Directions

From I-93 in Lincoln, take Exit 32 and head west on NH 112. In 11.5 miles follow NH 112 to the left as it is joined by NH 116. In 0.9 mile turn left onto NH 116. In another 1.7 miles turn left onto Long Pond Road (marked on some maps as North and South Road). Park at the trailhead for the Blueberry Mountain Trail, which will be on your right, 6.8 miles south of NH 116. Alternately, from the intersection of High Street and NH 25 in Glencliff, take High Street for 1.0 mile and turn left onto an unmarked dirt road following signs for the Appalachian Trail. The Blueberry Mountain Trail will be on the left in 0.7 mile.

Biking on Ski Trails

Attitash Bear Peak
Route 302, Bartlett
603-374-2368
www.attitash.com
Buy a lift ticket and ride down the slopes; 22 miles of trails are open to bikes.

The Balsams
Route 26, Dixville Notch
603-255-3921
www.thebalsams.com
Sixty-five kilometers of cross-country ski trails are open to bikes (sorry, no alpine trails). Maps are available at the center, which also has repair and rental services.

Bretton Woods
Route 302, Bretton Woods
603-278-3322
www.brettonwoods.com
One hundred kilometers of cross-country ski trails are open to bikes. No trail pass is required. Trails cross private property—please be respectful. Sorry, no downhill rides are open to bikes.

Franconia Village Touring Center
Route 116, Franconia
800-473-5299
www.franconiainn.com/ski-center
Eighty kilometers of cross-country ski trails are open to bikes. No trail pass is required.

Great Glen Trails

Route 16, Pinkham Notch
603-466-2333
www.mt-washington.com
Forty-seven kilometers of ski trails from beginner to technical expert
(cross-country only); a trail pass is required. New bikes can be rented
and a skills park is available for practice.

Loon Mountain

Route 112, Lincoln
603-745-8111
www.loonmtn.com
Lift tickets are available for 10.0 miles of expert-only downhill rides.
Fifteen miles of cross-country ski trails are open to beginners and
experts; no trail pass is required. Service is available to drop you off
at the Franconia Notch Bicycle Path, and a full service bike shop is
on the premise.

Waterville Valley

Route 49, Waterville Valley
603-236-8311
www.waterville.com
Take the lift up Snows Mountain or ride on the 100 kilometers of
cross-country ski trails. A trail pass is required, and a rental shop is
on the premise.

6
quietwater paddling

WHILE THE WHITE MOUNTAINS are not as rich in paddling opportunities as the Lakes Region to the south, a few ponds surrounded by beautiful scenery make for peaceful paddling. All of the trips in this chapter are suitable for both solo paddlers and families. These trips also provide excellent wildlife-watching opportunities: loons, ducks, beaver, and occasionally osprey, deer, moose, and river otters can be spotted in the waters within the White Mountain National Forest.

Safety and Etiquette

To ensure a safe and comfortable paddling experience, consider the following safety tips:

- Know how to use your canoe or kayak. Small lakes and ponds are the perfect place for inexperienced paddlers to learn, but if you are new to the sport, you should have someone show you some basic paddling strokes and impress upon you how to enter and exit your boat. New paddlers should consider staying close to shore until they are more comfortable with their paddling skills. Luckily, some of the most interesting aspects of the trips in this chapter are found along the shoreline.

- Turn around *before* the members of your party start feeling tired. Paddling a few miles after your arms are spent already can make for cranky travelers. All of the trips in this book start and end at the same location, so you can easily turn around at any time.

- Make sure everyone in your group is wearing a life jacket or personal flotation device (PFD) that fits properly and securely. It is easy to tip a canoe accidentally, especially if the notorious White Mountain winds kick up two-foot waves, since you can be as far as 0.5 mile from shore.

- Be cautious around motorboats on Conway Lake and Lake Tarleton, where large boats may create big wakes. Turn the bow of your boat into the waves if you are afraid of getting swamped by the wake of one of these larger boats; do not assume that bigger boats can see you. Kayaks especially can be hard to spot in bright sunlight or fog, so it might be up to you to get out of the way.

- Pay close attention to the winds. Winds as gentle as 10 MPH can create some fairly large waves on some of the ponds. With the mountains making their own weather, be prepared for a calm day to turn suddenly choppy. Bring a windbreaker, as it can get cold in a canoe in the lightest of winds. Long Pond and Upper Kimball Pond are small and narrow enough to paddle on windy days without too much difficulty.

- Stay off the water if thunderstorms are nearby. Lightning is a serious danger to boaters. If you hear a thunderstorm approaching, get off of the water immediately and seek shelter. For a current weather forecast, call the AMC weather phone at 603-466-2721 (option 4).

- Bring the following supplies along with you to make the trip more comfortable:
  Water—one or two quarts per person depending on the weather and length of the trip
  Food—Even for a short, one-hour paddle, it is a good idea to bring some high-energy snacks like nuts, dried fruit, or snack bars. Bring a lunch for longer trips.

Map and compass—and the ability to use them

Extra clothing—rain gear, wool sweater or fleece jacket, wool
or fleece hat in a waterproof bag

Flashlight

Sunscreen and hat

First-aid kit

Pocketknife

Binoculars for wildlife viewing

In addition to the no-impact techniques described in this
book's introduction, please keep the following things in mind while
paddling:

- Give wildlife a wide berth. Lakes and ponds are much different than forests in that wildlife has less of an opportunity to
  hide from humans. The summer months see numerous people
  in the water, and the ducks, heron, and loons waste a good
  deal of energy just swimming or flying away from curious
  boaters. If you spot wildlife, remain still and quiet and let the
  animals decide whether or not to approach you. Use binoculars if you want a closer view. In spring, steer clear of loons
  nesting along the shore.

- Respect private property. Much of the land surrounding the
  ponds in this chapter is private property. Most of the put-ins
  are on or adjacent to private property, so please act with
  respect in order to ensure future access for paddlers. Take a
  map that shows the national forest boundaries. Do not land
  your boat on private property, and speak quietly when paddling near homes and cottages.

- Respect the purity of the water. Some of the ponds in the White
  Mountains are used for drinking water by the surrounding
  communities. If you need to relieve yourself, try to do so on
  land, at least 200 yards from the shoreline.

- Sound carries a long way on the water, so try to keep your
  conversations quiet in order not to disturb other paddlers or
  nearby hikers.

- Boats are responsible for the movement of nonindigenous
  species, like the zebra mussel, between water bodies and river

systems. To prevent the spread of nonindigenous plants and animals, make it a habit to drain all of the water out of your canoe or kayak; visually inspect your boat for unwelcome hitchhikers; and rinse your boat off with a hose once you return home.

Paddling Times and Distances

The distances listed on our trips basically assume you will follow the shoreline of the pond for most of the trip. Trips will be shorter in distance if you paddle directly from point A to point B and back, but we expect that most people like to explore the shoreline for at least part of a trip to look for animals, flowers, and resting spots. Paddling times can vary widely based on paddlers' experience, physical conditioning, and curiosity. We have tried to come up with the time it would take a paddler of average strength and experience to complete these trips with only one short rest break to eat a snack. If you have a group of very curious paddlers, expect your trips to take longer.

Paddling in the White Mountains consists of misty mornings surrounded by water lilies and the cries of loons. The calm is often interrupted by the slap of a beaver's tail or the chattering of a kingfisher, sometimes so close and unexpected that you almost jump out of your boat. As the mist burns off you find yourself staring at a shoreline hemmed in by white pine, which are not quite tall enough to prevent you from looking upon the summits of Chocorua, Kearsarge, or Moosilauke. When you need a break from the rigors of hiking and the speed of mountain biking or whitewater kayaking, grab your boat and enjoy a lazy paddle on one of these sun-drenched ponds.

Upper Kimball Pond

> Distance: **3.4 miles round-trip**
>
> Estimated Time: **2 hours**
>
> Maps: **AMC White Mountain Map #5, USGS North Conway East Quadrangle**
>
> **An easy paddle with good mountain views and excellent bird-watching opportunities.**

UPPER KIMBALL POND is a small pond on the Maine-New Hampshire border south of Evans Notch. With a few unobtrusive camps, the pond is a relatively quiet place to spend a few hours dipping your paddles into the water while taking in the characteristically beautiful White Mountain scenery. A little more than 150 acres in size, the pond is small enough for a short family outing, but it has enough diversity to keep most people interested for at least a couple of hours. Motorboats and large waves are rarely a problem here. Most of the land surrounding this pond is private property, so please act in a respectful manner.

Put in next to the dam and paddle up a narrow passage before entering the main part of the pond. Find your way to the southern end of the pond by following either shoreline. The western shoreline is less developed, while the eastern shoreline has better views of Mount Kearsarge and other peaks. At the southern end of the pond you will enter a shallow, marshy area that bends to the right, leaving any signs of civilization behind. Here you can paddle among tall reeds, grasses, and cattails, and around the purple blooms of pickerelweed and the round, yellow flowers of water lilies. Larch trees and sheep laurel grow in the poor soils surrounding the marsh, and a variety of insect-loving birds feed on the bugs (that might be feeding on you). On a warm summer day you are bound to see a variety of swallows and flycatchers, as well as kingbirds and

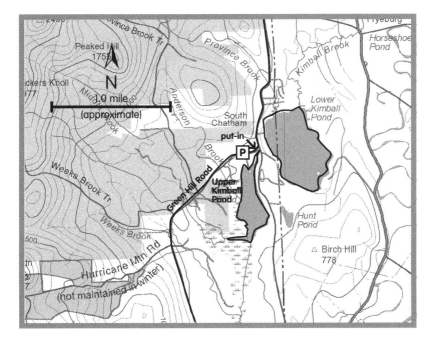

UPPER KIMBALL POND

cedar waxwings. During the twilight hours you might spot a beaver swimming or a mink patrolling the shore.

Once you can no longer find navigable water, just head back to the main part of the pond and follow either shore back to the parking area.

Directions

From the intersection of NH 16 and River Road in North Conway, head north on NH 16 for 1.8 miles and turn right onto Hurricane Mountain Road. Follow Hurricane Mountain Road until it ends in 6.0 miles. Turn left onto Green Hill Road, following the sign for Chatham. The put-in will be on the right in another 2.0 miles. Alternatively, from US 302 and ME 113 in Fryeburg, Maine, take ME 113 north. In 1.2 miles turn right, staying on ME 113. In another 0.9 mile turn left onto Green Hill Road. The put-in will be on the right in 5.5 miles.

Trip #52

Mountain Pond

> **Distance:** **1.7 miles round–trip plus a 0.3–mile portage**
>
> **Estimated Time:** **1 hour**
>
> **Maps:** **AMC White Mountain Map #5, USGS Chatham Quadrangle**
>
> **A paddle on a remote pond with excellent views of the surrounding mountains.**

THE FACT THAT YOU HAVE to carry your boat for about 0.3 mile before putting it in the water makes Mountain Pond the quietest of the quietwater trips in this book. It is worth the effort, as you will find solitude and excellent views on this small pond that sits 1,500 feet above sea level. The solitude is especially welcome if you had to fight the traffic through the nearby strip of outlet malls in North Conway. If you are looking for some pondside backcountry camping, you can spend the night in a lean-to on the northern side of the pond. As of 2000 primitive camping is allowed in the forest surrounding the pond. Be sure to practice no-impact camping techniques to ensure a pristine experience for the next visitor. For more information on camping in this area, contact the Saco Ranger District at 33 Kancamagus Highway, Conway, NH 03818; 603-447-5448.

From the parking area you will need to carry your boat to Mountain Pond via the Mountain Pond Trail. The trail is wide with good footing and reaches a fork just before the pond. Turn left and follow a side trail to the right in another 25 yards. This will take you to the put-in at the western edge of the pond. Near the put-in is a marshy area that is good habitat for ducks and frogs, especially bullfrogs and green frogs. The rest of the pond is surrounded by rocky shoreline, with sheep laurel, alder, and blueberries reaching out over the water. Bird watchers might spot northern bird species in

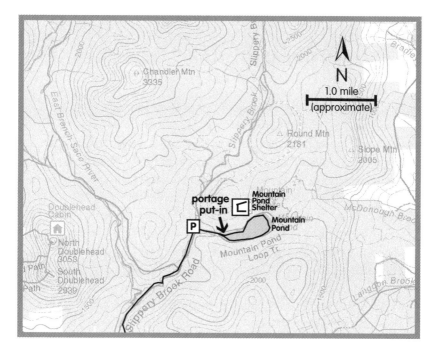

MOUNTAIN POND

the surrounding boreal forest when they are not gazing at the views of North and South Doublehead and South Baldface.

If you do not feel like carrying your boat to the put-in you can enjoy Mountain Pond on foot, as a hiking trail circles the pond. It takes about an hour and a half to complete this hike.

Directions

From the intersection of NH 16 and River Road in North Conway, drive north on NH 16 for 3.7 miles and turn right onto Town Hall Road. Go straight in 0.1 mile at a stop sign, follow the road until the 2.5-mile mark, and take the left fork. Go straight at an intersection 5.9 miles from NH 16, and take a right into a parking area in another 0.7 mile.

amphibious exploration

THE WHITE MOUNTAINS are home to a variety of toads, frogs, and salamanders, which can be found on virtually any trip into the mountains during spring and summer. Toads and frogs are the most commonly seen, particularly American toads, which seem to use hiking trails as their main habitat during the late summer months. Some amphibians breed in vernal pools, small ponds and pools that only fill with water for a few months in spring and early summer. These temporary bodies of water are relatively safe places for amphibians to breed, as they are devoid of fish that prey on the eggs and larvae of amphibians. Small frogs like spring peepers and wood frogs use vernal pools, as do spotted, Jefferson's, and blue-spotted salamanders. Larger frogs such as bullfrogs and green frogs do not use vernal pools, as their tadpoles can take more than a year to mature into adult frogs.

New Hampshire is home to eight species of frogs, two species of toads, ten species of salamanders, and one species of newts. While it is relatively easy to find toads and frogs, salamanders can seem nonexistent at times. Rest assured, they are plentiful — in fact if you gathered up all of the salamanders in the White Mountains, they would outweigh all of the moose. In the White Mountains the amphibians you are most likely to encounter are listed below:

Spring peepers are more likely to be heard than seen. Considered a chorus frog, but also exhibiting characteristics of tree frogs, spring peepers fill the night air in spring with their loud chorus of frog song. They prefer small, often temporary bodies of water near trees. These tiny frogs are less than an inch long and are usually brown or gray with a dark "X" on their backs.

Bullfrogs are the largest frogs in the United States, measuring from 3 1/2 to 6 inches in length. They are either green, or brown and gray with a green background. They can be

Red eft stage of the red-spotted newt

found in lakes, ponds, bogs, and streams, and have a voracious appetite, eating almost anything that they can swallow including small snakes.

Green frogs are smaller than bullfrogs, measuring 2 1/4 to 3 1/2 inches in length, and tend to be greenish-brown in color. In rare cases they may be blue. Green frogs tend to like shallower water than bullfrogs, spending their time in brooks, small streams, and along the edges of lakes and ponds.

Pickerel frogs are 1 3/4 to 3 inches in length and have square spots arranged in two parallel rows down their backs. They often have bright yellow or orange coloring on their hind legs. Pickerels prefer the clear, cold waters of sphagnum bogs, rocky ravines, and meadow streams.

Wood frogs are slightly smaller than pickerels but have an unmistakable robber's mask, a dark patch around the eye. Wood frogs are generally brown, blending in well with leaf litter on the forest floor. They spend a lot of their time in moist woods, away from water.

American toads are the only toads that live in the White Mountains, but they are very conspicuous on hiking and biking trails, especially in late summer when you might see dozens of young toads less than half an inch in length. They are 2 to 4 inches in length and generally tan or brown in color with a highly variable pattern of spots, ranging in color from gray, olive, and brown to brick red. One or two warts also appear on their larger spots.

Red-spotted newts and *red efts* are actually different forms of the same species. Red efts are the juvenile land form of the red-spotted newt, which can be seen hanging suspended in shallow ponds throughout the White Mountains. After a heavy rain red efts can be quite conspicuous, venturing out in broad daylight in large numbers. Red efts are bright orange-red in color with black-bordered red spots and range in size from 1 3/8 to 3 3/8 inches. Efts remain on land for one to three years before returning to the water and transforming into adult red-spotted newts.

Redback salamanders are common in leaf litter and under decaying logs in moist areas of the forest. They are 2 to 4 inches in length and dark gray in color with a wide red stripe down their back. Some members of this species do not have the red stripe and are called leadbacks. Like most salamanders, redbacks thrive on insects.

Frogs have been found recently throughout the United States (including New Hampshire) with severe physical deformities, most commonly having extra sets of legs. Scientists have discovered that one cause of these deformities is a parasitic flatworm. While it has yet to be proven, scientists believe that pollution may be an additional cause. Breathing through their moist skin, all amphibians may be especially susceptible to acid rain, airborne pollutants such as mercury, and chemicals that disturb the endocrine system like dioxin and PCBs.

Trip #53

Chocorua Lake

> **Distance: 3.3 miles round-trip**
>
> **Estimated Time: 2 hours**
>
> **Maps: AMC White Mountain Map #3, USGS Lake Quadrangle**
>
> **Loons, pine, and spectacular views of Mount Chocorua.**

CHOCORUA LAKE is familiar to travelers on NH 16 who approach the White Mountains from the south. The view of craggy Mount Chocorua from the lake is one of the most famous in all of New England. Despite the presence of NH 16 on the east and several well-concealed cottages on its western shore, Chocorua Lake manages to have a wild feel. While the mountain commands attention, paddlers on Chocorua Lake are soon drawn to the smaller details of nature—the colorful blooms of water lilies and sheep laurel, the calls of loons, and the swooping of swallows. At 220 acres the lake is relatively small, but winds can pick up and create some big waves, making it necessary to monitor the weather. In good weather, however, this is a great place for family paddling. Much of the western shore of Chocorua Lake is private property, so if you need to take a break and get out of your boat, do so on the conservation land on the eastern and southern shores.

Being somewhat pear shaped with no deep coves, navigation in Chocorua Lake is a simple task. By just following the shoreline in either direction you can see the whole lake in a couple of hours. While NH 16 borders the lake on the east, tall stands of red and white pine help to keep the road from your mind. Nature lovers will want to head to the western and northern shores of the lake where marshy coves are filled with lilies and pickerelweed. Loons nest here and insect-loving birds like tree swallows, flycatchers, and cedar

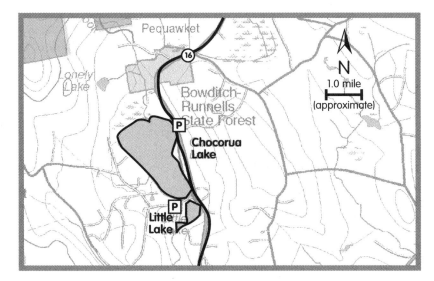

CHOCORUA LAKE

waxwings can usually be seen feeding above the lake on warm summer days. The north end of the lake is bordered by swampy land owned by The Nature Conservancy. Here you will find an old beaver dam, sheep laurel and other heaths, as well as small birds like swamp sparrows and yellowthroats flitting about the undergrowth.

At the southern outlet of the lake you can paddle under the bridge to Little Lake, a much smaller body of water that is a good place to watch for painted turtles and green frogs.

Directions

From the intersection of NH 16 and NH 113 in Tamworth, drive north on NH 16. There are two parking options. The first is to turn left in 1.6 miles onto Chocorua Lake Road and park in the lot on the left. This lot has a small picnic area on the lake as well as a portable toilet. The other option is to continue for an additional 0.6 mile and turn left onto a narrow road on conservation land that borders the eastern shore of the lake; park off to the side before reaching the signs that indicate parking for Tamworth residents only.

Trip #54

Conway Lake

> Distance: **7.5 miles round-trip**
>
> Estimated Time: **4 hours**
>
> Maps: **USGS Conway Quadrangle**
>
> **Mountain views and miles of varied wildlife-filled shoreline.**

CONWAY LAKE is a big lake by White Mountain standards, and provides miles of pine-covered shoreline filled with nooks and crannies that are fun to explore. This trip takes you to the southern half of the lake, which is well suited to quietwater paddling because of its two narrow and secluded fingerlike coves. Except for a 0.25-mile stretch of waterfront camps and a large commercial campground on the western shore, the lake is relatively undeveloped and provides excellent opportunities for bird watching and solitude. You might be lucky enough to spot a moose, beaver, or mink in the quieter coves. Since it is larger than other lakes in the region, Conway Lake does receive its share of motorboats that leave large wakes—on summer weekends plan an early morning paddle to avoid the noise. Its size also means fairly large waves can kick up on windy days, so check the weather forecast before you start your day and be prepared to turn around if the weather turns bad.

The fun starts as you launch into the larger, eastern finger at the southern end of the lake. The shallow, marshy area teems with insect-eating birds like swallows and kingbirds. As you get into the deeper water you will pass islands covered in red pine; at least one of these islands has a pair of nesting loons. If you stick to the left shore you will find yourself turning into the completely undeveloped western finger after about 1.2 miles. As you continue the forest begins to close in and you feel like you are on a remote stretch of river. It is a great place to watch for flycatchers, warblers, cedar waxwings,

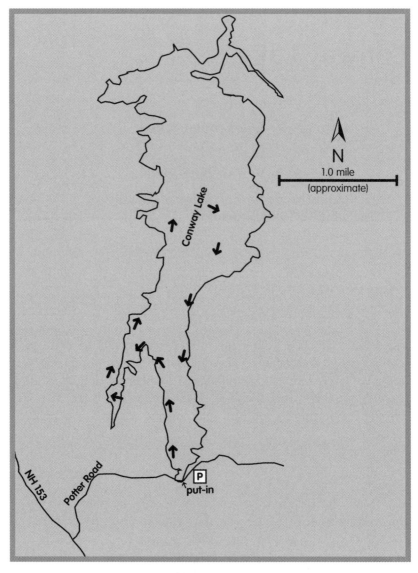

CONWAY LAKE

white-tailed deer, and moose. Near the southern end of the finger is a fairly large beaver lodge built on the bank of the lake. Early morning paddlers are likely to be startled by the loud slap of a beaver tail hitting the surface of the water.

Once you reach the end of the western finger, turn around and head up the left shoreline into the main part of the lake. This is the less-than-quiet stretch of developed shoreline, but quick paddling will put you back in quietwater territory in no time. You can explore this shoreline and its numerous coves for as long as you wish. One good turnaround spot is a large island, about an acre in size, that is covered by tall red pine with an understory of blueberries. Unless you plan to paddle most of the day, circle this island, head straight across the lake to the eastern shore, and follow the shore back to the put-in (keeping the shoreline on your left). Along the way you will be rewarded with scenic mountain views from the shade of tall white pine.

Directions

From the intersection of NH 16 and NH 153 in Conway, head south on NH 153. In 4.4 miles turn left onto Potter Road. The put-in will be on the left in 1.4 miles just beyond a small one-lane bridge.

the common loon: symbol of wilderness

Adult loon on a North Country pond

PERHAPS NO OTHER ANIMAL in New England symbolizes wilderness like the common loon, a bird known for its beauty and its calls, which include laughs, yodels, and wails. They are a primitive yet highly successful bird that has lived on earth for more than 50 million years. Once common on lakes and ponds across the northern United States, loon populations have declined dramatically in the last century — New Hampshire's population is only 50 percent of what it was 100 years ago. This decline is due to degradation of loon habitat through development and pollution. Loons are only slightly tolerant of human activities, and they are especially susceptible to lead poisoning (from fishing tackle) and mercury poisoning (from airborne pollutants). The common loon is currently listed as a threatened species in New Hampshire, where the population is thought to be around 450 adult birds. You are likely to see loons on any of the quietwater trips listed in this chapter.

Common loons are easy to identify. A common loon has a black head and bill, bright red eyes, a white and black striped collar, a white chest and belly, and a black and white checkered back. They are large, stout birds, about 32-inches long and weighing as much as 13 pounds. Unlike most birds, which have hollow bones for easy flight, loons have solid bones, giving them the mass needed to dive easily for fish. In addition, their feet are set far back on their bodies to help them dive, and internal air sacks allow them to control their diving speed and depth. Loons have been found diving to depths of 200 feet, as they search for fish, amphibians, crayfish, and even leeches. Adult loons prefer fish, especially perch, suckers, catfish, and sunfish. The same characteristics that make diving so easy for loons also make it hard for them to take off and fly. Without a breeze to fly into, a loon may need to run several hundred yards on the surface of a lake before it can become airborne.

Loons spend winters in waters along both the Atlantic and Pacific coasts, and fly to inland lakes and ponds as soon as the ice melts in early spring. Loons need a lot of space, and lakes smaller than about 100 acres can usually only accommodate one nesting pair. Loons are not very adept at moving on land and build their nests right on the shoreline, usually on islands or other places surrounded by water like partially submerged logs or muskrat lodges. These spots are prone to flooding and loons often lose their nests during periods of heavy rain. Loons usually lay two eggs in early June and the chicks hatch about one month later. Disturbing loons while they are incubating can cause them to leave the nest, which puts the eggs at risk for chilling (the embryo can die within thirty minutes if left unattended) or being taken by predators such as fox, raccoons, skunk, and crows. In June and July be especially careful not to disturb loons while enjoying your quietwater paddles.

Loon chicks can swim almost immediately, but they often ride on their parents' backs in order to rest and avoid predators like eagles, gulls, large fish, and snapping turtles. The parents feed the chicks until they start to dive for fish and other food at around eight weeks of age. By the time they are 12 weeks old they can usually fly, and they will often migrate a few weeks after their parents leave for the ocean in late October or early November. Wintering loons may be seen anywhere along the New England coast; young loons will remain at sea for three or four years before returning inland to breed.

Loons are cherished for their calls as much as their beauty. Common loons have four distinct calls: tremolo, wail, yodel, and hoot. The *tremolo*, which loons use when disturbed or annoyed, is a danger call that sounds similar to a human laugh. When intruders ignore a tremolo call, loons will stand up, violently kick the water, and flap their wings. The *wail* is the haunting cry often heard at night, which loons use to establish contact with a family member. This call is often the first contact humans have with loons, and it is forever etched in the memory of anyone who has attended summer camp on a lake in the North Country. Male loons use the *yodel* as a territorial song, warning intruding males that they have ventured into hostile territory. Each male has its own unique yodel, which is usually a long call that lasts up to six seconds and increases in volume. The last of the loon calls is the *hoot*, a short call used to locate other family members and check on their safety.

Four other species of loons live in North America, but the common loon is the only one that breeds south of Canada; however, it is possible to spot a red-throated loon off the New England coast, particularly in northern Maine. Red-throated loons have gray heads and a red throat patch and are slightly smaller than common loons.

Efforts to protect loons appear to be working, as their population seems to have stabilized in much of their range. New Hampshire recently banned anglers from using lead sinkers, and the preliminary results show that fewer loons are dying due to lead poisoning. Education efforts aimed at preventing the disturbance of loons while nesting also seem to be working. Often you will see buoys marking loon nesting areas in lakes with boat traffic—make sure to avoid these areas when you encounter them. Every little bit helps, and with wise pollution control measures and education efforts, we should be hearing loon calls for generations to come.

Trip #55

Long Pond

> Distance: **2.5 miles round–trip**
>
> Estimated Time: **1 hour 30 minutes**
>
> Maps: **AMC White Mountain Map #4, USGS East
> Haverhill Quadrangle**
>
> **An easy paddle on one of New Hampshire's
> most scenic ponds.**

LONG POND personifies quietwater paddling: it is remote, filled with wildlife, completely undeveloped, and surrounded by mountains. Despite its relatively small size (124 acres), Long Pond has plenty of shoreline to cover, since it is almost 1.0-mile long and has several spruce-covered islands. You easily can spend an entire morning or afternoon here exploring the coves, watching wildlife, and taking in the views of Mount Moosilauke. Backcountry camping is allowed in the surrounding forest, but not on the islands in the pond. (For more information about backcountry camping around Long Pond, contact the Ammonoosuc/Pemigewasset Ranger District at RFD # 3, Box 15, Route 175, Plymouth, NH 03264; 603-536-1310.)

There is really no need for us to explain a route in Long Pond, as it is small enough to just put your boat in and start paddling. The only thing to watch out for is the dam to the right of the put-in—do not paddle over it! The shorelines of the pond and its islands are a great place to watch for all kinds of wildlife—great blue heron, osprey, mergansers, otters, mink, and beaver. Surrounding the pond are a few marshy coves, but mostly you will find banks supporting tall spruce with an understory of sheep laurel, hobblebush, and alder. The slopes rising up beyond the shoreline are covered with hardwoods, putting on a brilliant display of color at the end of September and beginning of October.

LONG POND

If you are in the mood to tackle more than one trip in a day, Long Pond is relatively close to other trips in this book, including a paddle on Lake Tarleton (trip #56), a mountain-bike ride along Tunnel Brook (trip #50), and a hike up Mount Moosilauke (trip #19).

Directions

From I-93 in Lincoln take Exit 32 and head west on NH 112. In 11.5 miles follow the road to the left as it is joined by NH 116. In 0.9 mile turn left onto NH 116. In another 1.7 miles turn left onto Long Pond Road (marked on some maps as North and South Road). In 2.4 miles turn right, following a sign for Long Pond. The pond is at the end of this road in another 0.6 mile.

Lake Tarleton

Distance: **3.5 miles round–trip**

Estimated Time: **2 hours**

Maps: **AMC White Mountain Map #4, USGS Warren Quadrangle**

Views of Mount Moosilauke and a paddle along some of New Hampshire's most recently protected undeveloped shoreline.

LAKE TARLETON is located on the far western edge of the White Mountain National Forest, only a few miles from the Vermont border. While the western shore is home to a few houses and a large summer camp, the lake's eastern shore is undeveloped and fun to explore. In 1994 the undeveloped character of Lake Tarleton was threatened by plans to build a resort on the lake, which would have compromised both water quality and the viability of the surrounding forest as wildlife habitat. By the summer of 2000 more than 5,500 acres of the forest surrounding the lake (and three smaller nearby lakes) had been protected by a coalition of environmental groups, the federal government, and the state of New Hampshire. Due to these efforts, Lake Tarleton is home to loons and osprey, bears and moose.

Motorboats and waterskiing are allowed on the lake, but traffic is usually light on all but the busiest summer weekends. On busy days plan an early morning paddle to ensure a peaceful time on the lake. While you can choose any route, the most immediate rewards are found by following the shore to the right of the put-in. From here you soon will reach the eastern edge of the lake and encounter a few coves filled with pickerelweed and yellow water lilies. Most of the lake is surrounded by a northern hardwood forest, punctuated by the occasional tall white pine or spruce. You will hear bird song from the forest joined by the chatter of kingfishers and the

Canoeing Lake Tarleton.

calls of loons on the lake. Loons nest on the lake; take care not to disturb them, especially when they are nesting or with their young.

In addition to coves filled with heaths, frogs, and wild roses, Lake Tarleton provides good views toward Mount Moosilauke and the surrounding peaks. At the north end of the lake is a public beach, recently purchased by the state. Landing or launching a boat from the beach is prohibited, but if you feel like a swim after your paddle, drive 1.2 miles north to the beach parking area.

Direction

From the intersection of NH 25 and NH 25C in Warren, take NH 25C west for 5.0 miles and turn right onto a dirt road with a small sign that says "Road to Public Waters." The put-in is in a few hundred yards at the end of the road.

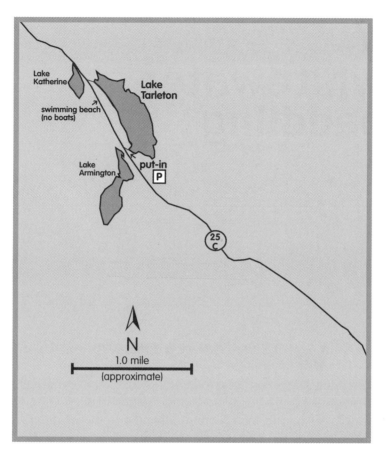

LAKE TARLETON

7
whitewater paddling

WHILE CLASSIC NEW ENGLAND whitewater rivers like the Deefield, Dead, and Penobscot are found in neighboring Maine and Massachusetts, whitewater enthusiasts can find many enjoyable paddling opportunities in the White Mountains. This chapter is merely an introduction to those opportunities, and the trips listed here were chosen mainly because these rivers often can be run later in the year. We have chosen runs with a maximum rating of Class II. Experienced paddlers looking to run Class III and higher whitewater should check out the *AMC Classic Northeastern Whitewater Guide* by Bruce Lessels, which explains in great detail the best whitewater in the Northeast. All of these trips require varying levels of experience on fast-moving water. Please read this introduction and the trip descriptions in detail before deciding if you have the skills necessary to complete a trip safely. River paddling is extremely rewarding, but it is a dangerous sport to participate in without the proper training.

Safety

Following these guidelines can save your life:

- Never paddle alone. American Whitewater recommends paddling with at least three people and two boats (www.americanwhitewater.org). The AMC suggests three boats.

- Dress for the water temperature. Water temperatures in the spring are often in the thirties and forties. Immersion in water this cold is a shock to your system and can cause rapid heat loss. Wear a wet suit or dry suit and pack warm clothes (in a dry bag) to change into in case you get cold.

- Always wear a life jacket or personal floatation device (PFD) even when scouting a river. Make sure your PFD is rated for turbulent water and allows freedom of movement for swimming and paddling.

- Boaters in kayaks or closed canoes should always wear a helmet—you **WILL** at some point hit your head on a rock while upside down in your boat. Open boaters should wear helmets in rapids rated Class II and higher.

- Outfit your boat with floatation, so that your boat will float if it gets swamped.

- Make sure you and your boat are outfitted in such a way that nothing can get tangled or hooked on the branches of fallen trees or other obstacles in the river. People drown because they get caught underwater on trees that have fallen into the river.

- Never stand up in whitewater; the power of whitewater should not be underestimated. Standing up puts you at risk for getting a foot caught between rocks on the bottom of the river. Once this happens, the force of the water can push you underwater—you can drown in less than two feet of water.

- Be practiced in self-rescue. Do **NOT** get in a boat on moving water unless you have practiced escaping from your boat. This is especially important for kayakers who must be able to wet-exit their boat in case they flip.

- Know how to paddle your boat in moving water. If you have never paddled on whitewater you should take a course in white-water techniques. Many of these techniques will help you enjoy your trip, while avoiding life-threatening situations. After some basic training all of the trips in this book are appropriate for beginning paddlers *who are paddling with a group of experienced whitewater paddlers.* The AMC New Hampshire Chapter has a whitewater school every spring that provides excellent training. Commercial outfitters with whitewater schools include Northern Waters and Great Glen Trails (see listings in Appendix). The AMC Workshops program also offers several whitewater courses.

- While moving downstream, always stay between the lead and sweep boats, and keep the boat behind you in sight.

- Learn to recognize and avoid these whitewater hazards:

High water—The more water in a river, the more powerful and dangerous it is. Do not attempt to paddle a river at or near flood stage. While we have given some guidelines to gauge each river by, we have not paddled these rivers in all conditions and you must use your own judgment in determining the safety of a river's water level. Streambeds also can change, making our gauge recommendations obsolete. If you are unsure of a river's safety, check with the Forest Service or local outfitters. Be aware that rivers can rise and fall considerably during the course of a few hours due to runoff and snowmelt. The National Oceanic and Atmospheric Adminstration (NOAA) and the National Weather Service publish current river flow data on the NOAA website at www.nws.noaa.gov/er/nerfc/gis_maps.

Strainers—Fallen trees and other obstacles that allow water to flow through them, but not you and your boat, are called strainers. Strainers are very dangerous as you can become pinned against the object and subjected to immense water pressure. Rescue from these situations can be very difficult or impossible. Learn to spot these obstacles well ahead of time, and be proficient enough to maneuver your boat around them.

Dams, ledges, reversals, holes, and hydraulics—Most of the holes and hydraulics encountered on the trips in this book are relatively benign; however, it is important to make a point not to approach dams or strong holes from either direction, as they can be impossible to escape in some circumstances.

Broaching—If your boat is pushed sideways against a rock by a strong current, you run the risk of being pinned against the rock and crushed by the current. This is an especially dangerous situation for kayakers, who can get trapped in their boat with no way to escape. To avoid being pinned in this situation you should throw your weight downstream, even going so far as to lean against the rock. This will allow the current to flow harmlessly under your boat.

To paddle whitewater safely everyone in your group should have rudimentary paddling skills. Kayakers should know how to use the following strokes/techniques: forward stroke, sweep, reverse sweep, draw, high brace, and low brace. Kayakers also should be able to exit a flipped boat safely and swim to safety. Canoeists should know how to use the following strokes: forward stroke, J stroke, back stroke, draw, cross draw, forward sweep, reverse sweep, low brace, and high brace. All boaters should know how to ferry, back ferry, and how to enter and exit an eddy safely. If any of these strokes/techniques are unfamiliar to you, get some training before risking your life on the river. For more information, check out the *AMC Whitewater Handbook, 3rd edition* by Bruce Lessels.

For additional safety and a more comfortable trip, bring the following:

Water—one or more quarts per person depending on the weather and length of the trip

Food—Even for a short, one-hour trip, it is a good idea to bring some high-energy snacks like nuts, dried fruit, or snack bars. Bring a lunch for longer trips.

Map and compass

Extra clothing in a waterproof bag—to warm up in after immersion in cold water

Flashlight

Sunscreen

First-aid kit

Pocketknife

Etiquette and the Environment

Like all outdoor sports, river paddling requires that we follow Leave No Trace techniques (see the introduction to this book) in order to prevent environmental degradation and preserve the wilderness experience for those who follow us. Please keep the following things in mind while on the river:

- Take great care when walking on shore, as the environment along the river banks can be especially fragile.

- All of the river trips in this book pass through private property for most of their length; please treat the environment with care and act with courtesy.

- If you are part of an especially large group (more than 12 boats), break your trip into two or more groups in order to relieve congestion.

- Get in and out of the water quickly—others may be waiting to use the put-in or take-out.

- Don't peel out in front of another boat.

- Don't hog eddies, surfing waves, or holes. Get your rest and have your fun, but others probably want to use the same river features you are enjoying.

- If you swim, use self-rescue skills as much as possible.

Local Paddling Groups

Joining a paddling club is a great way to enjoy whitewater safely. There are many clubs in New England. In New Hampshire the following groups always are willing to take on enthusiastic new paddlers:

- AMC New Hampshire Paddlers—AMC members can join this group by contacting the paddling co-chair (check the Chapter Activities section of *AMC Outdoors* for a current listing). Their website address is www.nhamcpaddlers.org.

- Merrimack Valley Paddlers—P.O. Box 233, Hollis, NH 03049; www.mvpclub.org.

- Mount Washington Valley Paddlers—Contact Canoe King in West Ossipee for information at 603-539-4799; or at www.w3.ime.net/~rivrrat/index.

Now that all those logistical issues are out of the way, get out on the river and have some fun. The five trips suggested in this book range from an easy day of primarily flatwater paddling on the Saco to a playful whitewater run on the Androscoggin, where you will want to get wet over and over again. The Saco trip is the most appropriate for beginner paddlers. The trip on the Pemigewasset River from Woodstock to Thornton is the best bet for those comfortable on fast-moving water and small rapids, but not yet trained in whitewater techniques. Paddlers experienced in Class II or higher water will find the remaining three trips to be a fun place to spend some time dodging rocks and surfing waves.

Pemigewasset River— Woodstock to Thornton

> Difficulty: **Flatwater, Quickwater, Class I**
>
> Distance: **12.3 miles**
>
> Estimated Time: **5 hours**
>
> Maps: **AMC White Mountain Map #4, USGS Woodstock and Plymouth Quadrangles**
>
> **A long, enjoyable paddle through the beautiful White Mountain countryside.**

PADDLING THIS SECTION of the Pemigewasset River requires that paddlers be comfortable maneuvering a boat on fast-moving water, but the rapids encountered on this trip are much easier than those on the Pemigewasset River—Woodstock Whitewater trip. This is also a much longer trip, requiring a fair amount of paddling just to keep moving forward. The reward for all of this paddling is a long day spent enjoying beautiful White Mountain scenery. This trip can get tedious during summer's low water levels, as you will have to get out and drag your boat over rocks in shallow sections. Plan your trip in spring or within a day or two of a heavy summer rain. To check the water level look for the gauge near the put-in; it is about 100 yards upstream on an old bridge abutment—a reading between three and six feet should make for decent paddling. A reading above six feet might make for stronger water conditions than are comfortable for many paddlers. If you are unsure of paddling conditions check with local outfitters in Lincoln.

The trip starts out with easy Class I rapids and a few rocks that require some maneuvering. These are the hardest rapids of the trip, and after passing a golf course at about the 2.0-mile mark, you

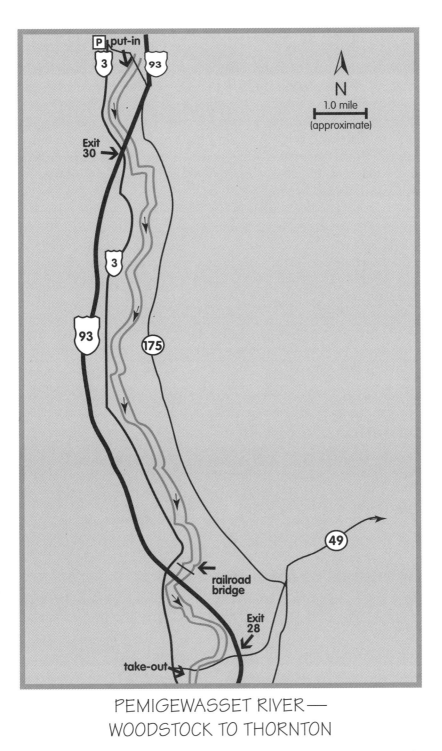

PEMIGEWASSET RIVER—
WOODSTOCK TO THORNTON

mostly encounter quickwater with a few short Class I sections usually confined to bends in the river and under bridges. Some of these river bends are tight with fast-moving water, creating the possibility of strainers on the outside bank. Start with your stern pointed at the inside bank of these turns and use a few back-paddle strokes to keep it there as the river pulls you toward the outer bank. For the most part this trip is an easy paddle; you can enjoy good views upstream of the western White Mountains while you float past a forest of northern hardwoods and tall white pine. You also will find plenty of beaches where you can rest in the sun.

After passing under a bridge at about the 5.0-mile mark you can expect the river to get flatter as you go, alternating between quickwater and flatwater sections. Navigation choices are easy, as you can choose to paddle safely on either side of any island you encounter. At about the 9.0-mile mark you will pass under an iron railroad bridge and then the two lanes of I-93. After I-93 the river splits—either direction is fine, but the right channel takes you past some interesting rock ledges as it winds through a series of narrow turns. After passing under another bridge at 12.3 miles the take-out is immediately on your right.

Directions to put-in

From I-93 take Exit 30 in Woodstock and drive north on US 3. In 1.1 miles turn right onto an unmarked side road. In another 0.3 mile turn right onto NH 175 and make an immediate right onto Death Valley Road. The put-in is at the end of the road.

Directions to take-out

From the put-in drive back to NH 175 and turn left (north). Take your first left, drive the 0.3 mile back to US 3 and turn left. Follow US 3 for 9.6 miles and turn left onto NH 49. The take-out is on the right in 0.2 mile just before NH 49 crosses the river.

the pemigewasset:
a river restored

THE PEMIGEWASSET RIVER is one of New Hampshire's cleanest and most popular big rivers, but this was not always the case. Like most parts of northern New England, the White Mountains were heavily logged during the late nineteenth and early twentieth centuries. The Pemigewasset was used extensively by the industry, to transport logs and as a sewer for pulp mill wastewater. Poor sewage treatment in communities along the river also contributed pollution, and by the 1960s the "Pemi" was a polluted stinking mess with less than 10 percent saturation of oxygen in its water—not conducive to supporting a healthy fish population. Improvement in wastewater treatment and the closing of paper mills has resulted in the Pemi being restored to a Class B river; safe for swimming and capable of supporting fish such as brook trout and Atlantic salmon.

Pemigewasset is an Abenaki word meaning "rapidly moving." The river certainly lives up to its name, beginning at Profile Lake at the base of Cannon Mountain and moving rapidly through Franconia Notch. The east branch of the river, which runs through Lincoln, has the most difficult rapids of the river, maintaining a solid Class IV rating for most of its length before it empties into the main branch in Woodstock. The river continues flowing south and follows I-93 for most of its length, picking up water from other rivers along the way such as the Mad, the Baker, the Newfound, and the Smith. At its confluence with the Winnipesaukee River in Franklin, the Pemi ends and the Merrimack River is born.

The Pemigewasset drains over 1,000 square miles of central New Hampshire, much of which was under the water of a large glacial lake at the end of the last ice age. This body of water known as Lake Merrimack began to drain approximately 10,000 years ago, leaving behind large deposits of gravel and sand that reach depths of 100 feet. Other glacial features evident along the Pemi include glacial erratics and gorges, the most famous of which is the Flume Gorge in Franconia Notch State Park. Native American tribes lived in the river valley, perhaps soon after the draining of Lake Merrimack. By the time of significant contact with Europeans in the sixteenth century, the Abenakis inhabited the area. This contact proved fatal, as up to 75 percent of the Native Americans in the area died in the sixteenth and early seventeenth century as a result of diseases such as smallpox and measles. In 1712 European soldiers on the Baker River killed several members of the Pemigewasset band of Abenakis; most Native Americans fled the Pemigewasset River valley soon after.

European settlement of the valley focused on agriculture on the southern half of the river and logging on the upper portions. By the turn of the twentieth century, most of the forest along the Pemi had been cleared of trees and burned. Below the steep slopes of Franconia Notch and around the towns to the south, this clogged the river with silt and created the potential for severe flooding. Poor forest conservation practices on rivers like the Pemigewasset was one of the major reasons groups like the AMC and Society for the Protection of New Hampshire Forests pushed Congress to pass the Weeks Act in 1911, creating the White Mountain National Forest.

The forest has since grown back and, despite the proximity of I-93, the river's watershed is relatively undeveloped. The river has been identified as eligible for inclusion in the federal Wild and Scenic Rivers program and, except for 10.0 miles in Lincoln and Woodstock, the Pemi is protected under the New Hampshire Rivers Management and Protection Program. Today kayakers, canoeists, swimmers, and fly fishers value the river's recreation value, while wildlife such as osprey, peregrine falcons, upland sandpipers, river otters, and snapping turtles depend on the river's resources to survive. In addition to the two trips listed in this chapter, kayakers seek out the Class II and III water of the Pemi just south of the Ayers Island Dam in Bristol.

Pemigewasset River— Woodstock Whitewater

> Difficulty: **Class I, Class II, one short Class III section (easily portaged)**
>
> Distance: **4.0 miles**
>
> Estimated Time: **2 hours 30 minutes**
>
> Maps: **AMC White Mountain Map #2, USGS Woodstock and Lincoln Quadrangles**
>
> **An adventurous stretch of whitewater with good views of Franconia Ridge.**

THIS SECTION of the Pemigewasset River is a good choice for paddlers who have experience in Class II whitewater and want to spend the day on a river, playing in eddies and searching out small waves to surf. The Pemigewasset is runnable throughout most of the year, though the low water levels in summer can make the trip fairly rocky (at times you might even need to get out and pull your boat over gravel bars). Late April through early June is the best time to enjoy big rapids, but be dressed for very cold water. An old gauge can be found at the take-out by walking upstream; look under the NH 175 bridge to an old bridge abutment. A gauge reading of four or five feet is a good indication that you will have a fairly rock-free run. If the gauge climbs much above the six-foot level, you should consider an alternate trip unless you are experienced in big water. When the Pemigewasset is running high it is a powerful river; its many winding turns create the possibility for dangerous situations, as trees can unexpectedly block the channel. The good news is that local outfitters do a good job at keeping the channel clear—if in doubt about

Whitewater kayaking on the Pemigewasset River.

river conditions check in with any of the outfitters in Lincoln to get an idea if current conditions are safe.

While you are checking the gauge, you should take a look at the only Class III rapids of the trip. In high water a few big waves and several holes are in these rapids, but usually several routes are available to choose from for getting through safely. Less experienced paddlers who want to avoid these rapids can just portage their boats from the bridge abutment (with the gauge) to the take-out. Play-boaters will find this to be the most exciting part of the trip. As with all whitewater trips, a run down this section of the Pemigewasset requires that open boats have flotation and closed boat paddlers are practiced at self-rescue.

Until you get to the ledges at the take-out the river can be run without any scouting. The trip is a good combination of quick-water, and Class I and Class II rapids for its entire length. The main threat to watch out for is strainers—fallen trees most common on the outside banks of bends in the river. Despite passing several houses and businesses this trip also provides some good scenery, particularly when looking back upstream toward Franconia Ridge.

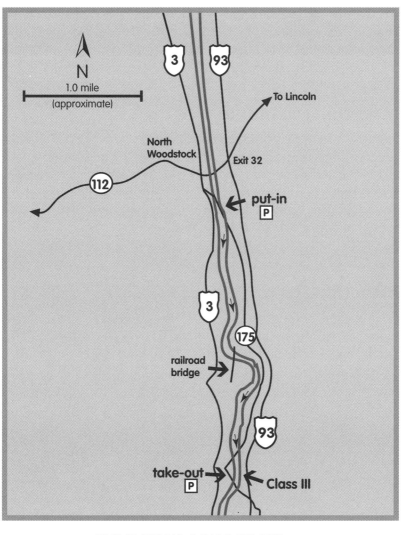

PEMIGEWASSET RIVER—
WOODSTOCK WHITEWATER

In between whitewater runs you might spot mergansers, kingfishers, and sandpipers. Except at the highest water levels, several large beaches along the way provide good places to take a rest or lunch break. Since this is a fairly short run, take your time playing in the small waves and eddies. You will reach the Class III ledges and the end of the trip when you pass an area of flatwater after going under

NH 175 for the second time—the gauge and scouting area will be on your right in just a few hundred yards. The take-out is on the right immediately after you pass under NH 175 for the third time.

Directions to put-in

From I-93, take Exit 32 in Lincoln and drive west on NH 112. In about 0.7 mile turn left onto US 3. In another 0.6 mile turn left onto NH 175, drive over the bridge, and make an immediate left onto Old Dump Road. In 0.1 mile turn left into a dirt parking area and park by the propane tanks. This is private property, so please act with respect to ensure access for future paddlers.

Directions to take-out

From the put-in drive back to NH 175 and turn left (south). In 3.5 miles just before the road crosses the river again, turn right onto Death Valley Road. Park at the end of the road.

Trip #59

Ammonoosuc River— Littleton to Lisbon

> Difficulty: **Quickwater, Class I, Class II**
>
> Distance: **6.8 miles (or 9.7 miles if alternate trip is followed)**
>
> Estimated Time: **3 hours**
>
> Maps: **USGS Lisbon, Sugar Hill, and Littleton Quadrangles**
>
> **Relatively easy rapids are followed by good bird–watching opportunities.**

THIS TRIP is less popular than the Saco, Pemigewasset, or Androscoggin River trips, probably due to the fact it is outside the normal tourist areas in the White Mountains. The Ammonoosuc River also tends to be too shallow for most of the summer, so plan to run this trip by Memorial Day in most years. Big-rapid paddlers know the Ammonoosuc for its Class III and IV rapids further upstream between Twin Mountain and Littleton. This section requires some experience maneuvering in technical Class II water, but its long stretches of rapid-free paddling make for a relaxing day in the White Mountains. While relatively easy, the rocks and rapids on this trip can create waves or tricky situations; it is a good idea for open-boat paddlers to use floatation in their boats and kayakers should be proficient at self-rescue. It is worth noting that both the put-in and the take-out for this trip are adjacent to private property, so please act in a respectful manner.

A gauge worth checking can be found on this trip. About 4.0 miles west of I-93, turn left onto Cedar Pond Road and park on the opposite side of the river; the gauge is on the bridge abutment. The

Ammonoosuc River, lower falls

trip is fairly rocky at any water level under a reading of about 1.5 feet. A water level less than one foot may be too rocky for an enjoyable trip. Above two feet expect to encounter more difficult rapids pushing Class III in spots. The river is divided in three places around small islands, creating the most difficult sections of the trip. These difficult places are easy to spot and each channel is usually runnable; however, they are worth scouting, as one option is usually easier to run than the others. The biggest waves will be encountered immediately after the Gale River joins the Ammonoosuc at about 4.0 miles. The last difficult rapid is about 1.0 mile beyond the Gale River, where an island extends most of the way across the river.

The scenery on this section of the Ammonoosuc is typical of rural New Hampshire—farms, houses, and northern hardwood forests. In spring birdlife is very active along the river and you are likely to see mergansers, swallows, and blackbirds. You should reach the take-out (on the left just before the US 302 bridge) near NH 117 in two or three hours.

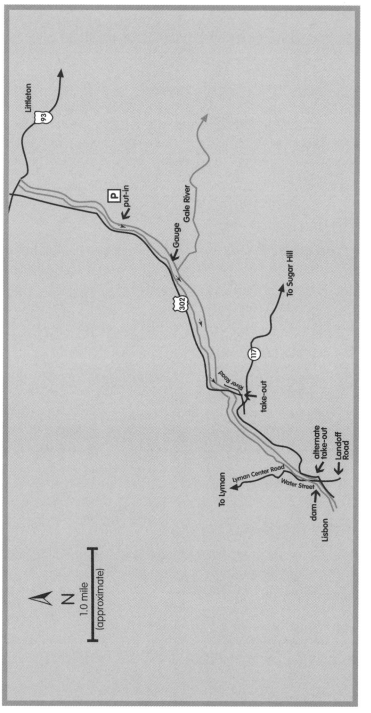

AMMONOOSUC RIVER—LITTLETON TO LISBON

Alternate trip

If you continue on to the alternate take-out you will get an extra 3.0 miles of paddling, mostly on flatwater through sandy, marshy habitat that teems with sandpipers, kingbirds, phoebes, and fly-catchers. An easy Class I rapid immediately follows after passing under US 302, and then the river bends to the left into the quiet backwater of the dam in Lisbon. When you see Lisbon encroaching on the river, keep an eye out for the dam. The take-out will be on the left about 50 yards before the dam.

Directions to put-in

From I-93 take Exit 42 in Littleton and drive west on US 302. In 0.5 mile turn left onto a dirt road and follow the power lines for a short distance to the river.

Directions to take-out

From the put-in turn left onto US 302, follow it for 7.4 miles, and turn left onto NH 117. Immediately take another left onto River Road; the take-out is on the left in 0.25 mile just before a small bridge. This is a small parking area with space for only four or five cars. If necessary, more cars can be parked in Lisbon (see alternate take-out).

Alternate take-out

From the put-in turn left onto US 302 and follow it for 9.6 miles into the center of Lisbon, New Hampshire. A public parking lot is on the right just before the dam in Lisbon, which is a convenient place to take out of the river. Parking is limited to two hours, so you will need to leave your cars in a lot on Moore Street. To get to Moore Street, continue through the center of town and turn left on Landaff Street. Moore Street will be the next left.

cold and fastwater: trout and salmon habitat

WHILE DODGING ROCKS or taking an unplanned swim in 40-degree water, you probably will not be thinking, "Hmm, this cold, well-aerated water is perfect trout habitat." Whitewater rivers and smaller mountain streams are in fact the perfect habitat for trout, which need cold, clean water with a high oxygen content. Do not be surprised to be sharing the river with fly fishers who love to use a fly rod in order to hook brook trout or one of the other introduced species in the area. The eastern brook trout is the only trout native to the streams in the White Mountains, although lakes and ponds may harbor the native lake trout. Rainbow and brown trout have been introduced to the area. In addition to trout, Atlantic salmon historically have inhabited the streams, although the salmon now found here are stocked. Trout feed on insects, leeches, crustaceans, and small fish, while young salmon tend to feed strictly on insects (adult salmon feed on fish, but only at sea). If you decide to try your luck at fishing in the White Mountains, you will need to pick up a New Hampshire state fishing license at area stores.

Eastern brook trout also are called squaretail or speckled trout, as their tails are almost square and their sides are usually sprinkled with red spots ringed in blue. Their bodies are brown or olive-green with dark wormlike markings. They can grow to weigh up to four pounds, though most brook trout in White Mountain streams are small and rarely exceed six inches in length. Besides being the only native trout in the White Mountains, eastern brook trout are the only naturally reproducing trout in the White Mountains, as rainbows and browns need to be stocked. "Brookies" thrive in water that stays below 68 degrees.

Rainbow trout are native to the western United States, but have been introduced to streams throughout the country. Rainbows are best identified by the broad, reddish band along their sides. They also have many black spots on their head, back, and tail. Most rainbow trout caught in rivers and streams are between 6 and 12 inches and weigh less than a pound. Since rainbows can survive in temperatures as warm as 77 degrees, they can reach weights of three to five pounds in lakes with warm, well-aerated water.

Brown trout were introduced to this country from Europe, and are found in slower moving water than rainbow and brook trout. They prefer water in the 65- to 70-degree range and tend to be found in deeper pools or the lower, quieter sections of streams. Brown trout are usually yellowish-brown in color and have large, dark spots on their sides, backs, and dorsal fins. Orange and/or red spots usually can be seen on their sides. Brown trout caught in New Hampshire are generally 7 to 14 inches in length and weigh less than a pound, although they can weigh up to four pounds.

Atlantic salmon are native to rivers and streams throughout New England. Due to the damming of rivers, however, only nine rivers and streams, all in Maine, currently have naturally occurring salmon runs (to learn more about wild Atlantic salmon, visit the website of the Downeast Salmon Federation at www.mainesalmonrivers.org). In the White Mountains, streams are stocked with young Atlantic salmon, which remain for one to three years before migrating to the Atlantic Ocean. Unlike Pacific salmon, which spawn once during their lifetime and then die, Atlantic salmon can survive to spawn multiple times. The young salmon found in streams are called parr and look similar to brown trout, except for a forked tail and a lack of spots on their dorsal fins. As the parr grow they become smolts, which have a silvery appearance.

A great way to see these fish up close is to visit a New Hampshire Fish and Game Department hatchery.

•Berlin Fish Hatchery—Off Route 110, Kilkenny Valley, Berlin, NH; 603-449-3412
•Twin Mountain Fish Hatchery—US Route 3, Twin Mountain, NH; 603-859-2041

Trip #60

Androscoggin River—
Northern Forest Adventure

> Difficulty: **Class I, Class II+**
>
> Distance: **2.0 miles**
>
> Estimated Time: **1 hour 30 minutes**
>
> Maps: **USGS Milan and Dummer Ponds Quadrangles**
>
> **A short but exciting stretch of almost nonstop rapids in the Great North Woods region of New Hampshire.**

THE ANDROSCOGGIN RIVER from Errol to Milan is popular with whitewater boaters because it has runnable rapids all summer long due to regular dam releases. This trip is short (many paddling groups run this trip more than once in a day), but it has a consistent stretch of Class II rapids full of powerful eddies, surfing waves, and small holes. It is a great place for intermediate boaters to hone their skills before moving up to more difficult water. Inexperienced paddlers are likely to fall out of their canoes or flip their kayaks, so self-rescue skills are a must. Dam releases occur on most summer days, resulting in medium flows with good rapids and rock clearance. You will want to make sure you time your trip with a dam release, which usually begins at 8 A.M. or 9 A.M.—a free dam release schedule can usually be picked up at Canoe King in Ossipee or Northern Waters in Conway and Errol.

While the river follows NH 16 you most likely will not notice, since you will be concentrating on paddling. Except for one 0.5-mile quickwater stretch, where the river gets close to the road, the Class I and II rapids are fairly constant. The most difficult rapids are soon after the aforementioned quickwater stretch, and big

Pontook Reservoir, Androscoggin River

standing waves provide plenty of excitement as the river's rating pushes close to Class III, especially in high water. Just before the end of the trip a large island divides the river. You can take either channel to the take-out, which will be on your right.

This section of the Androscoggin is too far north to be considered part of the White Mountains, but it makes a good day trip from the North Conway and Gorham areas. The river is a major watercourse in New Hampshire's Great North Woods, and it is a great place to watch for wildlife. While on the river you are likely to see mergansers, heron, and hawks such as osprey and sharp-shinned hawks. The drive up NH 16 from Milan past Errol to the Maine border is prime moose-watching habitat, especially at dawn and dusk with the Pontook Reservoir (above the dam at the put-in) being one of the best spots. For additional information on the Androscoggin River, check out the Androscoggin River Watershed Council at www.andro-watershed.org.

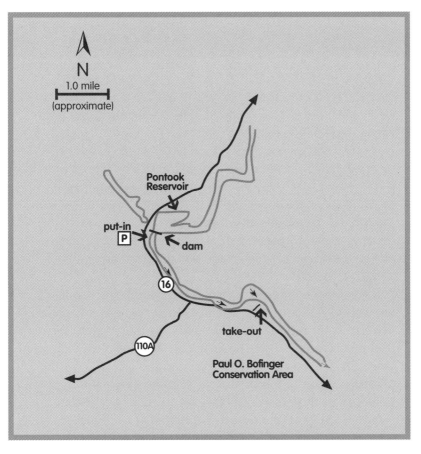

ANDROSCOGGIN RIVER

Directions to put-in

The put-in is in a parking area on the east side of NH 16, 1.6 miles north of NH 110A in Milan.

Directions to take-out

From the put-in drive south on NH 16 for 2.2 miles and turn left into the parking area for the Paul O. Bofinger Conservation Area.

the northern forest

LIKE MOST OF THE MAJOR RIVERS in the Northeastern United States, the Androscoggin River gets its start in a place called the Northern Forest (in New Hampshire, it is called the Great North Woods Region). The Northern Forest is a term used to identify a region that spans from the shores of Lake Ontario in northern New York across northern New England to Maine's border with New Brunswick. In this area are approximately 26-million acres of relatively undeveloped forest, surrounding small towns with traditionally forest-dependent economies. Today much of this forest is owned by paper and/or timber management companies, but many local economies are in transition away from extractive industries.

The Northern Forest is rich in recreation opportunities like hunting, fishing, hiking, and canoeing. Legendary places like Katahdin, Moosehead Lake, and Lake Placid are all part of the Northern Forest. The forest is rich in wildlife such as bears, moose, eagles, and coyote, and the last wild runs of Atlantic salmon in the U.S. occur in rivers in the Maine portion of the Northern Forest. Despite its relatively remote location, the Northern Forest is threatened by unsustainable logging practices and real estate development on sensitive lake and river shorelines.

You can find out more about the Northern Forest and how to protect it at the websites of the AMC, the Northern Forest Alliance, and the Northern Forest Center (see Appendix). An excellent book for learning about the Northern Forest is *The Northern Forest* by David Dobbs and Richard Ober, published by Chelsea Green Publishing Company.

Trip # 61

Saco River—North Conway
to Conway

> Difficulty: **Flatwater, Quickwater, Class I**
>
> Distance: **8.5 miles**
>
> Estimated Time: **4 hours**
>
> Maps: **AMC White Mountain Map #5, USGS Conway, North Conway East, and North Conway West Quadrangles**
>
> **An easy paddle close to town, with great scenery.**

THE SACO RIVER has something for everyone, from technical white-water diehards to flatwater enthusiasts paddling with boats full of tents and coolers. This trip is somewhere in between—an easy day trip that consists mostly of quickwater and flatwater paddling through the scenic countryside of North Conway and Conway. This is the easiest of the river trips in this book and is a good choice for beginners; however, one short stretch of Class I whitewater at the very end of the trip will require the ability to maneuver a fast-moving boat around a few rocks (follow the safety guidelines at the beginning of this chapter). This trip is best run at medium water levels in May and early June, or after a heavy summer rain. Later in the year the river can be very shallow, requiring paddlers to get out and drag their boats over sand and gravel bars. Unfortunately, there is no gauge for reading water levels at this time.

The paddle along this stretch of the Saco is a slow-moving, peaceful trip where you may be rewarded with wildlife sightings such as great blue heron, mergansers, kingfishers, and other birds. Besides invertebrates and other fish, these birds may be fishing for

Saco River

native eastern brook trout. If you want to try your luck at hooking a "brookie," take note that this part of the river is a fly-fishing-only area (and that you need a state fishing license). This trip follows the river as it meanders for 8.0 miles through northern hardwood forests and past farms, providing beautiful views of the surrounding hills and mountains. About 2.0 miles from the put-in you will pass the AMC Moose Campground (advanced reservations required). At about the halfway point you will pass under a railroad bridge. You know you have reached the end of the trip when the water gets bumpy and the Swift River enters on the right. The take-out will be on the left, immediately after you pass under the covered bridge.

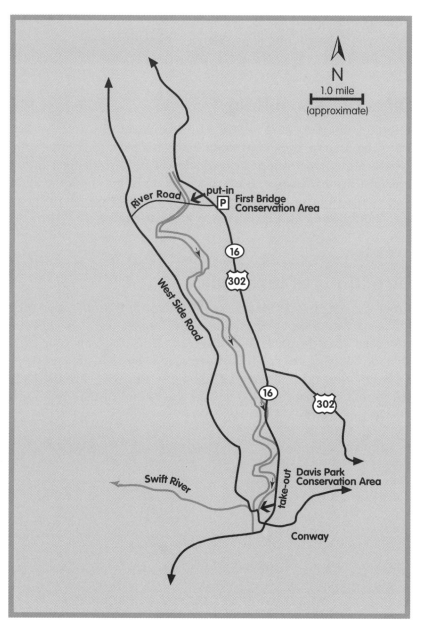

SACO RIVER—NORTH CONWAY TO CONWAY

If you are looking for an overnight camping adventure on the Saco, check out the opportunities offered by Saco Bound in

Conway (see Appendix). They provide boat shuttle services as well as private campgrounds along the river in nearby Maine.

Directions to put-in

From the intersection of NH 16 and River Road in North Conway (near the Eastern Slope Inn), head west on River Road. Park at the First Bridge Conservation Area, which will be on your right in 0.4 mile just before the river. It is actually easier to put in on the other side of the river on the left, but once you unload your boat there, you should park at the conservation area parking lot.

Directions to take-out

From the put-in head west on River Road for 0.6 mile, and turn left onto West Side Road. In another 6.1 miles turn left onto the first road after the Swift River covered bridge (also on your left). In about 50 yards turn left again at a stop sign. The take-out will be in another 0.1 mile on the right just after crossing the Saco River on a covered bridge. The take-out is part of the Davis Park Conservation Area.

8
other activities

THIS CHAPTER LISTS some things you can do to fill in the spaces between your hiking, bicycling, and paddling trips.

AMC Presentations and Nature Walks at Pinkham Notch Visitor Center

Evening programs and guided nature hikes. Call 603-466-2721 for more information.

Amusement Parks

Great entertainment for families with small children.

- *Attitash Bear Peak*—603-374-2368 or 800-223-SNOW; www.attitash.com. In summer this ski resort offers a thrilling ride down a mountain—on 1.0-mile-long alpine slides! They also have four waterslides, guided horseback tours, scenic chairlift rides, and children's adventure camps.

- *Clark's Trading Post*—Lincoln, NH; 603-745-8913. Perhaps most well-known for their live bear shows, you also will find exhibits of antique Americana, steam trains, a circus, and more.

- *Santa's Village*—Route 2, Jefferson, NH; 603-586-4445; www.santasvillage.com. An amusement park that brings the Christmas spirit to you in summer. Open: June 17 through Labor Day and again at Christmastime.

- *Six Gun City*—Route 2, Jefferson, NH; 603-586-4592. "The best of the west in the White Mountains." Old West entertainment and village, and a waterpark to cool you off on hot days.

- *Story Land*—Route 16, Glen, NH; 603-383-4186; www.storylandnh.com. An amusement park filled with rides, shows, and characters. Open: mid-June through Columbus Day.

- *Whales Tales*—Route 3, Lincoln, NH; 603-745-8810. The region's only full-size waterpark. Complete with wave pool, river, waterslides, and more.

Rides to the Top of a Mountain

Injured? Tired? Have young children? These are great opportunities to get all the view for none of the effort.

- *Cannon Mountain*—At parkway Exits 2 and 3 on I-93, Franconia Notch Parkway; 603-823-8800. Take the Aerial Tramway to the top of this 4,100-foot mountain. At the base of the mountain, you can enjoy Echo Lake Beach or their two museums: The Old Man of the Mountain Museum and the New England Ski Museum.

- *Loon Mountain* — Kancamagus Highway, Lincoln, NH; 603-745-8111; www.loonmtn.com. Loon Mountain offers a 1.5-mile Mountain Skyride up the ski mountain. At the top you can hear tales from "The Mountain Man," and check out glacial caves and a self-guided nature trail.

- *Mount Washington Auto Road at Great Glen*—Route 16 in Pinkham Notch, Gorham, NH; 603-466-3988; www.mt-washington.com. Enjoy the views from New Hampshire's highest mountain (6,288 feet) by driving yourself or by taking a guided tour. Open: mid-May through late-October.

- *Wildcat Mountain*—Route 16, Pinkham Notch, Jackson, NH; 603-466-3326; www.skiwildcat.com. Take a gondola ride to the 4,062-foot summit.

Museums and Historical Sites:

- *Eastman-Lord House Museum*—100 Main Street, Conway, NH; 603-447-5551. This house features 15 rooms ranging from 1818 to 1945.

- *The Frost Place*—Ridge Road, Franconia, NH; 603-823-5510. Poet Robert Frost's farmhouse and farm, with museum and nature trails.

- *Gorham Historical Society*—25 Railroad Street, Gorham, NH; 603-466-5570. This 1907 rail station gives you a chance to explore the early history of trains.

- *Heritage-New Hampshire*—Route 16, Glen NH; 603-383-4186; www.heritagenh.com. A walk-through adventure spanning 350 years of New Hampshire's happenings and events. Open: mid-June through mid-October.

- *Jackson Historical Society*—Jackson, NH; 603-383-4060. This museum contains documents, maps, deeds, genealogy, and more. Open all year.

- *Littleton Historic Sites*—Littleton, NH; 603-444-6561. Walking tours of 12 historic and architectural treasures along Main Street. A free brochure is available through the Chamber of Commerce.

- *Mount Washington Museum*—summit of Mount Washington; 603-356-2137. Run by the Mount Washington Observatory; accessible by the Auto Road (see page 324) or Cog Railway (see page 329). Open: mid-May through mid-October.

- *New England Ski Museum*—Franconia Notch Parkway, Franconia, NH; 603-823-7177. Exhibits of historic ski memorabilia, plus videos, books, and posters in museum shop.

- *Sugar Hill Historical Museum*—Main Street, Sugar Hill, NH; 603-823-5336. Changing exhibits reflect two centuries of North Country life and work.

Performing Arts

What a great way to spend a rainy day or a summer evening.

- *Arts Jubilee*—North Conway Village, NH; 603-356-9393. Summer family concert series under the stars.

- *Mount Washington Valley Theatre Company*—North Conway, NH; 603-356-5776. Enjoy professional live musical theatre, staged at the Eastern Slope Playhouse.

- *NCCA/Papermill Theatre*—603-745-6032. Summer theatre with three musical performances each summer, as well as a traveling children's theatre.
- *North Country Chamber Players*—Franconia, NH; 603-444-0309.

Rock Climbing

The White Mountains offer great opportunities for rock climbing. If you don't have a lot of experience, hire a guide to ensure total enjoyment and safety.

- *Adventures Vertical*—Intervale, NH; 603-356-3042; www.geocities.com/adventuresvertical.
- *Bartlett Backcountry Adventures*—Bartlett, NH; 603-374-0866; www.bartlettadventures.com.
- *Chauvin Guides International*—North Conway, NH; 603-356-8919; www.chauvinguides.com.
- *Eastern Mountain Sports Climbing School*—North Conway, NH; 800-310-4504; www.emsclimb.com.
- *International Mountain Climbing School*—North Conway, NH; 603-356-7064; www.ime-usa.com.
- *The Mountain Guides Alliance*—Intervale, NH; 603-356-5310; www.mountainguidesalliance.com
- *New England Mountain Guides*—207-935-2008 or 603-367-8486; www.climbnet.com/mga/index.
- *Profile Mountaineering*—North Woodstock, NH; 603-745-3106; www.profilemtneering.com.

Science and Nature Education

- *The Flume*—Franconia Notch State Park; 603-745-8391. Explore this natural gorge that extends for 800 feet.
- *SPNHF Lost River Reservation*—Route 112, Kinsman Notch, North Woodstock, NH; 603-745-8031; www.findlostriver.com. A self-guided tour follows Lost River as it winds its way through the narrow, steep-walled gorge. Open: mid-May through mid-October.

- *Polar Caves* — Route 25, Tenney Mountain Highway, Plymouth, NH; 603-536-1888 or 800-273-1886. Cave tours (continuously), nature trails, waterfowl and animal exhibits, Maple Sugar Museum, Rainbow Cascades, and the Glacial Boulder Maze.

- *Twin Mountain Conservation Center* — 603-447-6991. Nature programs on evenings and weekends promoting the appreciation of the environment, as well as a summer camp for children ages 4 to 16.

- *Twin Mountain Fish and Wildlife Center* — Route 3, Twin Mountain; 603-846-5108. Features interactive exhibits about watersheds and a 27-foot fish tank. Hatchery tours are available.

- *Warren Fish Hatchery and Education Center* — Route 25, Warren, NH; 603-764-8593. Interactive exhibits on wildlife habitat and the life cycle of the Atlantic salmon. Hatchery tours are available. Open: year-round.

- *The Weather Discovery Center* — Route 16, North Conway, NH; 603-356-2137; www.mountwashington.org. Interactive exhibits and presentations, on basic scientific concepts about weather observation, tools and technology, and how weather affects us.

Support New Hampshire Artisans
A great opportunity to appreciate talented artists and find a souvenir of your trip.

- *League of New Hampshire Craftsmen* — Route 16, North Conway, NH; 603-356-2441.

- *New Hampshire Homecraft Cooperative* — Campton, NH; 603-726-8626.

Swimming
The natural geology of the streams and rivers in the White Mountains provide countless opportunities for discovering natural swimming holes. If you are looking for a more structured experience, visit the beaches at these area ponds:

- *Russell Pond Campground*: Tripoli Road, Campton

- *Echo Lake*: Franconia Notch State Park

- *South Pond*: NH 16, Gorham

- *Lake Tarleton*: see trip #56

recommended reading

Guide Books

Bolnick, Bruce, Doreen, and Daniel. *Waterfalls of the White Mountains: 30 Hikes to 100 Waterfalls*. Backcountry Publications, 1999.

Daniell, Gene and Jon Burroughs. *White Mountain Guide, 26th Edition*. Appalachian Mountain Club, 1998.

Demrow, Carl and David Salisbury. *The Complete Guide to Trail Building and Maintenance, 3rd Edition*. Appalachian Mountain Club, 1998.

Jas, Victoria. *AMC River Guide: New Hampshire/Vermont, 2nd Edition*. Appalachian Mountain Club, 1989.

Lessels, Bruce. *Classic Northeastern Whitewater Guide: The Best Whitewater Runs in New England and New York—Novice to Expert, 3rd Edition*. Appalachian Mountain Club, 1998.

U'ren, Stephen B. *Performance Kayaking*. Stackpole Books, 1990.

Wilson, Alex. *AMC Quiet Water New Hampshire and Vermont: Canoe and Kayak Guide, 2nd Edition*. Appalachian Mountain Club, 2001.

History/Stories

Belcher, C. Francis. *Logging Railroads of the White Mountains*. Appalachian Mountain Club, 1980.

Brown, Dona. *A Tourist's New England: Travel Fiction 1820-1920*. University Press of New England, 1999.

Crawford, Lucy. *History of the White Mountains*. Durand Press, 1999.

Howe, Nicholas. *Not Without Peril: 150 Years of Misadventure on the Presidential Range of New Hampshire*. Appalachian Mountain Club, 2000.

Mudge, John T. B. *The White Mountains: Names, Places, and Legends*. Durand Press, 1995.

Stier, Maggie and Ron McAdow. *Into The Mountains: Stories of New England's Most Celebrated Peaks*. Appalachian Mountain Club, 1995.

Waterman, Laura and Guy. *Forest and Crag: A History of Hiking, Trail Blazing, and Adventure in the Northeast Mountains*. Appalachian Mountain Club, 1989.

Nature

Slack, Nancy G. and Allison W. Bell. *AMC Field Guide to the New England Alpine Summits*. Appalachian Mountain Club, 1995.

Steele, Fredric L. *At Timberline: A Nature Guide to the Mountains of the Northeast*. Appalachian Mountain Club, 1982.

Taylor, James, Thomas D. Lee and Laura Falk McCarthy. *New Hampshire's Living Legacy: The Biodiversity of the Granite State*. New Hampshire Fish and Game Department Nongame and Endangered Wildlife Program, 1996.

Thompson, Woodrow B., Brian K. Fowler and P. Thompson Davis. *Late Quaternary History of the White Mountains, New Hampshire, and Adjacent Southeastern Quebec*. Les Presses de l'Universite de Montreal, 1999.

VanDiver, Bradford. *Roadside Geology of Vermont and New Hampshire*. Mountain Press, 1987.

Waterman, Laura and Guy. *Backwoods Ethics: Environmental Issues for Hikers and Campers*. Countryman Press, 1993.

environmental organizations

Appalachian Mountain Club: 617-523-0655; www.outdoors.org

Appalachian Trail Conference: 304-535-6331; www.atconf.org

Friends of Tuckerman Ravine: 603-356-0131;
www.friendsoftuckerman.org

Leave No Trace: 303-442-8222; www.lnt.org

The Nature Conservancy: 603-224-5853; www.tnc.org

Northern Forest Alliance: 802-223-5256; www.thenorthernforest.org

Northern Forest Center: 603-229-0679; www.northernforest.org

Sierra Club, New Hampshire Chapter: www.sierraclub.org/chapter/nh

Society for Protection of New Hampshire Forests (SPNHF):
603-224-9945; www.spnhf.org

White Mountain Interpretive Association: 603-447-5448

The Wilderness Society: 617-350-8866; www.wilderness.org/ccc/northeast

appendix c
lodging

LITERALLY HUNDREDS of choices for lodging exist in and around the White Mountains. They range from basic campgrounds to very expensive, luxurious hotels and inns. Here are some resources to help you find the place that's right for your needs:

State of New Hampshire Division of Tourism: 800-FUN IN NH; www.visitnh.gov

Bethlehem Chamber of Commerce: 603-869-3409

Conway Village Chamber of Commerce: 603-447-2639

Country Inns in the White Mountains: 603-447-2818

Franconia Notch Chamber of Commerce: 800-237-9007

Jackson Chamber of Commerce: 800-866-3334

Lincoln/Woodstock Chamber of Commerce: 800-227-4191; www.linwoodcc.org

Lisbon Chamber of Commerce/White Mountain Lodging Bureau: 603-838-6673

Littleton Chamber of Commerce: 603-444-6561

Mount Washington Valley Chamber of Commerce: 800-367-3364; www.mtwashingtonvalley.org

Northern White Mountain Chamber of Commerce: 800-992-7480; www.northernwhitemountains.com

White Mountain Attractions: 800-346-3687 www.visitwhitemountains.com

national forest campgrounds

NAME	LOCATION	OPEN SEASON	SITES	HIKING	SWIMMING
Basin	Saco Ranger Station: Rt. 113, 15 mi. North of Fryeburg, ME	mid-May to mid-Oct.	21	*	
Big Rock	Pemigewasset Ranger Station: Kancamagus Hwy., 6 mi. east of Lincoln, NH	mid-May to mid-Oct.	28	*	
Blackberry Crossing	Saco Ranger Station: Kancamagus Hwy., 6 mi. west of Conway, NH	year-round	26	*	
Campton Family	Pemigewasset Ranger Station: Rt. 49 (Exit 28 off I-93)	mid-May to mid-Oct.	58	*	
Cold River	Saco Ranger Station: Rt. 113, 15 mi. north of Fryeburg, ME	mid-May to mid-Oct.	14	*	
Covered Bridge	Saco Ranger Station: Kancamagus Hwy, 6 mi. west of Conway, NH	mid-May to mid-Oct.	49		*
Crocker Pond	Rt. 5 South of Bethel, ME	mid-May to mid-Oct.	7		
Dolly Copp	Androscoggin Ranger Station: Rt. 16, 6 mi. south of Gorham, NH	mid-May to mid-Oct.	176	*	
Hancock	Pemigewasset Ranger Station: Kancamagus Hwy., 12.5 mi. west of Conway, NH	year-round	56	*	*
Hastings	Androscoggin Ranger Station: Rt. 113, 3 mi. south of Rt. 2, Gilead, ME	mid-May to mid-Oct.	24	*	
Jigger Johnson	Saco Ranger Station: Kancamagus Hwy., 12.5 mi. west of Conway, NH	late-May to mid-Oct.	76	*	

BOATING	FISHING	TOILETS	SHOWERS	UNIVERSAL ACCESS	RESERV.	OTHER
*	*	Flush		*	*	
	*	Vault				
*	*	Vault		*		Visitor programs; winter walk-in access half price
*	*	Flush	*	*	*	Visitor programs
*	*	Vault		*	*	12 RV sites
	*	Vault	*		*	Near Albany covered bridge
*		Vault				
	*	Flush		*	*	Visitor programs
	*	Vault– tent sites flush–RV sites		*		35 RV sites
	*	Vault		*	*	
	*	Flush	*			Visitor programs

national forest campgrounds

NAME	LOCATION	OPEN SEASON	SITES	HIKING	SWIMMING
Passa-conaway	Saco Ranger Station: Kancamagus Hwy., 15 mi. west of Conway, NH	mid-May to mid-Oct.	33	*	
Russell Pond	Pemigewasset Ranger Station: Tripoli Rd., Campton, NH, 3.7 mi. off I-93 at Exit 31	mid-May to mid-Oct.	86	*	*
Sugarloaf I	Ammonoosuc Ranger Station: Twin Mtn., NH, 3 mi. east of Rt. 302 then 5 mi. south on Zealand Rd.	mid-May to mid-Oct.	29	*	
Sugarloaf II	Ammonoosuc Ranger Station: Twin Mtn., NH, 3 mi. east of Rt. 302 then 5 mi. south on Zealand Rd.	mid-May to mid-Dec.	32	*	
Waterville	Pemigewasset Ranger Station: Waterville, NH, 8 mi. northeast on Rt. 49 from I-93 Exit 28	mid-May to mid-Nov.	27	*	
White Ledge	Saco Ranger Station: Rt. 16, Albany, NH, 5 mi. south of Conway, NH	mid-May to mid-Nov.	28	*	
Wild River	Androscoggin Ranger Station: 5 mi. on Wild River Rd., off Rt. 113, 3 mi. south of Rt. 2, Gilead, ME	mid-May to mid-Oct.	12	*	
Wildwood	Ammonoosuc Ranger Station: Rt. 112, 7 mi. west of Lincoln, NH	mid-May to mid-Dec.	26	*	
Zealand	Ammonoosuc Ranger Station: Rt. 302, 2 mi. east of Twin Mtn., NH	mid-May to mid-Oct.	11	*	

To make WMNF campground reservations call 877-444-6777 or visit ReserveUSA.com.

BOATING	FISHING	TOILETS	SHOWERS	UNIVERSAL ACCESS	RESERV.	OTHER
	*	Vault		*		
*	*	Flush	*	*		Visitor programs
	*	Flush			*	
	*	Vault		*	*	
	*	Vault		*	*	
		Vault		*	*	
	*	Vault		*		3 RV sites
	*	Vault		*		
	*	Vault		*		

state park campgrounds

NAME	LOCATION	OPEN	SITES
Cannon Mountain RV Park; 603-823-8800	I-93/Rt. 3 Franconia Notch Pkwy.	7	year-round
Crawford Notch State Park; 603-374-2272	Rt. 302, Harts Location, 12 mi. northwest of Bartlett, NH	31	May–Dec.
Franconia Notch State Park: Lafayette Campground; 603-823-9513	I-93/Rt. 3 Franconia Notch Pkwy.	98	mid-May–Columbus Day
Moose Brook State Park; 603-466-3860	Off Rt. 2, Jimtown Rd., Gorham, NH	58	mid-May–mid-Oct.

For more information on state parks call 603-271-3556 or visit www.nhparks.state.nh.us. For reservations call 603-271-3628.

For private campgrounds try these resources:

New Hampshire Campground Owners Association: 800-222-6764; www.ucampnh.com

KOA Kampgrounds: 406-248-7444; www.koakampgrounds.com

New Hampshire Division of Tourism: 800-FUN IN NH; www.visitnh.gov

HIKING	SWIMMING	BOATING	FISHING	TOILETS	SHOWERS	UNIVERAL ACCESS
*	*	*	*	Flush	*	*
*			*	Vault		with
*			*	Flush	*	with assistance
*	*		*	Flush	*	with assistance

backcountry campsites

SHELTER	APPROACH/TRAILS
Beaver Brook Shelter	Via Beaver Brook Trail: 0.3 mi.; Trailhead: Rt. 112 opposite Kinsman Ridge Trail (AT).
Black Mountain Cabin	Via Black Mt. Ski Trail: 1.4 mi.; Trailhead: Carter Notch Rd. Reservation only; call Saco Ranger Station at 877-444-6772.
Black Mt. Pond Shelter*	Via Guinea Pond Trail to Black Mt. Pond Trail: 2.4 mi.
Blue Brook Shelter	Via Basin Trail: 2.0 mi. to side trail, 0.3 mi. to shelter; Trailhead: Wild River Campground
Cabot Cabin	Via Mt. Cabot Trail: 3.5 mi.
Camp Heermance*	Via Blueberry Ledge Trail near summit of Mt. Whiteface
Camp Penacook*	Via Piper Trail 3.1 mi.; take spur trail 0.2 mi.; Trailhead: Rt. 16, behind Piper Trail Cabins & Restaurant
Camp Rich*	Via Dicey's Mill Trail: 3.9 mi. 25 yards, left on side trail; Trailhead: Old Mast Rd. Parking Area
Camp Shehadi*	Via Rollins Trail: 2.0 mi. from Mt. Whiteface; via Downes Brook Trail: 6.0 mi.
Camp 13 Falls*	Via Franconia Brook Trail: 5.1 mi.; via Twin Brook Trail: 2.7 mi. from Galehead Hut
Camp 16	REMOVED
Caribou Shelter*	Via Mud Brook Trail: 3.0 mi. 70 yards to the right.
Carlo Col Campsite (Mahoosuc Range)	Via Carlo Col Trail: 2.3 mi.; via Mahoosuc Trail from Gentian Pond Shelter: 3.7 mi. (AT).
Coppermine Shelter	Via Coppermine Trail: 2.5 mi.; Trailhead: Coppermine Rd.
Crag Camp	Via Randolph Path, Hincks Trail, and Spur Trail: 3.2 mi.; Trailhead: Appalachia on Rt. 2
Desolation Shelter*	Via Signal Ridge Trail to Carrigain Notch Trail: 5.1 mi.; via Wilderness Trail: 9.3 mi.

FACILITIES	FEE	CAPACITY
Lean-to	No	6
Cabin w/stove; *spring not reliable	Yes	8
Lean-to	No	8
Lean-to	No	6
Cabin; no water	No	8
Lean-to; no water	No	6
Lean-to; tent platforms	No	8/4
Lean-to	No	8
Lean-to; water 0.5-mi.	No	6
Tent platforms	No	36
Lean-to; tent platforms; *spring not reliable	No	6/4
Cabin; tent platforms	No	14/6
Lean-to; tenting permitted	No	7
Cabin; caretaker in summer	Yes	14; groups limited to 10
Lean-to; tenting permitted	No	8 (tenting)

backcountry campsites

SHELTER	APPROACH/TRAILS
Doublehead Cabin	Via Doublehead Ski Trail: 1.8 mi.; Trailhead: east side of Dundee Rd. in Jackson, 2.9 mi. from Rt. 16
Dry River Shelter #2	REMOVED
Dry River Shelter #3*	Via Dry River Trail: 6.3 mi.; Trailhead: US 302, Crawford Notch
Edmunds Col Emergency Shelter	REMOVED
Eliza Brook Shelter	Via Kinsman Ridge Trail to Eliza Brook Shelter Spur: 7.5 mi.; Trailhead: hiker parking lot near Tramway I-93 (AT)
Ethan Pond Campsite	Via Ethan Pond Trail: 2.8 mi. from Willey House Station on Rt. 302 (AT)
Flat Mt. Pond Shelter	Via Flat Mt. Pond Trail: on the shore of Flat Mt. Pond
Franconia Brook Campsite	Via the Eastside Trail: 3.0 mi. from the Lincoln Woods Trailhead, on the east side of the Pemigewasset River
Full Goose Shelter (Mahoosuc Range)	Via Mahoosuc Trail: between Fulling Mill Mt. and Goose Eye Mt. (AT)
Garfield Ridge Campsite	Via Garfield Ridge Trail: 3.9 mi.; via Franconia Brook Trail to Garfield Ridge Trail: 7.9 mi. (AT)
Gentian Pond Campsite (Mahoosuc Range)	Via Mahoosuc Trail: 11.4 mi.; via Mahoosuc Trail from Mt. Hayes: 8.3 mi., on Gentian Pond (AT)
Gray Knob Cabin	Via Lowe's Path: 3.2 mi.; Trailhead: US 2 near Lowe's store
Guyot Shelter & Campsite	Via Twinway Trail from Galehead Hut: 3.6 mi.; via Wilderness Trail and Bondcliff Trail: 11 mi. (AT)
Harvard Cabin	Via Tuckerman Ravine and Huntington Ravine Trails: 1.8 mi.; Dec. 1–March 31 only

FACILITIES	FEE	CAPACITY
Cabin; no water	No	8
Lean-to	No	8
Lean-to; tenting permitted	No	8+
Lean-to; tent platforms	No	8/20
Lean-to; tenting permitted	No	8
16 tent platforms	No	64
Lean-to; spring 30 yards east	No	8
Lean-to; 7 tent platforms; caretaker in summer	Yes	12/28
Lean-to; tent sites	Yes	20
Winterized cabin; caretaker year-round	Yes	15
Lean-to; 6 tent platforms; caretaker in summer	Yes	12/24
Cabin; some tenting permitted	Yes	12

backcountry campsites

SHELTER	APPROACH/TRAILS
Hermit Lake Shelters (Tuckerman Ravine)	Via Tuckerman Ravine Trail: 2.4 mi.; Trailhead: AMC Pinkham Notch Visitor Center, Rt. 16; also accessible by Boott Spur Link and Lion's Head Trail
Imp Campsite	Via Carter-Moriah Trail and Spur: 6.8 mi. from spur trail; 2.0 mi. from Mt. Moriah; 2.0 mi. via Carter-Moriah Trail (AT)
Isolation Shelter	REMOVED
Jeffers Brook Shelter	Via AT: north 1.1 mi. from Rt. 25
Jim Liberty Cabin	Via Liberty Trail: 3.3 mi.; Trailhead: parking area at Paugus Mill Road in Chocorua
Kinsman Pond Campsite	Via Kinsman Ridge and Kinsman Pond Trails: 11.6 mi.; via Lonesome Lake, Fishin' Jimmy, and Kinsman Pond Trails: 3.6 mi.
Liberty Springs Tentsite	Via Liberty Springs Trail: 2.4 mi. (AT)
The Log Cabin	Via Lowe's Path: 2.5 mi.; from Mt. Adams summit via Lowe's Path: 2.3 mi.
Mizpah Tentsites (near Mizpah Hut— a.k.a. Nauman)	Via Crawford Path–Mizpah Cutoff: 2.5 mi.; from Lakes of the Clouds Hut: 5.7 mi. (AT)
Moose Mountain Shelter	Via Clark Pond Loop from Goose Pond Rd.: 0.5 mi. from AT
Mt. Langdon Shelter	Junction of Mt. Langdon and Mt. Stanton Trails
Mountain Pond Cabin	REMOVED
Mountain Pond Shelter	Via Mt. Pond Loop Trail: 0.6 mi. (taking a left at the fork); Trailhead: Slippery Brook Rd.
Old Shag Camp	REMOVED
Osgood Campsite	Via the Great Gulf Trail and Osgood Trail: 2.5 mi. (AT)

FACILITIES	FEE	CAPACITY
12 lean-tos; 3 tent platforms; caretaker year-round	Yes; tickets sold at Pinkham Notch Visitor Center only	86
Lean-to; tent platforms; caretaker in summer	Yes	12/20
Lean-to	Yes	8
Cabin	No	9
Lean-to; 3 tent platforms; caretaker in summer	Yes	22
12 tent platforms; caretaker in summer	Yes	48
Cabin semi-enclosed; caretaker in summer	Yes	8
7 tent platforms; caretaker in summer	Yes	30
Lean-to	No	5
Lean-to	No	5
Lean-to	No	8
3 tent platforms	No	12

backcountry campsites

SHELTER	APPROACH/TRAILS
The Perch	Via Randolph Path and Perch Path: 5.3 Mi., near (AT)
Perkins Notch Shelter	Via Wild River Trail, south of No-Ketchum Pond, southeast side of Wild River: 7 mi.
Province Pond Shelter	Via Province Brook Trail: 1.6 mi. at Province Pond
Rattle River Shelter	Via Rattle River Trail: 1.7 mi. from US Rt. 2 (AT)
Resolution Shelter*	Via Davis Path: 3.7 mi.; via Mt. Langdon and Mt. Parker Trails: 6.8 mi.
Rocky Branch Shelter #1	Via Rocky Branch Trail: 1.7 mi. from Jericho Rd.
Rocky Branch Shelter #2*	Via Rocky Branch Trail: 3.7 mi., at the junction of Rocky Branch Trail and Isolation Trail
Sawyer Pond Shelter	Via Sawyer Pond Trail: 4.5 mi., on Sawyer Pond
South Baldface Shelter	Via Baldface Circle Trail: 2.5 mi.; just below ledges on South Baldface
Speck Pond Shelter (Mahoosuc Range)	Via Mahoosuc Trail: 26.1 mi.; via Speck Pont Trail: 3.7 mi., on Speck Pond (AT)
Spruce Brook Shelter	Via Wild River Trail: 3.2 mi. from Wild River Campground
Three Ponds Shelter	Via Three Pond Trail: 2.5 mi., on knoll above Middle Pond on side trail
Trident Col Tentsites (Mahoosuc Range)	Via side path from Mahoosuc Trail: 6.6 mi.; Trailhead: Rt. 16, Gorham (AT)
Valley Way Tentsite	Via Valley Way: 3.1 mi.

*In designated wilderness areas, a facility or shelter is scheduled for removal when in need of major repair. Information gathered from *On Foot in the White Mountains* by the U.S. Forest Service.

FACILITIES	FEE	CAPACITY
Lean-to; 4 tent platforms; caretaker in summer	Yes	6/16; groups limited to 10
Lean-to	No	6
Lean-to	No	6
Lean-to	No	10
Lean-to; water scarce in dry season	No	8
Lean-to; 5 tent platforms	No	8/20
Lean-to	No	8
Lean-to; 5 tent platforms	No	8/20
Lean-to; spring unreliable	No	6
Lean-to; tent platforms; caretaker in summer	Yes	12/10
Lean-to; tent platforms	No	6/4
Lean-to	No	10
4 tent sites; water 50 yards west below tent sites	No	20
2 tent platforms	No	8

outfitters

NAME	ADDRESS	PHONE	SEASON	OPEN BIKES	RENT BIKES	FIX BIKES
Canoe King	2340 White Mtn. Hwy, W. Ossipee	603-539-4799	all year	yes	no	no
Franconia Sport Shop	Main St., Franconia	603-823-5241	all year	yes	yes	yes
Greasey Wheel Bikes	40 S. Main St., Plymouth	603-536-3655	all year	yes	yes	yes
Joe Jones Ski & Sports	Rt. 49, Campton	603-726-3000	fall & winter	no	no	no
Joe Jones Ski & Sports	2709 Main St. Conway	603-356-9411	all year	yes	yes	yes
Kayak Jack's Fun Yak Rentals	558 White Mtn. Hwy., Conway	603-447-5571	seasonal	no	no	no
Littleton Bike Shop	87 Main St. Littleton	603-444-3437	all year	yes	yes	yes
Lone Wolf Canoe	Rt. 3A, Plymouth	603-536-1885	seasonal	no	no	no
Loon Mtn. Bike Center	Kancamagus Hwy., Lincoln	603-745-8111	seasonal	yes	yes	yes
Moriah Sports	101 Main St. Gorham	603-466-5050	all year	yes	yes	yes
Northern Extremes	Rt. 302, Glen	603-383-8117	seasonal	-no	no	no

SELL KAYAKS	RENT KAYAKS	SELL TOURS	KAYAK CANOES	RENT CANOES	SELL WINTER SPORTS	OTHER
no	yes	yes	yes	yes	Snowmobile tours	Paddling accessories
no	no	no	no	no	Rent & sell alpine and cross-country skis, snowshoes, snowboards & skates	Hiking apparel, boots & accessories; camping gear and necessities
no	no	no	no	no	no	Full-service bike shop; group rides
no	no	no	no	no	Skis, snowboards & apparel	
no	yes	no	no	yes	Skis, snowboards	Skateboards, inflatables, summer apparel & Ski demos
yes	end of season	no	yes	end of season	no	Shuttle service to river; sell kayaks & canoes after Labor Day
no	no	no	no	no	no	Field hockey, indoor fitness equipment
no	yes	no	no	yes	no	
no	no	no	no	no	no	Inline skate park, rock-climbing wall
no	yes	no	no	no	Alpine & cross-country skis & snowshoes	Accessories & apparel; guided snowshoe treks
yes	yes	yes	yes	no	no	

outfitters

NAME	ADDRESS	PHONE	OPEN SEASON	RENT BIKES	FIX BIKES	SELL BIKES
Northern Extremes	Rt. 16, North Conway	603-383-8117	all year	no	no	no
Outback Kayak Co.	104 Main St., Woodstock; Mill Front Plaza, Lincoln	603-745-2002	all year	no	no	no
Outdoor Outfitters	Rt. 112, Lincoln	603-745-4806	seasonal	no	no	no
Pemi-Baker River Adventures	33 Sanborn Rd., Plymouth	603-536-5652	seasonal	no	no	no
Red Jersey Cyclery	Rt. 302, Bartlett	603-383-4660	Feb.–Dec.	yes	yes	yes
Rhino Bike Works	95 Main St., Plymouth	603-536-3919	all year	yes	yes	yes
Saco Bound Canoe & Kayak Rental	Rt. 302, Center Conway; Rt. 16, Conway	603-447-3002	seasonal	no	no	no

RENT KAYAKS	SELL KAYAKS	KAYAK TOURS	RENT CANOES	SELL CANOES	WINTER SPORTS	OTHER
yes	yes	yes	yes	no	Snowmobiles	
yes	yes	yes	yes	yes	Snowshoes, cross-country skis, snowmobiles & snow tubes	AMC members 15% discount with verification; ATVs, llama trekking, summer & winter apparel, camping gear, handmade quilts & alpaca & llama sweaters
yes	yes	yes	yes	yes	no	Outdoor clothing, accessories for canoes and kayaks; operate a 7-acre island you can stay at on your tours
yes	no	no	yes	no	no	Inflatable tubes, shuttle service to river
no	no	no	no	no	no	All biking accessories; sponsor weekly group rides on Wed. & Sat.
no	no	no	no	no	cross-country ski equipment	Accessories & apparel
yes	yes	yes	yes	yes	no	Guided canoe & kayak trips; full-service paddling shop; info on all rivers in area

outfitters

NAME	ADDRESS	PHONE	OPEN SEASON	RENT BIKES	FIX BIKES	SELL BIKES
Saco Valley Canoe	Rt. 302, Center Conway; Rt. 302, Fryeburg	603-447-2444	seasonal	no	no	no
Ski & Bike Warehouse	Main St., Lincoln	603-745-3164	all year	yes	yes	yes
Ski Fanatics	Rt. 49, Campton	603-726-4327	all year	yes	yes	yes
Sports Outlet	Main St., North Conway	603-356-3133	all year	yes	yes	yes
The Bike Shop	Mountain Valley Mall Blvd., North Conway	603-356-6089	all year	no	yes	yes
Umbagog Outfitters	P.O. Box 268, Errol	603-356-3292; www.umbout. com	seasonal	no	no	no
Village Ski & Snowboard	Main St., Lincoln	603-745-8852	winter season	no	no	no
Zeil Schuss Ski Shop	24 Glen Rd., Gorham	603-466-5756	all year	no	yes	yes

RENT KAYAKS	SELL KAYAKS	KAYAK TOURS	RENT CANOES	SELL CANOES	WINTER SPORTS	OTHER
yes	yes	no	yes	yes	no	Shuttle service to Saco River; campground on the Saco
no	no	no	no	no	Snowshoes, cross-country & alpine skis, snow boards	
yes	yes	yes	yes	yes	Snowshoes, alpine & cross-country skis, snowboards	
no	no	no	no	no	Cross-country skis	Accessories, apparel, shoes
no	no	no	no	no	no	
no	end of season	no	no	end of season	no	Teach all levels of whitewater & touring canoeing & kayaking; provide all equipment
no	no	no	no	no	Sell & rent new snowshoes, alpine & cross-country skis, snow-boards, all accessories	AMC members 15% discount with verification
no	no	no	no	no	Alpine & cross-country skis	

about the authors

JERRY AND MARCY MONKMAN specialize in ecophotography, creating images that depict nature and man's interaction with nature. From their home base in Portsmouth, New Hampshire, they spend as much time as possible hiking, biking, and paddling around New England with their daughter, Acadia, capturing it all on film. Their photos of the Northeast are published regularly by the Appalachian Mountain Club, the Northern Forest Alliance, and the Appalachian Trail Conference. Their work has also appeared in *Backpacker, Outdoor Photographer, Outdoor Explorer, Canoe and Kayak, Conservation Sciences, Yankee Magazine, Country Discoveries,* and *Natural History,* as well as in National Audubon Society and National Geographic field guides. They maintain a website full of pictures and travel essays at www.ecophotography.com. *Discover the White Mountains* is the second in their "Discover" series. *Discover Acadia National Park* was published in 2000.

about the amc

SINCE 1876, the Appalachian Mountain Club has helped people experience the majesty and solitude of the Northeast outdoors. We offer outdoor skills workshops, guided trips, and lodging options for all levels of outdoor adventuring. Our programs include trail maintenance, air and water quality research, and conservation advocacy work to preserve the special outdoor places we love and enjoy for future generations.

We believe that people who enjoy breathing fresh air, climbing mountains, splashing in streams, and walking on trails have more fun and take better care of the outdoors. Join the fun today. Call 617-523-0636 for membership information.

From beginner backpacking to advanced backcountry skiing, we teach outdoor skills workshops to suit your interest and experience, and offer guided hiking and paddling trips. Our four outdoor education centers guarantee year-round adventures. And with accommodations throughout the Northeast, you don't have to travel to the ends of the earth to see nature's beauty and experience unique wilderness lodging.

We can lead you to the best hiking, biking, skiing, and paddling destinations from Maine to North Carolina. With more than 50 books and maps published, we're your definitive resource for discovering wonderful outdoor places. For ordering information call 800-262-4455.

Appalachian Mountain Club
5 Joy Street
Boston, MA 02108-1490
617-523-0636
www.outdoors.org

leave no trace

The Appalachian Mountain Club is a national educational partner of Leave No Trace, a non-profit organization dedicated to promoting and inspiring responsible outdoor recreation through education, research, and partnerships. The Leave No Trace Program seeks to develop wildland ethics—ways in which people think and act in the outdoors to minimize their impacts on the areas they visit and to protect our natural resources for future enjoyment. Leave No Trace unites four federal land management agencies — the U.S. Forest Service, National Park Service, Bureau of Land Management, and U.S. Fish and Wildlife Service—with manufacturers, outdoor retailers, user groups, educators, organizations like the AMC and the National Outdoor Leadership School (NOLS), and individuals.

The Leave No Trace ethic is guided by these seven principles:

- Plan ahead and prepare
- Travel and camp on durable surfaces
- Dispose of waste properly
- Leave what you find
- Minimize campfire impacts
- Respect wildlife
- Be considerate of other visitors

The AMC has joined NOLS — a recognized leader in wilderness education and a founding partner of Leave No Trace—as the only sole national providers of the Leave No Trace Master Educator course through 2004. The AMC offers this five-day course, designed especially for outdoor professionals and land managers, as well as the shorter two-day Leave No Trace Trainer course, at locations throughout the Northeast.

For Leave No Trace information and materials contact:
Leave No Trace, P.O. Box 997, Boulder, CO 80306; 800-332-4100; www.LNT.org

index

A

Albany Brook, 184–85
Ammonoosuc Lake & Trail, 20–21, 40
Ammonoosuc River, 15
  Littleton to Lisbon, 32–33, 309–312
Androscoggin River, 241
  Errol to Milan, 32–33, 315–17
Appalachian Mountain Club,
  82–83, 174, 356
Appalachian Trail, 82, 100,107,
  110, 124, 128–30, 146
Arethusa Falls, 55–57
Attitash Bear Peak, 268
Avalanche Brook & Camp, 248–49

B

Baldface Range & Circle
  Trail, 24–25, 137–40, 241
Bartlett Experimental Forest,
  26–27, 183–85
Basin-Cascade Trail, 47–50
Basin, the, 47–50, 131, 215
Bear Notch Road, 183–85,
  223, 225, 237, 239
Beebe River & Road, 30–31,
  250, 260–62
Birch Hill & Trail, 237–40
Bog Brook & Trail, 88–91
Bog Brook Eddy, 28–29, 230–32
Boott Spur & Trail, 26–27,
  111, 156–60, 162
Bretton Woods, 16, 268
Bumpus Brook & Trail, 51–54

C

Cannon Mountain, 57, 62,
  213, 215, 303
Caribou Mountain & Trail,
  24–25, 95–98, 140
Caribou–Speckled Mountain
  Wilderness, 95, 97, 255–56
Carlo Col Campsite & Trail, 124, 127
Carter Dome & Trail, 26–27, 144–47
Carter Lakes, 146–47
Carter Notch Hut (AMC), 91, 146–47
Carter-Moriah Trail, 144, 146
Carter Range, 139, 146, 241
Cascade Brook & Trail, 20–21,
  47–50, 58–60, 62, 63
Cascade Path, 20–21, 58–60

Chocorua–Tamworth Loop,
  26–27, 195–97
Chocorua Lake, 30–31, 281–82
Cloudland Falls, 57, 152
Cohos Trail, 85–86
Cold River Camp (AMC), 137
Conway Lake, 30–31, 283–85
Conway Recreation Trail,
  26–27,186–88
Coosauk Fall, 20–21, 51–55
Coppermine Brook & Trail, 57
Crawford Notch, 12, 14, 16,
  56–57, 66–68, 85, 172–73, 194
  Depot Visitor Center, 66, 173
  Hostel (AMC), 40
Crawford Path, 16, 158, 169, 172
Crystal Cascade, 57, 157

D

Davis Path, 85–87, 158
Diana's Baths, 57, 141, 143
Dickey Mountain & Trail, 22–23, 80–84

E

East Branch, Pemigewasset River,
  17, 39, 100–101, 208–11
Elephant Head, 116–17
Elephant Rock & Path, 58–60
Ellsworth Pond, 26–27, 198–201
Ethan Pond Trail, 100–101, 104,
  106
Evans Brook, 44–46
Evans Notch, 44, 91, 137, 274

F

Falling Waters Trail, 57, 149, 151–52
Falls Pond, 20–21, 40, 225
Fishin' Jimmy Trail, 50, 62
Flat Mountain Pond & Trail, 30–31,
  250–54
Flume & Trail, 20–21, 39, 132, 134
Flume Gorge Visitor Center, 39,
  72, 131, 215
Franconia Brook & Campsites,
  39, 189, 191–92
Franconia Falls, 39, 189
Franconia Notch, 14, 39, 47, 50, 57
  Bicycle Path, 28–29, 50, 72,
  131, 212–15
  State Park, 61, 132
Franconia Range, 153–155
Franconia Ridge & Trail, 26–27,
  131, 134, 148–52, 192
Franconia Village Touring Center, 268

G

Goose Eye Mountain & Trail, 124–27
Gorge Brook & Trail, 107–10
Great Glen Trails, 269
Great Gulf Wilderness & Trails,
  20–21, 39, 76, 111, 115,
  166, 255–56
Greeley Ponds & Trail, 22–23,
  69–71, 247
Greenleaf Hut (AMC), 148, 150
Guinea Pond Trail, 250–51, 254
Gulfside Trail, 115, 167–69

H

Hermit Lake & Shelters, 111, 158–60
Hitchcock Fall, 20–21, 51–55
Howker Ridge Trail, 51–54

K

Kearsarge North & Trail, 16, 22–23,
  92–94
Kinsman Falls & Pond, 47–48, 55

L

Lafayette Campground, 50, 61,
  63, 215
Lakes of the Clouds Hut (AMC),
  164, 167–69, 172
Lake Tarleton, 32–33, 291–93
Liberty Spring Tentsite & Trail,
  131–134, 215
Lincoln Woods & Trail, 17,
  26–27, 39, 189–92
Livermore Road & Trails, 30–31,
  247–49
Lonesome Lake & Trail, 22–23,
  47, 50, 61–63
  Hut (AMC), 50, 61, 63
Long Pond, 32–33, 289–90
Loon Mountain, 28–29, 208–11, 269
Lost Pond & Trail, 20–21, 40, 41
Lowe's Bald Spot, 22–23, 74–76
Lower Nanamocomuck Ski Trail,
  28–29, 217, 223–25, 239

M

Mad River, 70, 248
Madison Gulf & Trail, 14, 76,
  111, 166, 168
Madison Spring Hut (AMC), 164–68
Mahoosucs & Trail, 24–25,124–27
Mizpah Spring Hut (AMC),
  119, 164, 169, 172

Moat Mountains & Trail, 13, 16, 28–29, 226–29
  North Moat, 24–25, 141–43, 226, 228
  Smoky Quartz Area, 226–29
Moose Brook State Park, 28–29, 202–204
Moose Campground (AMC), 320
Mount Adams, 74, 111, 167
Mount Carrigain, 216
Mount Carlo, 24–25, 124–27
Mount Chocorua & Trails, 13, 24–25, 120–23, 195–97, 282
Mount Clay & Loop Trail, 168
Mount Crawford & Trail, 18, 22–23, 85–87
Mount Eisenhower & Loop Trail, 169, 172
Mount Flume, 134, 191
Mount Hight, 26–27, 144–47
Mount Hope, 86
Mount Israel, 22–23, 77–79
Mount Jackson, 24–25, 57, 116–19, 172–73
Mount Jefferson & Trails, 24–25, 112–15, 168
Mount Kancamagus, 69–71
Mount Kineo, 198, 201
Mount Lafayette, 16, 149–50
Mount Liberty, 24–25, 131–34, 151
Mount Lincoln, 150–51
Mount Madison, 54–55, 166–67
Mount Monroe Loop Trail, 169
Mount Moosilauke and Trails, 16, 24–25, 107–10, 263–265, 292
Mount Moriah, 16, 146
Mount Osceola & Trail, 16, 69
Mount Pemigewasset & Trail, 22–23, 72–73, 194
Mount Pierce, 165, 172
Mount Tripyramid & Trail, 247–49
Mount Washington & Trails, 16, 26–27, 76, 115, 156–63, 169
  Auto Road, 76, 158
Mount Webster, 24–25, 116–19, 172–73
Mount Willard & Trail, 22–23, 66–68, 194
Mountain Pond & Trail, 30–31, 233, 234, 276–77

N
Nineteen-Mile Brook Trail, 144–47
North & South Baldface. See Baldface Range.

Norway Rapids & Trail, 59, 248

O
Old Bridle Path, 149–50, 152
Old Jackson Road, 74–76

P
Parapet Brook & Trail, 166–67
Peabody River, 39, 166
Pemigewasset River, 15, 39, 47, 72, 108, 181, 189–92, 215, 303–304
  Woodstock to Thornton, 32–33, 300–302
  Woodstock Whitewater, 32–33, 305–308
Pemigewasset Wilderness, 17, 39, 55, 100, 104–105, 191, 255–56
Pinkham Notch, 14, 42, 158, 159, 160, 165
  Visitor Center (AMC), 40, 41, 74, 157
Presidential Range, 26–27, 164–73
Presidential Range–Dry River Wilderness, 86, 116, 119, 255–56
Profile Lake, 214, 303
Province Pond & Trail, 30–31, 182, 257–59

R
Red Ridge & Trails, 141–43, 226, 228
Rob Brook Road, 28–29, 237–40
Rocky Glen Falls, 49, 55
Rocky Gorge & Scenic Area, 40, 57, 223, 225
Roost & Trail, 20–21, 44–46, 194

S
Sabbaday Falls, 20–21, 39, 57
Saco River, 15, 85, 186–88, 228
  North Conway to Conway, 32–33, 319–22
Sandwich Range Wilderness, 120, 123, 253, 255–56
Sawyer Pond & Trail, 237–40
Sawyer River, Road & Trail, 28–29, 178, 216–19
Silver Cascade & Brook, 56–57, 118, 173
Slippery Brook, Road & Trail, 28–29, 233–35

Smith-Eastman Recreation Area, 186
Snows Mountain & Ski Trail, 58–60
Speckled Mountain, 95, 97, 140, 255–56
Square Ledge & Trail, 20–21, 41–43, 194
Stairs Fall (Randolph), 20–21, 51–55
Stairs Falls (Franconia Range), 57, 152
Swift River, 40, 216, 223–25, 237, 239, 240, 321
Swiftwater Falls, 57, 152

T
The Balsams, 268
Thoreau Falls & Trail, 24–25, 55, 99–101, 106
Tuckerman Ravine & Trail, 12, 14, 57, 74, 111, 156–60
Tunnel Brook & Trail, 30–31, 178, 182, 263–67, 290

U
Upper Kimball Pond, 30–31, 274–75

V
Valley Way Trail, 111

W
Waterville Valley & Trails, 55, 58, 80, 247–48, 270
Webster Cliffs & Trails, 68, 116–19, 172–73
Welch and Dickey Mountains & Trail, 22–23, 80–84
West Branch, Pemigewasset River, 131–32
Whitewall Mountain, 99–100
Wild River Camp (AMC), 91
Wild River, Road & Trail, 28–29, 44, 140, 241–44
Wildcat Mountain, 41–42, 90, 147
Wildcat River & Trail, 22–23, 88–91
Wilderness Trail, 17, 20–21, 39

Z
Zeacliff & Trail, 18, 24–25, 102–106
Zealand Falls & Trail, 24–25, 55, 99–106
  Hut (AMC), 102, 104
Zealand Pond, 100, 104
Zealand River & Road, 99, 103